Springer Compass International

Series Editors
Steven S. Muchnick
Peter Schnupp

C. Lins

The Modula-2
Software Component Library

Volume 1

With 21 Illustrations

Springer-Verlag
New York Berlin Heidelberg
London Paris Tokyo

Charles Lins, Apple Computer, Inc., Cupertino, CA 95014, USA

Editors

Steven S. Muchnick, SUN Microsystems, Inc., Mountain View, CA 94043, USA
Peter Schnupp, InterFace Computer GmbH, D-8000 München 81, West Germany

All of the Modula-2 software in this book was written by C. Lins. Copyright © 1988 by Charles A. Lins. 5063 Clairemont Mesa Blvd. # 6, San Diego, CA, USA 92117.
MacMETH, by Werner Heiz, Neugasse 71, CH-8005, Zürich, Switzerland. Copyright © 1986, Institut für Informatik Eidgenössische Technische Hochschule (ETH) Zürich, Clausiusstr. 55, CH-8096 Zürich, Switzerland.
TML Modula-2 Compiler, by Robert R. Campbell. Copyright © 1987, Robert R. Campbell.
Ada is a registered trademark of the U.S. Government (Ada Joint Program Office).
Apple, the Apple logo, AppleTalk, LaserWriter, and Lisa are registered trademarks of Apple Computer, Inc.
ImageWriter, MacDraw, Macintosh, MacPaint, and MacWrite are trademarks of Apple Computer, Inc.
Motorola is a trademark of Motorola, Inc.
UNIX is a trademark of AT&T Bell Laboratories.

Cover: Pastel on paper (1984), John Pearson

Library of Congress Cataloging-in-Publication Data
Lins, C. (Charles)
    The Modula-2 software component library.
    (Springer compass international)
    Bibliography: v. 1, p.
    1. Modula-2 (Computer program language)
I. Title.   II. Series.   QA76.73.M63L56   1988   005.13'3   88-24956

Camera-ready copy provided by the author.

9 8 7 6 5 4 3 2 1

ISBN-13: 978-1-4684-6370-5   e-ISBN-13: 978-1-4684-6368-2
DOI: 10.1007/978-1-4684-6368-2

To Doris Regina
whose love made this possible

Contents

11   Set Abstraction   201

Appendices

Bibliography

Abbreviations

ADS	Abstract Data Structure
ADT	Abstract Data Type
ASM	Abstract State Machine
Avg	Average
Def	Definition
Imp	Implementation
Max	Maximum
Min	Minimum
Msg	Message
No	Number
Proc	Procedure
Str	String

Introduction

The reusable software components in Modula-2 described in this book resulted from the author's software development efforts over many years in constructing software artifacts, especially with regard to data structures and their use in building reliable application software. The components provide a library of tested software building blocks covering the elementary data structures that form the foundation of computer science. Such a library is useful to software developers (both professional and hobbyist), educators, students, and programmers wanting to learn about and study examples of well-engineered software products using Modula-2.

Reusable Software

The concept of reusing software in order to increase productivity, has been around at least since 1968 when M. D. McIlroy presented a paper, "Mass-Produced Software Components," to the NATO conference on software engineering. The many benefits of software reuse derive from increased software development productivity and quality. The advantages resulting from reuse have long been recognized by software engineers, but the bright promise of reusable software is mostly unrealized. It has been estimated that as little as 15% of the billions of lines of source code created worldwide over the years may be suitable for widespread reuse. The continual shortage of software engineers, the great variation in capability and productivity between individuals, and the scarcity of highly productive programmers make it surprising that the practice of software reuse is not widespread throughout the software industry.

Within the past several years researchers have investigated the factors responsible for limiting practical software reuse. These studies implicate several managerial and technical issues. The researchers agree on several factors bearing upon the problem, which can be categorized into three main groups: *economic*, *managerial* and *technical*.

Factors in the economic area include the initial capital investment required to create software for reuse, the tendency of business economics to work against reusability, and the nature of reuse as multi-organizational. Management, both project and corporate, provides few rewards for reuse, while the numerous approaches toward reuse, with no single *best* method, inhibits management from actively pursuing a particular strategy.

The primary technical issues include organizational problems of cataloging and retrieval of reusable software, variations in level of reuse (object code, source code, design), lack of suitable design techniques applicable to reusable software, few programming languages supporting reuse, and the difficulties encountered in attempting to write reusable software. This last factor should not be underestimated; the amount of extra effort required from the beginning to produce software that can later be reused may combine with the reality of project deadlines to kill chances for developing reusable software.

The economic and managerial factors of software reuse are probably over-emphasized in the current literature. The technical issues are most relevant, especially the simple reality of the difficulty of writing reusable software. By presenting complete examples of software designed and written for reuse, our presentation provides an incentive for others in developing reusable software.

The components developed in this series can be reused in more than one way. Once compiled, the object code may be reused within a single software system and across many software systems. The source code may be reused to provide a foundation for the construction of a variant of the component. And finally, the design and documentation supporting the components may be reused. Each of these methods for reusing software is shown in operation throughout the books.

This series helps remedy the unrealized promise of reusable software by providing a library of reusable components and demonstrating techniques and methods used to construct them.

Modula-2

Professor Niklaus Wirth of ETH (Eidgenossische Technische Hochschule) Zürich developed Modula-2 as a successor to Pascal. Modula-2 extends Pascal in two directions — downward *towards* the machine architecture and upward *away from* the machine architecture. The language incorporates features supporting *systems programming*, where low-level access to the machine is often necessary or required. Modula-2 specifically provides three features:

- language facilities for direct access and manipulation of the hardware;
- the ADDRESS and WORD data types; and
- controlled relaxation of the language's strict type checking.

In the other direction, Modula-2 allows and encourages module development by providing a mechanism for separating interfaces from their implementations. Furthermore, Modula-2 cleans up various syntactic problems in Pascal and enhances the syntax. Facilities provided by the module concept allow Modula-2 to implement abstract data structures effectively. They also facilitate information hiding and object-oriented principles. Modula-2 is faithful to its Pascal ancestry by lending itself to the construction of well-written, well-documented programs.

Modula-2 supports the development of software using modern concepts of software engineering and has advantages over many other languages which do not support present-day software engineering principles. The language's syntax is simple, having only 38 reserved words. It is mostly machine-independent, and the machine-dependent facilities are localized in a module called SYSTEM. Because of its simplicity and its descent from Pascal, the language is easily learned by many programmers; compilers have been implemented for many popular microcomputers and larger computer systems.

Software is composed of layers which form a hierarchy of modules; Modula-2 directly supports this paradigm by providing separate compilation of modules with full type and interface checking across module boundaries. This facility can save significant recompilation time and effort during the testing and maintenance phases of a software project. These factors make the language available to a wider spectrum of programmers than a larger language (such as Ada®).

Our implementations in Modula-2 make it easier for others to port the modules to another language (such as Pascal or C) than doing so from Ada. Many language features of Ada (for example, exception handling, instantiation, generic packages, tasking, etc.) are not present in other languages and so modules employing these constructs would have to be coded explicitly — which is not always easy to accomplish.

These are the reasons for selecting Modula-2 as the implementation language for the components in this series.

Orientation

A series on reusable software and data structures must choose between emphasizing theoretical and practical aspects. A theoretical inclination can be interesting in itself (the subject of algorithms and data structures is a vein of knowledge worth mining), but the author felt the practical issues would appeal to a wider audience.

Once the decision for a practical approach had been made, it was necessary to determine the specific method to be used in defining generic, reusable modules. Several articles have recently (early to mid-1987) been published in *BYTE* and the *Journal of Pascal, Ada, and Modula-2* on techniques for constructing generic modules, similar to Ada generics and generic packages, using the language Modula-2. Each technique has its own advantages and disadvantages regarding simplicity, (type-checking) safety, generality, efficiency, and ease of reuse. The author does not intend to discuss the theoretical issues but to provide practical software components that may be reused. For simplicity and consistency, therefore, the series uses only one of the several available techniques.

We recognize the importance of reading programs as well as writing them. Considerable benefit and experience can be gained through careful examination of modules presented within these pages. Each module can be reused *as is*. However, it may be a valuable learning experience to modify the module to provide an alternate implementation for a data structure or algorithm, to experiment with other methods of providing generic facilities, or for any of many other reasons.

Big O Notation

The analysis of algorithms is a "well developed area of study in computer science" [1, pg. 12]. In choosing an algorithm for the solution of a given problem, one is interested in having an idea of how long the algorithm requires for execution and the amount of space it uses. The answer depends on four factors:

- the volume and type of input,
- the compiler,
- the hardware, and
- the time complexity of the algorithm.

An algorithm's time complexity, in some cases, can be determined only by sophisticated mathematical analysis. This measurement of an algorithm's time complexity is typically given in what is known as asymptotic, or Big-O, notation describing the running time of the algorithm as a function of the input (N) with all machine dependencies (hardware and compiler) factored out.

The derivation of complexity measures and the mathematical foundations of this area of computer science are well beyond the scope of this work, but some quantitative guidelines can be given in this regard.

Notation	Running Time
O(1)	Constant
O(log log N)	Log Log
O(log N)	Logarithmic
O(N)	Linear
O(N log N)	Linearithmic
O(N^2)	Quadratic
O(N^3)	Cubic
2^N	Exponential

The term *Linearithmic* is borrowed from Sedgewick [2] which, along with reference [3], contains more extensive coverage of this subject.

Implementing Algorithms

When an algorithm is implemented using a real compiler and hardware, its running time is affected by inherent machine dependencies, including the amount of code generated for the algorithm. This factor, c, is the *constant of proportionality* and is a hidden factor in Big-O notation. Depending on the machine operations used, there may be situations (over a particular range of values for N, for example) of an O(N^2) algorithm running *faster* than an O(N) or O(log N) algorithm! Of course, after some value of N the better algorithm will yield a result in less time, but depending on the requirements of the application this may not be relevant to the task at hand. A helpful principle is to first implement a simple, but potentially slower, algorithm and later incorporate the more complex solution, if necessary.

Organization of the Series

This work is divided into pieces which are more manageable than a single monolithic document would be. The division into four volumes allows for full exposition of each module and concept, while providing for rapid retrieval of specific information, depending on the reader's requirements. The volumes' contents are grouped by data structure, as follows:

Volume 1
- Stacks
- Strings
- Sets
- Bags (a.k.a. Multisets) (Disk only)

Volume 2
- Lists
- Queues
- Deques

Volume 3
- Mappings
- Trees
- Graphs

Volume 4
- Hashing
- Searching
- Sorting

Prerequisites

The series assumes the reader to possess a certain amount of information, though the author has attempted to keep the prerequisites to a minimum. Knowledge of a high-level language such as Pascal, Ada, or (ideally) Modula-2 is expected. C programmers should have little difficulty understanding the concepts presented here since Modula-2 shares many similar facilities, though the operator set of Modula-2 is not as rich as C's. For anyone not familiar with programming in Modula-2, Niklaus Wirth's book *Programming in Modula-2* should be used alongside these volumes. An introductory text on Modula-2 would also be beneficial. Some knowledge of elementary data structures will be helpful but should not be essential to understanding the components and associated documentation. In any case, many references are provided to direct readers in their own research, since the subjects of data structures and software engineering encompass a wide range of knowledge. Finally, access to a Modula-2 compiler and suitable hardware on which to run it will be required for readers to conduct their own experiments in modifying components, extending their utility, and constructing other modules and applications of the components.

How to Use this Book

Chapters One through Four should be read before the others since they discuss design and implementation issues that pertain to the components. Prior to examining a particular component's implementation, the chapter on the abstraction should be read or reviewed. This chapter contains a specification for the abstraction and associated routines, plus information specific to the abstraction and information common to all its implementations. Finally, the specific component chapter may be studied. The component chapter contains information specific to that component's implementation. It is divided into two sections: the first covering the definition module, which contains documentation necessary to utilizing the module; the second covering the actual implementation details.

Source Code Availability

All source code presented in this series is available from the author on diskette for a nominal charge. Versions for the TML Modula-2 and MacMETH compilers for the Macintosh are available on 3.5-inch disks. The disks include versions of the modules customized for the basic data types such as characters, integers, reals, etc., and also incorporate use of Macintosh-specific features where necessary for the most efficient implementations possible. Versions of these modules may be available for other Macintosh compilers and other hardware; so it would be best to contact the author regarding disk formats not covered here. The author's address is:

C. Lins
Modula-2 Software
c/o *Springer Verlag*
815 De la Vina St.
Santa Barbara, CA, USA 93101

The software was developed on the Macintosh but machine-dependencies have been kept to a minimum to keep conversion to other systems relatively painless. Memory allocation and deallocation is one area of difference between the Macintosh and other hardware due to the presence of the ROM-based Memory Manager. Display of error messages is another area of machine-dependence due to the Macintosh graphic interface; this has been localized in the low-level error-handling modules. The implementation of the Modula-2 equivalent of the *Raise* statement, developed and presented in Volume One, is left to the user since it can be as simple or complex as one desires.

Development Environment

The modules presented in this series were initially developed on the author's Macintosh computer using the MacMETH and TML Modula-2 compilers. The development hardware configuration consisted of 512K bytes of memory, one 800K-byte internal disk drive, and an ImageWriter I printer. The system software was System 3.2 and Finder 5.3. The *Macintosh Programmer's Workshop* (MPW) software development system (version 1.0.1) from Apple Computer was used to generate source and cross-reference listings, and provided useful general tools for the software development process. *FastEddie2* by Cottage Software was the editor used to enter the source programs along with the built-in editing facilities of the MPW system.

The actual manuscript was written using MacWrite® distributed by Claris, and diagrams were drawn with MacDraw®. It was typeset using ReadySetGo4® and printed using Times Roman and Courier fonts.

Acknowledgements

Many people over the years through their own written works have influenced the author's concepts and ideas on software engineering and programming practice. Many of these printed resources will be found in the references.

Several individuals deserve special mention:

- David Parnas deserves particular credit for his ideas on information hiding. There are also those many individuals who worked in the Naval Research Laboratory's Software Cost Reduction project for the A7-E avionics software.

- Grady Booch provided inspiration through his recent (1987) book *Software Components in Ada* which demonstrates that Ada®, if nothing else, is an excellent language for describing algorithms. This author considers the algorithms, identifier naming conventions and layout presented there worthy of serious study by all programmers.

- Jon Bentley through his "Programming Pearls" column, in *Communication of the ACM* provided the author with many ideas, (and reinforced my own existing concepts of software design). This is the best column on programming to appear in any magazine or journal, and the author highly recommends it.

- Niklaus Wirth and his associates at ETH Zürich labored to bring first Pascal and now Modula-2 to reality. Without his insight and endeavors this series might have been suffixed "in Fortran"!

- On a more personal note, I would like to thank Jeff Meyerson of Computer Science Corporation and Dr. Steve Muchnick of Sun Microsystems for their willingness to review this work while it was in manuscript form.

- Also many thanks to the publisher and many individuals at Springer-Verlag who provided many insights into the publishing business, while always providing encouragement and assistance.

- Thanks also to Don and Rae Huntington of Production Services who put in many hours on editing, proofreading and typesetting the manuscript.

- Last, but not least my agent, William Gladstone, was able to make the necessary contacts, initiating the process of bringing my ideas to fruition.

A Few Words from the Lawyers

The author and publisher make no warranties, expressed or implied, that the software contained in this volume is free of error, or is consistent with any particular standard of merchantability, or that it will meet your requirements for any particular application. The software should not be relied upon for solving a problem whose incorrect solution could result in injury to a person or loss of property. If you use the software in such a manner, you do so at your own risk. The author and publisher disclaim all liability for direct or consequential damages resulting from the use of the software.

The author has extensively tested all modules contained in this volume, including all error conditions and exception handling. The source code for the test programs is included on the source code disk. As is well known, all the testing in the world cannot prove a program to be error-free. Furthermore, no software can operate with guaranteed correctness under conditions of failed hardware. However, the author has done his best to bring you high-quality, reliable software and trusts you will find it useful for your applications.

References

[1]   J. Bentley, *Programming Pearls*, Addison-Wesley, Reading, MA 1986.

[2]   R. Sedgewick, *Algorithms*, Addison-Wesley, Reading, MA 1983.

[3]   A.V. Aho, J.E. Hopcroft, and J.D. Ullman, *Data Structures and Algorithms*, Addison-Wesley, Reading, MA 1983.

1 Reusable Software Components

Communication necessarily involves interpreting the meaning of words in an agreed-upon way. This is especially important in written communication, since readers cannot ask the author, "What do you mean by...?" "Could you elaborate more fully on...?"

Chapter One provides a common framework for subsequent chapters. It defines fundamental terms used throughout the series. The chapter also reviews the concept of data abstraction, since the book emphasizes data structures. These topics form the subject material found in Section 1.1.

Section 1.2 summarizes the importance of reusable software components as a justification for much of the subsequent material. Several attributes used in categorizing various component implementations become issues in an actual implementation. Section 1.3, therefore, extensively presents this theme.

1.1 Components and Data Abstraction

1.1.1 Data Abstraction

"*Abstraction* is the act or process of separating the inherent qualities or properties of something from the actual physical object or concept to which they belong [21]." When applied to data structures, abstraction involves the precise set of operations applied to a given instance of the data structure. *Object*, in this context, refers both to abstraction of the data and to its internal representation. A data structure may then be treated as an entity separate from its physical manifestation. Individual data elements entered into and retrieved from an object can also be abstracted and generically named as an *item*.

An *abstract data* type combines objects and operations in a single, unified form that may be used as if the objects were elementary data types. In other words, an abstract data type consists of a set of run-time objects characterized by the operations available on it and the properties of the operations.

Abstraction is a powerful technique for managing complexity and is, therefore, especially important to the complex tasks of software development. Data abstraction is closely related to the principle of information hiding [Parnas] which separates data from its environment by encapsulating it within a module. *Access procedures* become the sole means of retrieving and changing the data by strictly controlling access to data within the module from outside the module.

These techniques provide increased reliability, safety, and security of the data by preventing direct manipulation of the underlying representation which would possibly create erroneous results by violating (implicit) assumptions or invariants. Reducing the number of details that must be understood facilitates comprehension of software design. Localizing representation details and related code simplifies software maintenance, since changes in representation are also localized and not spread across the software. These advantages are purchased at the price of loss of execution efficiency due to procedure call overhead.

1.1.2 Components

Component is defined as "A simple part, or a relatively complex entity regarded as a part, of a system" [21]. A *reusable software component* can then be defined as, "A simple part, or a relatively complex entity regarded as a part, of a software system that can be readily employed within other software systems."

From this definition it can be seen that a module provides an excellent mechanism for storing concrete realizations of software parts. If our definition is constrained within the domain of data structures then a reusable software part becomes a module encapsulating a specific implementation of an abstract data type (or abstract state machine). It may, therefore, be viewed as an abstraction of an object or entity having defined operations that may be applied to instances of that object. This is essentially the same definition as for a data abstraction, except that there are many ways to produce a concrete realization of such an abstraction. Thus, a module is used to distinguish one realization from another.

1.2 Importance of Reusable Software Components

The development of software systems, especially complex ones, has been fraught with problems: software delivered late or not at all; software that does not meet the user's requirements, functional or otherwise; software that is unreliable; and software that is inordinately difficult to maintain. Sommerville notes [19] that "many software systems are still being built which are unreliable, over budget, poorly documented, and not well suited to the user."

The ongoing RISKS forum in Software Engineering Notes (published by the Special Interest Group on Software Engineering, SIGSOFT, of the ACM) has identified and reported many systems failures. Hardware costs have been decreasing and software costs escalating. Sometimes 80% or more of the total development cost is budgeted toward software. Software development in the US today (1987) may be in excess of $100 billion annually. Obviously, any technique that can be applied to reduce this great outlay of money will result in enormous cost savings, even if productivity is improved by only a few percentage points.

The problems and expense in software development have led to much research attempting to identify the reasons and potential solutions. The technique of software reuse has been discussed since the late 1960s. T. C. Jones lists the results of several studies that indicate from 40 to 75% of all software developed before 1983 was not application specific [12]. Standish notes [20] that, "Software reuse has the same advantage as theft over honest toil."

1.3 Component Forms

The structure or form of a software component will vary depending on how one wishes to balance its operation with regard to space, time and environment. Goguen [8] and Booch [2] use the term *form*, while Knuth [13,22] uses the term *property* in this context to refer to the variations in internal structure and operational semantics in a module.

Four major properties can be used to categorize a component and its objects:

- concurrent operation or environment,
- object size or space used,
- memory management, and
- iteration or traversal over the items of an object.

Each of the above properties is discussed briefly below using terminology borrowed from Booch [2] and is used with permission of the publisher.

1.3.1 Concurrency

"Does the component behave properly in the presence of only one or more than one task?"

Sequential   The semantics of the object are preserved only in the presence of one thread of control.

Guarded   The semantics of the object are preserved in the presence of multiple threads of control, and mutual exclusion is enforced by all clients of the object.

Concurrent   The semantics of the object are preserved in the presence of multiple threads of control. The object itself enforces mutual exclusion. Access by multiple clients is sequentialized.

Multiple   The semantics of the object are preserved in the presence of multiple threads of control, and mutual exclusion is enforced by the object itself. Multiple simultaneous readers are permitted, but writers are sequentialized.

The classic issue here, *Mutual exclusion*, occurs when more than one task has access privileges to a data object. Each operation on the data in this situation must be indivisible (atomic). The data is thus ensured to be in a consistent state whenever accessed. Booch [2, pg. 42] provides information concerning how Ada's tasking mechanisms support the construction of components for these forms.

Modula-2 provides the *coroutine* for simulating concurrent execution at a lower level of abstraction. Unfortunately, a particular compiler is not required to support many low-level features of Modula-2. The Macintosh hardware and operating system does not support the coroutine feature. Refer to the Modula-2 language definition for specific details on coroutines.

No protection within the *sequential* form component is available to guarantee mutual exclusion, and therefore only one task may have access to the structure.

The client modules that access the component in the *guarded* form must cooperate to achieve mutual exclusion through the use of a semaphore or signal. Modula-2 achieves this by exporting the routines Seize and Release (equivalent to Dijkstra's P and V), which simply make calls to *Processes.WAIT* and *Processes.SIGNAL*. The guarded form is the most flexible of the three component forms that support concurrent operations, allowing construction of critical regions of arbitrary complexity.

The *concurrent* form may be derived from the *guarded* form by hiding and encapsulating the semaphore within the component. This is equivalent to a *monitor* module which enforces mutual exclusion (c.f. [23,24]).

1.3.2 Space

The space property describes whether the object size is fixed or, over its lifetime, varies the amount of memory used by the object.

Bounded   Denotes that an object's (maximum) size, once created, remains fixed.

Unbounded   Denotes that an object's size varies dynamically as items are inserted and removed.

Bounded components are by definition managed, since this may be accomplished by the compiler. Unbounded components may be managed or unmanaged, which leads to the next section on memory management and garbage collection.

1.3.3 Garbage Collection & Memory Management

An unbounded component may dynamically allocate and deallocate memory resources so the question becomes one of how memory management is handled for such objects. The root question is, What are the semantics of the component regarding release of previously allocated resources?

Unmanaged   The underlying runtime system and compiler provide automatic garbage collection.

Managed   The component itself provides garbage collection.

Controlled   The sequential component provides garbage collection, even for multiple tasks sharing the component.

Garbage collection crosses all component instances and tasks within a system. Modula-2 does not define garbage collection; since almost nothing is implicit in Modula-2.

The component in an *unmanaged* form never disposes of dynamically allocated objects and no mechanism is provided to release allocated resources associated with items stored within the component. Such a form must assure that space requirements for a component instance are not exceeded prior to completion of its task. The unmanaged form may be trivially derived from the managed form by removing all (direct and indirect) references to SYSTEM.DEALLOCATE (equivalent to Pascal's *Dispose*). The unmanaged form in a Modula-2 environment is of minimal utility and is not considered further in this series.

A *managed* form component releases any and all dynamically allocated resources associated with an item. This common situation in a Modula-2 program makes the component responsible for recovery of all heap space allocated. A module may use SYSTEM.DEALLOCATE to return recovered space to the underlying run-time system; or, alternately, the module may provide a local memory management scheme for the so-called free list.

The *controlled* form protects access to the free list of deallocated resources when operating with multiple tasks. Modula-2 lacks true concurrency so operation of the managed and controlled forms is similar. A more extensive discussion is found in Booch [2].

1.3.4 Iterators

The object may or may not export an operation that can be applied to an object to visit its parts, depending upon its design:

Non-iterator   No iterator operations are provided for this object.

Iterator   Iterator operations are provided for this object.

Practitioners will appreciate the ability to invoke an iterator; not providing the feature lessens the usefulness of the component. To derive the non-iterator form it is necessary merely to remove the Iterator routine(s) from the Definition and Implementation Modules for a given component. Therefore, the non-iterator forms will not be considered further.

1.3.5 Variations in Form

A software component may be classified according to the various combinations of the component's four properties and their associated attributes. The classification forms a hierarchy of possible attributes and forms. All component forms are possible, though some are not very useful. The Bounded Unmanaged form (as noted by Booch [2]) is one such instance, and thus is not covered, even though Modula-2 allows one to create such a form.

This classification covers a broad range of components but is not comprehensive, for two reasons:

- some structures and abstractions may have additional properties that introduce new component forms; and

- there is more than one way to implement a component form resulting from variations and trade-offs in algorithmic complexity, implementation difficulty, space usage, and execution speed. These trade-offs appear especially in the unbounded component forms.

Obviously, there are many ways to implement a data structure.

References

[1]   F. B. Bastani and S. S. Iyengar, "The Effect of Data Structures on the Logical Complexity of Programs," *Communications of the ACM*, Vol. 30(3), (Mar. 1987), pp. 250-259.

[2]   G. Booch, "Software Components With Ada Structures," *Tools, and Subsystems*, Benjamin/Cummings, Menlo Park, CA 1987.

[3]   M. H. Brown and R. Sedgewick, "Techniques for Algorithm Animation," *IEEE Software*, Vol. 2(1), (Jan. 1985), pp. 28-39.

[4]   J. Bruckner and J. Harp, "Implementing Opaque Types in Generic Data Structures in Modula-2," *Journal of Pascal, Ada, & Modula-2*, Vol. 6(4), (Jul./Aug. 1987), pp. 14-30.

[5]   J. Bruckner and J. Harp, "Macro Modules in Modula-2," *Journal of Pascal, Ada, & Modula-2*, Vol. 6(6), (Nov./Dec. 1987), pp. 5-10.

[6]   A. L. Crawford, "An Extension to Modula-2 For Generic Types," *Journal of Pascal, Ada, & Modula-2*, Vol. 6(6), (Nov./Dec. 1987), pp. 11-16.

[7]   G. Ford and R. S. Wiener, *Modula-2 A Software Development Approach*, John Wiley & Sons, New York, NY 1985 pp. 289-317.

[8]   J. Gougen, "Parameterized Programming," *IEEE Transactions on Software Engineering*, SE-10(5), (Sept. 1984), pg. 138.

[9]   K. J. Gough, "Writing Generic Utilities in Modula-2," *Journal of Pascal, Ada, & Modula-2*, Vol. 5(3), (May/Jun. 1986), pp. 53-62.

[10] C. A. R. Hoare, *Communicating Sequential Processes*, Prentice-Hall International, Englewood Cliffs, NJ 1985.

[11] E. Horowitz and J. B. Munson, "An Expansive View of Reusable Software," *IEEE Transactions on Software Engineering*, SE-10(5), (Sept. 1984), pp. 477-487.

[12] T. C. Jones, "Reusability in Programming: A Survey of the State of the Art," *IEEE Transactions on Software Engineering*, SE-10(5), (Sept. 1984), pp. 488-494.

[13] D. Knuth, *The Art of Computer Programming, Fundamental Algorithms*, Vol. 1, Ch. 2, Addison-Wesley, Reading, Mass., 1972.

[14] B. Liskov and J. Guttag, *Abstraction and Specification in Program Development*, The MIT Press and McGraw-Hill, Cambridge, MA 1986.

[15] H. Oktaba and R. Berber, "Crafting Reusable Software in Modula-2," *BYTE*, Vol. 12(10), (Sept. 1987), pp. 123-128.

[16] G. Pomberger, *Software Engineering and Modula-2*, Prentice-Hall International, Englewood Cliffs, NJ 1984.

[17] C. Reynolds, "On Implementing Generic Data Structures in Modula-2," *Journal of Pascal, Ada, & Modula-2*, Vol. 6(5), (Sept./Oct. 1987), pp. 26-38.

[18] R. F. Sincovec and R. S. Wiener, *Data Structures Using Modula-2*, John Wiley & Sons, New York, NY 1985.

[19] I. Sommerville, *Software Engineering*, Second Edition, Addison-Wesley, Reading, MA 1985.

[20] T. A. Standish, "An Essay on Software Reuse," *IEEE Transactions on Software Engineering*, SE-10(5), (Sept. 1984), pp. 494-497.

[21] *The American Heritage Dictionary of the English Language*, Houghton Mifflin Company, Boston, 1976.

[22] C. R. Vick and C. V. Ramamoorthy, eds., "Handbook of Software Engineering," Ch. 12, *Data Design*: Types, Structures, and Abstractions, Van Nostrand Reinhold, 1984.

[23] N. Wirth, *Programming in Modula-2*, 3rd. ed., Springer-Verlag, New York, NY 1985, pp. 128-135.

[24] N. Wirth, *Algorithms and Data Structures*, Prentice-Hall, Englewood Cliffs, NJ 1986, pp. 49-52.

2 Specification

An abstraction provides a conceptual entity, devoid of tangible substance, and so eliminates unnecessary complexity. Data structures are very tangible quantities. Abstract data structures are a class of objects and a set of operations applicable to an object of that class. Therefore, there must be a vehicle for describing the object and the behavior of the operations towards the object. A specification has the primary purpose of defining "the behavior of an abstraction" [10].

The remainder of this chapter details the content, format and notation of the specification documents.

2.1 Requirements for Specifications

The task of creating a specification document raise a fundamental question, What format shall this take? Informal, English prose documents are sources of ambiguity and error. On the other hand, highly formal, rigorous formats are difficult to write and understand by the uninitiated. This series uses a format that lies between the two extremes. Our method provides a complete, unambiguous specification, as formal and rigorous as possible, without being overly mathematical to reach the widest possible audience. The specification technique is readily learned and understood.

The specification document and format will be applicable to specification of abstract data types and associated operations.

The format, adapted from that developed by Guttag and Liskov [10] for the language CLU, consists of relatively few constructs. It rigorously defines the syntax and semantics of operations, and provides powerful facilities for defining abstract data types.

2.2   Specification of Abstractions

2.2.1   Procedure Abstractions

A procedure is a form of abstraction accepting a set of input arguments which it transforms into a set of output results. The transformation may modify one or more inputs, while either the input or output set may be empty. A procedure is a mapping in which the set of inputs form the *domain*, and the set of outputs the *range*. A procedure is *partial* when its behavior is defined for only those arguments in a subset of the domain. Arguments not members of this subset spawn *undefined* behavior (and possibly results). A *total* procedure has its behavior defined for all arguments in its domain.

2.2.2   Specifying Procedure Abstractions

Specification of a procedure requires a description of both its syntax and semantics. Syntax identifies the procedure by name — the name and type of each argument or result — and the order in which the arguments and results occur. Semantics delineates the procedure's meaning and behavior, together with any constraints on the arguments that may be necessary to ensure the specified behavior.

A template of the format used in procedure abstraction specifications follows:

\<Section#\>   \<procedure name\>   \<arguments and results\>

Requires	lists constraints that insure the defined behavior
Where	describes arguments of procedural parameters
Modifies	lists all modified input arguments
Effects	describes the procedure purpose and effects visible as normal behavior
Signals	identifies exception conditions and behavior under those conditions

2.2.2.1   Header Section

The first line, the header, identifies the beginning of a procedure specification with the section number, followed by the procedure name, and the list of arguments and results. Parameters are identified by special arrow symbols: an input argument (↓), modified input argument (↕), or result (↑), followed by the name and type.

2.2.2.2 Requires Section

The *requires* section describes constraints the routine imposes on its caller to ensure that the behavior will be as specified. Failure to do so results in undefined behavior. A requires section containing the key word **nothing** indicates a total procedure — one whose behavior is specified for all input values.

2.2.2.3 Where Section

The *where* section lists each procedure parameter to the routine together with the order and type of its arguments. This section may be omitted when a routine does not require procedure parameters.

2.2.2.4 Modifies Section

The *modifies* section lists the names of all inputs that may be modified by the routine. The key word **nothing** indicates that none of the input arguments are modified by the routine.

2.2.2.5 Effects Section

The *effects* section provides a brief description of the purpose or function of the routine and the behavior of the routine in the normal case (i.e., when no error conditions occur). The section defines output(s) produced by the routine and any modifications made to the inputs listed in the modifies clause. An argument followed by a single quote mark indicates its value on exit from the routine. Examples used to clarify the intended behavior are identified by the symbol 'e.g.,' or the word 'Example'.

2.2.2.6 Signals Section

The *signals* section identifies possible exception conditions. An exception is a condition that causes the routine to initiate an alternative behavior (to the normal behavior). It labels each exception with an identifying name, the key word **when** followed by the conditions which raise the exception, and the key word **ensuring** followed by the behavior and effects that result in each case. The key words **modifies nothing** indicate that the behavior of a routine in an exception condition does not modify any of its inputs.

2.2.3 Data Abstractions

2.2.3.1 Abstract Data Structures

Pomberger [12] defines an *abstract data structure* as "... a set of objects (its components) and a set of operations, which can be applied to the components or to the data structure as a whole."

Object in the definition refers to the entities named items in this book.

According to this definition, a module implementing an abstract data structure permits a single instance of an abstract object.

2.2.3.2 Abstract Data Types

Pomberger [12] adds to his definition of abstract data type: "An *abstract data type* defines a set of objects, which all have the same abstract data structure, by the operations applicable to them."

Thus, an Abstract Data Type is an extension of the Abstract Data Structure. In this instance, however, in addition to employing the principle of *information hiding* (also called data hiding), Modula-2 provides client modules with facilities for creating new abstract variables. Abstract variables of the data type are independent of each other. In other words, the state of an abstract data type variable is unaffected by the state of, or operations applied to, any other abstract data type variable. This is similar to declarations of program variables from Modula-2's primitive data types. If one declares two variables, X and Y, both of type CHAR, for example, the assignment statement X := "a"; will not effect the value (or state) of the variable Y.

(Of course, there may be *indirect* implementation effects; such as, an operation on ADT variable, α, consuming enough memory resources causing operations on another ADT variable, β, to fail due to lack of memory. In such a situation, the state of β does not change due to the failure.)

Abstract Data Structures differ from *Abstract Data Types* in that a module implementing an Abstract Data Structure provides only *one* data structure (and therefore one variable — possibly hidden in the implementation module), while a module providing an Abstract Data Type permits creating *many* data structures of the data type along with a set of operations that may be applied to variables of that type. (An Abstract Data Type is similar to the *class* concept of languages such as SIMULA, SmallTalk, and Object Pascal, for those familiar with these languages. The difference here is that Modula-2 Abstract Data Types do not directly support the concept of *inheritance*.)

2.2.4 Specifying Data Abstractions

The two sections below define and describe data abstractions.

Overview

The Overview section describes the data type and objects of that type. It provides a model of the data type detailing static relationships between dependent data associated with an object of the type. The term *attribute* in this series refers to these data items, recording the state of an object, and provides an essential aspect of the data type abstraction.

Operations

The Operations section spells out each operation that may be applied to an object of the data type and the operation's behavior. The specification format is described above for procedural abstractions. This accomplishes the same thing as a Modula-2 Definition Module.

2.2.5 Special Symbols

Several symbols simplify descriptions in the specifications and program documentation. Some are unique but most are taken from the realm of mathematics.

↓ Input parameter	↑ Output parameter	↕ input-output parameter
¬ NOT	& AND	I OR
≠ not equal	≤ less than or equal to	≥ greater than or equal to
∈ is an element of	∉ is not an element of	∅ the empty set
∀ for all	∃ there exists	≡ If and only if
↯ Exception		

2.3 Abstract Data Type Operations

Operations associated with an abstract data type can be classified according to their effect on the internal state of the object. Figure 2.1 shows a hierarchical taxonomy for abstract data type operations. The leaves of the tree are standard operations required for a generalized implementation. Authors of literature on abstraction and abstract data types use a variety of terms to refer to these operations and minor variations in the classification presented here may occur.

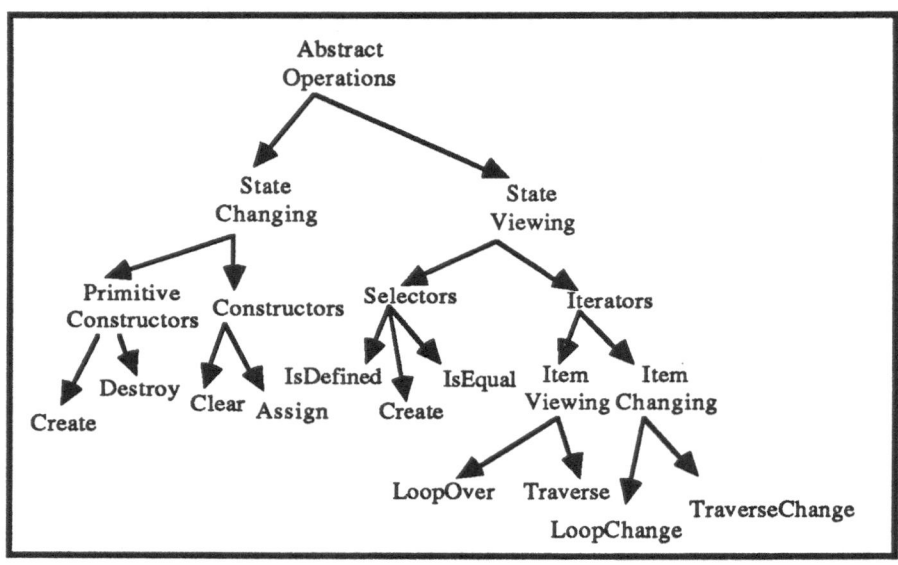

FIGURE 2.1 Hierarchy of Abstract Operations

Primitive Constructors   create new objects and destroy old objects.

Constructors   modify objects by adding or removing items, or create objects from other objects.

Selectors   examine objects, returning items (without changing state) or information on the state of an object.

Iterators   provide looping facilities over some or all the items of an object.

2.3.1   Standard Specifications of Primitive Constructors

2.3.1.1   Create ()↑TheObject

Requires	**nothing**
Modifies	**nothing**
Effects	Attempts to create a new abstract data type object.
Signals	Overflow **when** unable to create new object **ensuring modifies nothing** and returning the null object.

2.3.1.2   Destroy (↕TheObject)

Requires	**nothing**
Modifies	**at most** TheObject
Effects	Removes all items from TheObject, if any, and deallocates TheObject. The Destroy operation is the inverse of Create. Once destroyed, TheObject may only be used as an input parameter to the IsDefined operation, or the result parameter to another Create operation.
Signals	Undefined **when** a given object has not been created, or has been destroyed **ensuring modifies nothing**

2.3.2   Standard Specifications of Constructors

2.3.2.1   Clear (↕TheObject)

Requires	**nothing**
Modifies	**at most** TheObject
Effects	Removes any items from TheObject making TheObject empty.
Signals	Undefined **when** ¬IsDefined(TheObject) **ensuring modifies nothing**

2.3.2.2   Assign (↓SourceObject ↕DestinationObject)

Requires	**nothing**
Modifies	**at most** DestinationObject
Effects	Attempts to create to duplicate of the SourceObject in the DestinationObject. If the destination object if not defined on entry to the

routine, it is created using the attributes of the source object. If the destination object is defined, it is cleared prior to the assignment.

Signals   Overflow **when** unable to complete the assignment of the source to the destination object **ensuring modifies at most** DestinationObject

Signals   Undefined **when** ¬IsDefined(SourceObject) **ensuring modifies nothing**

2.3.3 Standard Specifications of Selectors

2.3.3.1 IsDefined (↓TheObject)

Requires   **nothing**

Modifies   **nothing**

Effects   Returns the logical value of True only if TheObject has been properly created and has not yet been destroyed.

Signals   **nothing**

2.3.3.2 IsEmpty (↓TheObject) ↑Boolean

Requires   **nothing**

Modifies   **nothing**

Effects   Returns the logical value of True only if TheObject contains no items.

Signals   Undefined **when** ¬IsDefined(TheObject) **ensuring** returns True

2.3.3.3 SizeOf (↓TheObject) ↑Cardinal

Requires   **nothing**

Modifies   **nothing**

Effects   Returns the current maximum size for a given bounded object.

Signals   Undefined **when** ¬IsDefined(TheObject) **ensuring** returns zero (0).

2.3.3.4   IsEqual (↓LeftObject ↓RightObject) ↑Boolean

Requires	**nothing**
Modifies	**nothing**
Effects	Returns the logical value of True only if LeftObject and RightObject contain the same items and states.
Signals	Undefined **when** ¬IsDefined(LeftObject)	¬IsDefined(RightObject) **ensuring** returns False.

2.3.4   Standard Specifications of Iterators

2.3.4.1   LoopOver (↓TheObject ↓LoopAccessProcedure)

Requires	LoopAccessProcedure ≠ NIL
Where	LoopAccessProcedure = **procedure** (↓Item) ↑Continue [Boolean]
Modifies	**nothing**
Effects	Passes each item of TheObject to a given Loop Access Procedure in turn. The exact order depends on the abstraction. An item's value may not be changed during the traversal, including calling operations that add (remove) items to (from) TheObject, which should not be invoked. The Loop Access Procedure is allowed control over the continuation of the iteration. The iteration may be terminated before all items have been processed by returning a function result of False. A result of True causes the iteration to continue to the next item, if any.
Signals	Undefined **when** ¬IsDefined(TheObject) **ensuring modifies nothing**

2.3.4.2   LoopChange (↓TheObject ↓LoopChangeProcedure)

Requires	LoopChangeProcedure ≠ NIL
Where	LoopChangeProcedure = **procedure** (↕Item) ↑Continue [Boolean]
Modifies	**at most** items contained in TheObject
Effects	Passes each item of TheObject to a given Loop Change Procedure in turn. The exact order depends on the abstraction. An item's value may be changed during traversal but other operations adding items to or removing items from TheObject should not be invoked. The Loop Change Procedure is allowed control over the

continuation of the iteration. The iteration may terminate before all items have been processed by returning a function result of False; while a result of True causes the iteration to continue to the next item, if any.

Signals   Undefined **when** ¬IsDefined(TheObject) **ensuring modifies nothing**

2.3.4.3   Traverse (↓TheObject ↓AccessProcedure)

Requires   AccessProcedure ≠ NIL

Where   AccessProcedure = **procedure** (↓Item)

Modifies   **nothing**

Effects   Passes every item of TheObject in turn to a given Access Procedure. The exact order depends on the abstraction. An item's value may not be changed during the traversal, including calling operations that add (remove) items to (from) TheObject which should not be invoked.

Signals   Undefined **when** ¬IsDefined(TheObject) **ensuring modifies nothing**

2.3.4.4   TraverseChange (↓TheObject ↓ChangeProcedure)

Requires   ChangeProcedure ≠ NIL

Where   ChangeProcedure = **procedure** (↕Item)

Modifies   **at most** items contained in TheObject

Effects   Every item of TheObject is passed to a given Change Procedure in turn. The exact order depends on the abstraction. An item's value may be changed during traversal but operations should not be invoked that add items to or remove operations from TheObject.

Signals   Undefined **when** ¬IsDefined(TheObject) **ensuring modifies nothing**

Further Reading

The following works examine the subject of software requirements:

B. Liskov and J. Guttag, *Abstraction and Specification in Program Development*, The MIT Press, Cambridge, MA 1986.

IEEE *Guide to Software Requirements Specifications*, ANSI/IEEE Std 830-1984

References

[1]   F.L. Bauer (ed.), *Software Engineering An Advanced Course*, Springer-Verlag, Berlin, Germany 1975.

[2]   D.M. Berry, "Towards a Formal Basis for the Formal Development Method and the Ina Jo Specification Language." *IEEE Transactions on Software Engineering*, Vol. SE-13(2), (Feb. 1987) pp. 184-201.

[3]   G. Booch, "Object-Oriented Development." *IEEE Transactions on Software Engineering*, Vol. SE-12(2), (Feb. 1986) pp. 211-221.

[4]   D.N. Card, F.E. McGarry, and G.T. Page, "Evaluating Software Engineering Technologies." *IEEE Transactions on Software Engineering*, Vol. SE-13(7), (Jul. 1987) pp. 845-851.

[5]   P. Freeman, "A Conceptual Analysis of the Draco Approach to Constructing Software Systems." *IEEE Transactions on Software Engineering*, Vol. SE-13(7), (Jul. 1987) pp. 830-844.

[6]   J.D. Gannon, R.G. Hamlet, and H.D. Mills, "Theory of Modules." *IEEE Transactions on Software Engineering*, Vol. SE-13(7), (Jul. 1987) pp. 820-829.

[7]   N. Gehani and A.D. McGettrick, *Software Specification Techniques*, Addison-Wesley, Reading, MA 1986.

[8]   A.N. Habermann and D. Notkin, "Gandalf: Software Development Environments." *IEEE Transactions on Software Engineering*, Vol. SE-12(12), (Dec. 1986) pp. 1117-1127.

[9]   E. Horowitz and R.C. Williamson, SODOS: "A Software Documentation Environment - Its Use." *IEEE Transactions on Software Engineering*, Vol. SE-12(11), (Nov. 1986) pp. 1076-1087.

[10] B. Liskov and J. Guttag, *Abstraction and Specification in Program Development*, The MIT Press, Cambridge, MA 1986.

[11] K. Matsumura, H. Mizutani, and M. Arai, "An Application of Structural Modeling to Software Requirements and Design." *IEEE Transactions on Software Engineering*, Vol. SE-13(4), (Apr. 1987) pp. 461-471.

[12] G. Pomberger, *Software Engineering and Modula-2*, Prentice-Hall International, New York, NY 1984.

[13] R.S. Pressman, *Software Engineering: A Practitioner's Approach*, McGraw-Hill, New York, NY 1982.

[14] V. Rajlich, "Refinement Methodology for Ada." *IEEE Transactions on Software Engineering*, Vol. SE-13(4), (Apr. 1987) pp. 472-478.

[15] R.S. Wiener and R. Sincovec, *Software Engineering with Modula-2 and Ada*, John Wiley & Sons, New York, NY 1984.

3 Module Guide

3.1 Purpose

The module guide is a road map for someone travelling the module roadways to locate the relevant module(s). For anyone taking a 'Sunday drive' among the modules, the document acts as a tour guide — pointing out interesting features dotting the modular landscape.

The guide contains a description of each module, identifying its role within the software and its 'secrets.' The guide defines services provided by a module and describes how other modules make use of these services. A module's secrets consist of a set of assumptions that cannot be made by client modules (and programmers) using the module. Clients may use and depend upon only those facts about the module provided through its interface.

This guide is divided into three major sections:

Section One   All modules related to error or exception handling.

Section Two   All general support modules used by the abstract data structure modules.

Section Three   Abstract data structure modules grouped by data structure, (e.g., Stack, Lists, etc.).

Modules are ordered alphabetically by name within each section. Module Import Graph diagrams (see Appendix E) support the Module Guide. These reveal the hierarchical structure of the modules through the 'imports' relation.

3.2 Exception Handling Modules

3.2.1 Error Handling

The Error Handling module defines data types and routines for signaling occurrence of an error condition and invoking an error handler in response to the error. The module provides for indicating three pieces of information:

1. the module raising the exception,
2. the routine raising the exception, and
3. the exception itself.

The exported type defines the parameter requirements of the general error handler routine.

The Raise routine provides for signaling an error and invocation of an error handler. Two error handlers are used by other modules:

1. a null handler that does nothing, and
2. a handler that reports the exception to the user's terminal display and then exits the program.

3.3   Generic Item Support Modules

3.3.1 Items

The Items module exports an abstraction of a data item along with procedure types describing the standard operations of:

- assignment (:=),
- equality comparison (=),
- establishing the ordering relation between two abstract items,
- logical relational expressions between two abstract items (e.g., x < y), and
- a routine to dispose of the item (for dynamically allocated items).

The Items module also provides several useful constants for representing such frequently needed values as:

- a default value for a *Null*, or empty, data item;
- a *do nothing* dynamic memory deallocation routine;
- a procedure constant for the Modula-2 assignment operator; and
- a procedure constant for the Modula-2 equality comparison operator.

The Items module provides the three procedure constants above for use as parameters to the Create operation for objects comprised of statically allocated data of the Type Manager module items (e.g., CHARs, INTEGERs, etc.).

The secret of the Items module is the internal representation of the Item abstraction (as an ADDRESS).

3.3.2 Item Operations

The ItemOperations module provides predefined assignment, equality testing, and comparison routines for the standard Modula-2 data types CHAR, INTEGER, CARDINAL, LONGINT, LONGCARD, and REAL. The ItemOperations routines are provided as a convenience for using the standard types as items in a generic abstract data type module.

The secret of the module involves the details of translating an abstract Item to one of the standard types and the Modula-2 operations for assignment and comparison.

3.3.3 Relations

Provides a common definition of two enumerations, Relation and RelOps, for ordering (respectively) relations (<, =, >) and standard relational operators (<, ≤, =, ≠, ≥, >). Because of the remote possibility of a failure resulting from a (user defined) comparison operation, each enumeration type has, as its last value, a constant representing such a condition. A failure could occur when a comparison routine's parameters were, for some reason, determined to be incomparable or unordered. The extension of a failure value is also conceivably compatible with the IEEE Standard for Binary Floating-Point Arithmetic (ANSI/IEEE Std 754-1985).

Routines are exported supporting conversion between the two enumeration types using a simple array mapping. Facilities are provided for determining the NOT of a relational operator and for determining the logical truth of other relational operators implied by a given relation being true.

The secrets of this module are mappings between Relations to RelOps, RelOps to the corresponding ¬RelOps, and RelOps to implied RelOps.

3.3.4 Type Manager

The TypeManager module provides facilities for associating assignment, comparison and disposal of generic items with a unique identifier. An object being created is given this identifier so that type-checking may be carried out on operations involving multiple generic objects. The module also ensures that procedure parameters for assignment and disposal operations are non-NIL, since a NIL procedure cannot be called.

3.4 Bags (Disk Only)

The various Bag modules are contained on the souce disk for Volume 1.

3.4.1 Bag Enumerations

The Bag Enumerations module does not hide anything since only enumeration types are exported. The module identifies operations relevant to bag objects and the exception conditions that may occur as a result of a bag operation.

The name of this module is abbreviated *BagEnum.*

3.4.2 Bag-Sequential Bounded Managed Iterator

This module provides an implementation of the bag abstraction. As the title indicates, the module may be used only in a non-tasking environment. Bags are bound to the specific size (i.e., maximum number of items) provided by the client when a bag is created.

The module manages bag objects in two ways:

1. by returning dynamically allocated space for a bounded bag to the system heap (when an object is destroyed), and
2. by detecting attempts to use a bag object that the Create operation has not defined.

The Bag-Sequential Bounded Managed Iterator module provides iterator operations that permit accessing the value of an item in the bag. Items of the bag are not constrained by an ordering relation; in other words, the items are unordered and operations on items such as < or > are meaningless.

The secrets of this module are:

- the internal structure used to implement a bounded bag,
- the internal representation invariants and how these are enforced,
- the algorithms used to implement bounded bag operations,
- how to detect undefined bag objects, and
- how to raise bag exceptions.

The name of this module is abbreviated as *BagSBMI.*

3.4.3 Bag-Sequential Unbounded Managed Iterator

This module provides an implementation of the bag abstraction. As the title indicates, the module may only be used in a non-tasking environment. Bags are not bound to a specific size (i.e., maximum number of items) when a bag is created. The module manages bag objects in two ways:

1. by returning dynamically allocated space for items of an unbounded bag (when the last of a particular item is removed from the bag) and recovering dynamically allocated space for the unbounded bag object to the system heap (when an object or item is destroyed), and
2. by detecting attempts to use a bag object not defined through the Create operation.

The Bag-Sequential Unbounded Managed Iterator module provides iterator operations that permit accessing the value of an item in the bag. Items of the bag are not constrained by an ordering relation; in other words, the items are unordered and operations on items such as < or > are meaningless.

The secrets of this module are:

- the internal structure used to implement an unbounded bag,
- the internal representation invariants and how these are enforced,
- the algorithms used to implement unbounded bag operations,
- how to detect undefined bag objects, and
- how to raise bag exceptions.

The name of this module is abbreviated as *BagSUMI*.

3.4.4 Bag-Discrete Sequential Bounded Managed Iterator

This module provides an implementation of the bag abstraction. As the title indicates, the module may only be used in a non-tasking environment, and only with items with a discrete range of values (e.g., characters, cardinal numbers, enumerations, etc.). Bags are bound to the specific size and range provided by the client when a bag is created. Bag objects are managed in two ways:

1. by returning dynamically allocated space for a bounded bag to the system heap (when a bag object is destroyed), and
2. by detecting attempts to use a bag object not defined through the Create operation.

The Bag-Discrete Sequential Bounded Managed Iterator module provides iterator operations that permit accessing the value of an item in the bag. By definition, a discrete bag is also an ordered bag.

The secrets of this module are:

- the internal structure used to implement a discrete bounded bag,
- the internal representation invariants and how these are enforced,
- the algorithms used to implement discrete bag operations,
- how to detect undefined bag objects, and
- how to raise bag exceptions.

The name of this module is abbreviated as *BagDSBMI*. There may be specific modules for characters, integers, etc.

3.5 Sets

3.5.1 Set Enumerations

This module does not hide anything since only enumeration types are exported. Set Enumerations identifies the operations relevant to set objects and the exception conditions that may occur as a result of a set operation. The module name, abbreviated *SetEnum*, is found in Section 12.1.

3.5.2 Set-Sequential Bounded Managed Iterator

This module provides an implementation of the set abstraction. As the title indicates, the module may only be used in a non-tasking environment. Sets are bound to the specific size (i.e., maximum number of items) provided by the client when a bag is created.

Set objects are managed in two ways:

1. by returning dynamically allocated space for a bounded set to the system heap (when a set object is destroyed), and
2. by detecting attempts to use a set object not defined by the Create operation.

The Set-Sequential Bounded Managed Iterator module provides iterator operations that permit accessing the value of an item in the set. Items of the set are not constrained by an ordering relation; in other words, the items are unordered and operations on items such as < or > are meaningless.

The secrets of this module are:

- the internal structure used to implement a bounded set,
- the internal representation invariants and how these are enforced,
- the algorithms used to implement bounded set operations,
- how to detect undefined set objects, and
- how to raise set exceptions.

The name of this module is abbreviated as *SetSBMI*. Definition and implementation modules for this abstraction form are found in Chapter 12.

3.5.3 Set-Sequential Unbounded Managed Iterator

This module provides an implementation of the set abstraction. As the title indicates, the module may only be used in a non-tasking environment. Sets are not bound to a specific size (i.e., maximum number of items) when a set is created. Set objects are managed in two ways:

1. by returning dynamically allocated space for the items of an unbounded set (when an item is removed from the set) and recovering dynamically allocated space for the unbounded set object to the system heap (when an object is destroyed), and
2. by detecting attempts to use a set object not defined through the *Create* operation.

The Set-Sequential Unbounded Managed Iterator module provides iterator operations that permit accessing the value of an item in the set. Items of the set are not constrained by an ordering relation; in other words, the items are unordered and operations on items such as < or > are meaningless.

The secrets of this module are:

- the internal structure used to implement an unbounded set,
- the internal representation invariants and how these are enforced,
- the algorithms used to implement unbounded set operations,
- how to detect undefined objects, and
- how to raise set exceptions.

The name of this module is abbreviated *SetSUMI* and is the topic of Chapter 13.

3.5.4 Set-Discrete Sequential Bounded Managed Iterator

This module provides an implementation of the set abstraction. As the title indicates, the module may only be used in a non-tasking environment, and only with items with a discrete range of values (e.g., characters, cardinal numbers, enumerations, etc.). Sets are bound to the specific size and range provided by the client when a set is created. Set objects are managed in two ways:

1. by returning dynamically allocated space for a bounded set to the system heap (when an object is destroyed), and
2. by detecting attempts to use a set object not defined through the Create operation.

The Set-Discrete Sequential Bounded Managed Iterator module provides iterator operations that permit accessing the value of an item in the set. By definition, a discrete set is also an ordered set.

The secrets of this module are:

- the internal structure used to implement a discrete bounded set,
- the internal representation invariants and how these are enforced,
- the algorithms used to implement discrete set operations,
- how to detect undefined set objects,
- how to raise set exceptions.

The name of this module is abbreviated as *SetDSBMI*. There may be specific modules for characters, integers, etc. A sample definition and implementation module for character data types is discussed in Chapter 14.

3.6 Stacks

3.6.1 Stack Enumerations

This module does not hide anything since only enumeration types are exported. The operations relevant to stack objects and the exception conditions that may occur as a result of a stack operation are identified. The name of this module is abbreviated *StackEnum*. Its definition is found in Chapter 6.

3.6.2 Stack-Sequential Bounded Managed Iterator

This module provides an implementation of the stack abstraction. As the title indicates, the module may only be used in a non-tasking environment. Stacks are bound to the specific size provided by the client when a stack is created. Stack objects are managed in two ways:

1. by returning dynamically allocated space for a bounded stack to the system heap (when an object is destroyed), and
2. by detecting attempts to use a stack object not defined through the Create operation.

The Stack-Sequential Bounded Managed Iterator module provides iterator operations that permit changing the value of an item on the stack at other than the top.

The secrets of this module are:

- the internal structure used to implement a bounded stack,
- the internal representation invariants and how these are enforced,
- the algorithms used to implement bounded stack operations,
- how to detect undefined stack objects, and
- how to raise stack exceptions.

The name of this module, abbreviated as *StackSBMI*, is the topic of Chapter 6.

3.6.3 Stack-Sequential Unbounded Managed Iterator

This module provides an implementation of the stack abstraction. As the title indicates, the module may only be used in a non-tasking environment. Stacks are unbounded and therefore may grow to any size limited only by the amount of memory available. Stack objects are managed in two ways:

1. by returning dynamically allocated space to a locally maintained free list of nodes, and
2. by detecting attempts to use a stack object not defined through the Create operation.

The Stack-Sequential Unbounded Managed Iterator module provides iterator operations that permit changing the value of an item on the stack at other than the top.

The secrets of this module are:

- the internal structure used to implement an unbounded stack,
- the internal representation invariants and how these are enforced,
- the algorithms used to implement unbounded stack operations,
- how to detect undefined stack objects,
- how to raise stack exceptions, and
- how to manage the list of freed stack nodes.

The name of this module is abbreviated as StackSUMI. Chapter 7 provides details of its definition and implementation form.

3.7 Strings

3.7.1 String Enumerations

This module does not hide anything since only enumeration types are exported. The operations relevant to string objects and the exception conditions that may occur as a result of a string operation are identified. *StringEnum* is the abbreviated name for this module, as found in Chapter 9.

3.7.2 String-Sequential Bounded Managed Iterator

This module provides an implementation of the string abstraction. As the title indicates, the module may only be used in a non-tasking environment. Strings are bound to the specific maximum size provided by the client when a string is created. String objects are managed in two ways:

1. by returning dynamically allocated space for a bounded string to the system heap (when an object is destroyed), and
2. by detecting attempts to use a string object not defined through the Create operation.

The String-Sequential Bounded Managed Iterator module provides iterator operations that permit changing the value of an item in the string.

The secrets of this module are:

- the internal structure used to implement a bounded string,
- the internal representation invariants and how these are enforced,
- the algorithms used to implement bounded string operations, and
- how to detect undefined string objects, and
- how to raise string exceptions.

The name of this module is abbreviated as *StringSBMI*. Chapter 9 comprises the necessary definition and implementation modules.

3.7.3 String-Sequential Unbounded Managed Iterator

This module provides an implementation of the string abstraction. As the title indicates, the module may only be used in a non-tasking environment. Strings are unbounded and therefore may grow to any size limited only by the amount of memory available. String objects are managed in two ways:

1. by returning dynamically allocated space to a locally maintained free list of strings, and
2. by detecting attempts to use a string object not defined through the Create operation.

The String-Sequential Unbounded Managed Iterator module provides iterator operations that permit changing the value of a string item.

The secrets of this module are:

- the internal structure used to implement an unbounded string,
- the internal representation invariants and how these are enforced,
- the algorithms used to implement unbounded string operations,
- how to detect undefined string objects,
- how to raise string exceptions, and
- how to manage the list of freed strings.

The name of this module is abbreviated as *StringSUMI*. Definition and implementation modules are found in Chapter 10.

3.8 Module Names

The method used to form module names is summarized below, in EBNF-like format.

ModuleName	ComponentName + (ComponentSpecificFormCode) + ConcurrencyForm + SpaceForm + GarbageCollectionForm + IteratorForm + ModuleSuffix.
ConcurrencyForm	[Sequential I Guarded I Concurrent I Multiple].
SpaceForm	[Bounded I Unbounded] .
GarbageCollection Form	[Managed I Unmanaged I Controlled].
IteratorForm	[Noniterator I Iterator].
ModuleSuffix	[DefinitionSuffix I ImplementationSuffix I ProgramSuffix].
DefinitionSuffix	".DEF."
Implementation Suffix	".IMP."
ProgramSuffix	".MOD."

Concurrency Forms	**Space Forms**
Sequential = *S* Guarded = *G* Concurrent = *C* Multiple = *M*	Bounded = *B* Unbounded = *U*
Iterator Forms	**Garbage Collection Forms**
Noniterator = *N* Iterator = *I*	Managed = *M* Unmanaged = *U* Controlled = *C*

For example: Stack Module-Sequential, Bounded, Managed, Iterator -> StackSBMI.

References

[1] D.L. Parnas and K.H. Britton, *A-7E Software Module Guide* (NRL Memorandum Report 4702), Naval Research Laboratory, Washington D.C., 1981.

[2] D.L. Parnas, *On the Criteria To Be Used in Decomposing Systems into Modules, in Tutorial on Software Design Techniques Fourth Edition* (P. Freeman and A.I. Wasserman, eds.), IEEE Computer Society Press, Silver Spring, MD, 1983, pp. 304-309. (Reprinted from Communications of the ACM, December 1972, pp. 1053-1058).

[3] D.L. Parnas, *Designing Software for Ease of Extension and Contraction, in Tutorial on Software Design Techniques Fourth Edition* (P. Freeman and A.I. Wasserman, eds.), IEEE Computer Society Press, Silver Spring, MD, 1983, pp. 310-320. (Reprinted from IEEE Transactions on Software Engineering, Vol. SE-5, No. 2, March 1979, pp. 128-138).

[4] R.H. Wallace, J.E. Stockenberg and R.N. Charette, *A Unified Methodology for Developing Systems*, Intertext Publications, Inc., New York, NY, 1987.

4 Generic Items

This chapter considers more deeply the individual module specifics presented in overview by the Module Guide in the previous chapter.

Chapter One, in presenting reusable software components and data abstraction, couched the definition of a generic item in abstract terms. It is time to demonstrate concretely the realization of an abstract idea within the context of real data structures.

The chapter adopts a bottom-up approach investigating items — entities used in comprising objects. Section 4.1 first investigates items at the language level. Then Section 4.2 presents the specification for a generic item; followed in Section 4.3 by modules that implement the ideas discussed in the first two sections.

4.1 Items

An abstract data type will potentially deal with a great variety of data. Each instance of the data type (object) may be bound to a different base type — for example, a Stack of INTEGERs, or a Set of CHARs. Modula-2 permits the programmer to create new data types from existing, elementary data types; the number of base types is (potentially) infinite. This variety may appear to present a problem when attempting a generic representation of all these types. But it is possible to reduce all these types to a relatively small number of categories.

4.1.1 Kinds of Items

Modula-2 classifies data types according to the data type construction facilities of the language. The taxonomy has three elements:

Primitive   These are the elementary data types of the language, CHARs, INTEGERs, etc. Items described by primitive data types are usually created at compile-time by means of variable declarations.

Structured   Data types are those formed using the data type composition operators, RECORD and ARRAY.

Dynamic   These are data types which reference other structures, e.g., the POINTER and ADDRESS types.

4.1.2 Static vs. Dynamic Items

Another classification for items considers how and when items are created and destroyed. The Modula-2 compiler handles storage requirements for a *static* item when the variable is declared. The scoping rules of Modula-2 manage access to such items. Programmers explicitly handle storage requirements for *dynamic* items through calls to SYSTEM.ALLOCATE and SYSTEM.DEALLOCATE.

The semantics of operations applicable to an item should remain the same regardless of whether the item is static or dynamic. The semantics of assignment, equality and comparison in Modula-2 differ between static and dynamic items, however. Static items require direct manipulation (or accessing) of the item's *value*, whereas only *pointers* to a dynamic item's value may be manipulated.

The difference between the two kinds of items in Modula-2 is the primary source of the "dangling pointer" insecurity problem and is the main reason why beginning programmers have such difficulty when first encountering pointers. An example will clarify this discussion.

The component items of two generic stacks, which we shall call S and T, are pointers to (dynamically allocated) objects of the same base type. An assignment operation could have one of two possible meanings:

1. Duplicate the pointer S into T, this is the same as the Modula-2 assignment statement, T := S; or
2. Create a copy of the stack S and store the reference to this copy in the stack T.

In the first case, both S and T *share* a common, associated underlying structure: actions changing the stack S implicitly change the stack T! The second instance avoids such structural sharing and either object can be safely manipulated without affecting the other. A similar situation occurs with individual data items created dynamically.

4.1.3 Operations on Items

Modula-2 requires certain elementary operations on generic items regardless of the implementation technique selected. Typically, these operations are the same as those defined for the primitive data types.

Access   ↓Item — Allows the value of an item to be referenced.

Assignment   ↓Item ↑Item — Enforces equality between two items.

Equality   ↓Item ↓Item ↑Boolean — Tests for equality between two items.

Comparison   ↓Item ↓Item ↑OrderingRelation — Evaluates the ordering rela-
                  tion between two items. The OrderingRelation consists of the re-
                  lational operators of the language (<, ≤, =, ≥, >, ≠). The subset
                  (<, =, >) may suffice since the other relations may be derived
                  from these three.

Creation   ↑Item — Brings a new item into existence. Items may be created
                  at either compile-time (on the stack) or run-time (on the heap).
                  A newly created item does not have a value until it becomes the
                  target of an assignment operation. The item's value is said to be
                  Undefined until the moment of the first assignment.

Disposal   ↕Item — Causes an item, already in existence, to cease to exist.
                  All attempts to operate on an item after it has ceased to exist are
                  illegal. The compiler will ensure the validity of compile-time
                  items by the scoping rules of Modula-2. The validity of opera-
                  tions on items created at run-time is the responsibility of the
                  programmer.

4.1.4 Generic Items

When creating reusable software components it is desirable to separate the data
abstraction from the actual data values managed by that abstraction. For example, the abstraction of a stack defines the same operations regardless of whether
data type(s) manipulated by the stack are of the primitive data types of the language (characters, integers, etc.) or are themselves more complex structures.
Building components in this manner can simplify the implementation. Several
approaches can achieve this goal in Modula-2, each having unique advantages and
disadvantages regarding simplicity, efficiency, and security. We will not argue
the merits and demerits of the various approaches, but will present one that suits
our needs. For other proposed solutions refer to references [2-3, 6-11].

This series treats Items as an Abstract Data Type using facilities provided by
opaque types. This extends the ideas presented by Gough in [8], though here we
have gathered together the operations related to generic items into a closely knit
group of modules.

The advantages and disadvantages of this approach are summarized below:

+ Relatively strong type checking, since user must explicitly perform type
   transfer.

+ Fully generic, since the item type can be anything.
+ Item operations are encapsulated, separated from other ADT structures.
- The user must make an effort to provide routines to implement type transfer and possibly type conversion.
- Some loss of efficiency since procedures may be necessary to implement elementary operations (:=, =, relational operators).
- Actual items must be compatible with SYSTEM.ADDRESS. Because of this restriction, the SIZE of the actual item must be less than or equal to SIZE(SYSTEM.ADDRESS). Record and array structures will need to be passed by address (using the ADR function), or allocated to the heap and passed by a pointer to the structure.

4.1.5 Defining Generic Items

Depending on the item category, the following operations must be provided to a module using generic items:

Primitive Items   Standard Modula-2 assignment and relational operators Assignment and Equality (= and ≠) are implemented. The client module must implement any comparison operations needed since the relational operators < and > are not supported for opaque types. Do not attempt dynamic disposal of a statically allocated primitive item. Depending on security built into the Modula-2 storage management module(s), results could range from no observable effect to complete system breakdown.

Structured Items   The client module must provide Assignment and Comparison operations. The Disposal operation is not required unless the structure is also dynamically allocated.

Dynamic Items   All operations must be provided by the client module.

4.2 Generic Item Specifications

4.2.1 Relations

The Relations module provides a central repository defining the standard relational operators and their common operations. The basic relations and their associated symbols are: less than (<), equal to (=), and greater than (>). In addition to these, the relational operators also include the following symbols: less than or equal to (≤), not equal to (≠), greater than or equal to (≥), and unordered (no symbol). Two enumerations, *Relation* and *RelOp*, define each group of symbols.

4.2.1.1 RelToRelOp (↓Relation) ↑RelOp

Requires	**nothing**
Modifies	**nothing**

Effects Maps a given Relation to the corresponding RelOp. Specifically:

Relation	*RelOp*
less	lt
equal	eq
greater	gt
incomparable	unordered

Signals **nothing**

4.2.1.2 RelOpToRel (↓RelOp) ↑Relation

Requires	**nothing**
Modifies	**nothing**

Effects Maps the given RelOp to the corresponding Relation, if any. Specifically:

RelOp	*Relation*
lt	less
le	incomparable
eq	equal
ne	incomparable
gt	greater
ge	incomparable
unordered	incomparable

Signals **nothing**

4.2.1.3 NotRelOpOf (↓RelOp) ↑RelOp

Requires	**nothing**
Modifies	**nothing**

Effects Maps the given RelOp to the corresponding ¬RelOp. Specifically:

RelOp	*¬RelOp*
lt	ge
le	gt
eq	ne
ne	eq
gt	le
ge	lt
incomparable	incomparable

Signals **nothing**

4.2.1.4   ImpliesB   (↓RelOp ↓RelOp) ↑BOOLEAN

Requires	**nothing**
Modifies	**nothing**
Effects	Returns the logical value True if the first RelOp when True implies that the second RelOp would also be True. For example, given two (compatible) variables, x and y, of a base type having an ordering relation between the values of that type:

when x < y is True, x ≤ y would also be True, while x = y would be False.

when x = y is True, both ≤ and ≥ would also be True between x and y.

RelOp Index	*Set of Relations Mapping*
≤	{≤, <, =}
<	{≤, <, ≠}
=	{≤, =, ≥}
≠	{<, ≠, >}
>	{≠, >, ≥}
≥	{=, >, ≥}
?	{}

Signals	**nothing**

4.2.2   Items

A module is required to abstractly define generic items and to provide procedure templates for the allowable operations. This module relegates to the client module the creation of items and associating the declaration of an item with a value.

4.2.2.1   Assignment   (↓Item) ↑Item

Requires	**nothing**
Modifies	**nothing**
Effects	Returns a copy of the source item in the target item. Assignment enforces equality between items.
Signals	**nothing**

4.2.2.2   Equality   (↓Item ↓Item) ↑BOOLEAN

Requires	**nothing**
Modifies	**nothing**

Effects   Returns the logical value True if and only if the two given items contain the same value.

Signals   **nothing**

4.2.2.3 Comparison (↓Item ↓Item) ↑Relation

Requires   **nothing**

Modifies   **nothing**

Effects   Returns the ordering relation, (<, =, or >), that holds between the two given items.

Signals   **nothing**

4.2.2.4 Disposal (↕Item)

Requires   **nothing**

Modifies   **nothing**

Effects   Destroys the item so that it no longer has a value.

Signals   **nothing**

4.3 Implementing Generic Items

4.3.1 Relations Definition Module

This module provides definitions for the standard Modula-2 relations and relational operators, routines for mapping one type to the other, deriving the NOT of a relational operator, and testing whether a given relational operator implies that another relational operator may also be true.

```
DEFINITION MODULE Relations;
(*================================================================
   Version   : 1.00 09 Oct 1987 C. Lins
   Compiler  : TML Modula-2 Compiler for the Apple Macintosh
   Component : Tool - Relational Operators Utility

   REVISION HISTORY
   v1.00 09 Oct 1987 C. Lins:
      Initial TML Modula-2 implementation
================================================================*)
```

```
TYPE Relation =        (               (*-- Ordering Relations *)
                       less,           (*-- < less than          *)
                       equal,          (*-- = equal to           *)
                       greater,        (*-- > greater than       *)
                       incomparable (*-- ? failure result    *)
                       );
TYPE RelOp     =       (               (*-- Relational Operators    *)
                       lt,             (*-- < less than             *)
                       le,             (*-- ≤ less than or equal to  *)
                       eq,             (*-- = equal to              *)
                       ne,             (*-- ≠ not equal to          *)
                       gt,             (*-- > greater than          *)
                       ge,             (*-- ≥ greater than or equal to *)
                       unordered (*-- ? failure result       *)
                       );
PROCEDURE RelToRelOp ( theRelation : Relation (*-- in  *))
                                   : RelOp    (*-- out *);
PROCEDURE RelOpToRel ( theRelOp    : RelOp    (*-- in  *))
                                   : Relation (*-- out *);

   (*-----------------------*)

PROCEDURE NotRelOpOf ( theRelOp    : RelOp    (*-- in  *))
                                   : RelOp    (*-- out *);
PROCEDURE AImpliesB  ( left        : RelOp    (*-- in  *);
                       right       : RelOp    (*-- in  *))
                                   : BOOLEAN  (*-- out *);
END Relations.
```

4.3.2 Relations Implementation Module

This module provides definitions for the standard Modula-2 relations and relational operators, routines for mapping one type to the other, deriving the NOT of a
relational operator implies that another relational operator may also be true.

```
IMPLEMENTATION MODULE Relations;
(*================================================================
   Version : 1.00a 22 Oct 1987 C. Lins
   Compiler : TML Modula-2 Compiler for the Apple Macintosh
   Code Size: R- 326 bytes
   Component: Tool - Relational Operators Utility

   REVISION HISTORY
   v1.00a 22 Oct 1987 C. Lins:
       Initial TML Modula-2 implementation
=================================================================*)
```

```
(*
```

4.3.2.1 Local Data Types

RelSet   Defines a set of relational operators.

4.3.2.2 Local Variables

mapToRelOp   Simple mapping from Relation to RelOp.

mapRelation   Simple mapping from RelOp to Relation.

relMap   Maps array of relational operators to a RelSet. It is used by
                         the relational expression routines to easily determine whether
                         the result from a comparison routine meets the expression re-
                         lation. The mapping is described above in the specification,
                         section 4.2.1.4.

notRelOp   Maps relational operators to its opposite, i.e., = yields ≠.
```
*)
```

```
VAR mapToRelOp : ARRAY Relation OF RelOp;

PROCEDURE RelToRelOp ( theRelation: Relation (*-- in  *))
                                  : RelOp    (*-- out *);

BEGIN
  RETURN mapToRelOp [ theRelation ];
END RelToRelOp;
(*--------------------------*)

VAR mapRelation : ARRAY RelOp OF Relation;

PROCEDURE RelOpToRel ( theRelOp : RelOp    (*-- in  *))
                                 : Relation (*-- out *);
BEGIN
  RETURN mapRelation [ theRelOp ];
END RelOpToRel;
(*--------------------------*)

VAR notRelOp : ARRAY RelOp OF RelOp;

PROCEDURE NotRelOpOf ( theRelOp : RelOp (*-- in  *))
                                 : RelOp (*-- out *);

BEGIN
  RETURN notRelOp [ theRelOp ];
END NotRelOpOf;
(*--------------------------*)
```

```
TYPE RelSet = SET OF RelOp;
VAR  relMap : ARRAY RelOp OF RelSet;

PROCEDURE AImpliesB     (left : RelOp   (*--in*);
                         right: RelOp   (*--in*))
                              : BOOLEAN (*-- out *);

BEGIN
  RETURN left IN relMap [ right ];
END AImpliesB;
(*---------------------------*)


(*~~~~~~~~~~~~~~~~~~~~~~~~~~~~~*)
(*   MODULE INITIALIZATION    *)

BEGIN
   relMap [ lt ] := RelSet {le, lt, ne};
   relMap [ le ] := RelSet {le, lt, eq};
   relMap [ eq ] := RelSet {le, eq, ge};
   relMap [ ne ] := RelSet {lt, ne, gt};
   relMap [ gt ] := RelSet {ge, gt, ne};
   relMap [ ge ] := RelSet {eq, ge, gt};
   relMap [ unordered ] := RelSet {};
   notRelOp [ lt ] := ge;
   notRelOp [ le ] := gt;
   notRelOp [ eq ] := ne;
   notRelOp [ ne ] := eq;
   notRelOp [ gt ] := le;
   notRelOp [ ge ] := lt;
   notRelOp [ unordered ] := unordered;
   mapToRelOp [ less ]    := lt;
   mapToRelOp [ equal ]   := eq;
   mapToRelOp [ greater ] := gt;
   mapToRelOp [incomparable] := unordered;
   mapRelation [ lt ] := less;
   mapRelation [ le ] := incomparable;
   mapRelation [ eq ] := equal;
   mapRelation [ ne ] := incomparable;
   mapRelation [ gt ] := greater;
   mapRelation [ ge ] := incomparable;
   mapRelation [ unordered ] := incomparable;

END Relations.
```

4.3.3 Items Definition Module

```
DEFINITION MODULE Items;
(*================================================================
    Version   : 1.07 04 Dec. 1987 C. Lins
    Compiler  : TML Modula-2 Compiler for the Apple Macintosh
    Component : Structure - Generic Item Types
```

4.3.3.1 Introduction

Provides the abstract data type, Item, which has the operations Assignment (:=), (In)Equality (=,#), Comparison (<,≤,=,≠,≥,>), Disposal, and iterator support routines. Actual routines providing these facilities must be imported from the predefined ItemOperations module (for the standard types) or be provided by the programmer.

4.3.3.2 Interface Design Issues

The primary task is to provide generic facilities by furnishing operations equivalent to the standard operations for assignment (:=), (in)equality comparison (=,≠) and for ordered data types, the relational operators (<,=,>). These minimum operations must be available in order to have a functional data type.

Standard Modula-2 facilities for these operations on an opaque type would involve semantics for assigning and comparing the opaque type itself, this typically being a pointer type. Standard operators would suffice to permit non-pointer types as legitimate values for an item. But to attempt to use abstract data structures and dynamically allocated variables as items would result in the standard operators operating on the ADDRESS of or the POINTER TO the value of an item instead of the value itself. This is sufficient for (in)equality comparisons but assignment of pointer types results in sharing the pointer rather than copying its value. Furthermore, relational comparisons (< or >) are meaningless, since we only know the ADDRESS of the value, not the value itself. (Modula-2 does not perform these operations on opaque types anyway.)

```
================================================================*)

FROM Relations IMPORT
    (*--Type*) Relation, RelOp;


(*
```

This module provides support for generic data items. This is accomplished by providing an opaque type "Item" representing an arbitrary data type. This technique permits the creation of modules that can manipulate generic data structures with a minimum of knowledge about the actual data being manipulated permitting a single module to implement specific forms of a data structure. Plus the module need only be concerned with actual implementation issues regarding that structure — there need be only one unbounded stack module, one bounded stack module, etc. If necessary, type-specific modules can be built on top of the generic module. Of course, constraints must be placed on the client module(s) to insure proper usage of a generic item:

1. The actual data type mapped to an Item must be compatible with SYSTEM.ADDRESS. Specifically, the relation SIZE(DataType) $\leq$ SIZE(SYSTEM.ADDRESS) must be true. If this condition is not met, (e.g., a record or array structure), then the client module must use a pointer to the actual data.

2. Modula-2 supports only two standard operations for opaque types — assignment (:=) and the test for (in)equality (=,#). The relational operators <, <=, >, and >= are not supported for opaque types. The client module must provide any necessary relational operators to the generic module.

```
*)

TYPE Item;                        (*-- The generic data type *)
CONST NullItem = VAL(Item, NIL);  (*-- An 'empty' value for an
                                      item *)

(*--
```

4.3.3.3 Constructors

AssignProc   ($\downarrow$Item) $\uparrow$Item — Defines a generic function procedure type representing equivalent semantics as the standard Modula-2 assignment operator. A generic module must have a mechanism for assigning generic items to efficiently implement the standard Assign operation. The assignment operator accomplishes this for the simple data types (CHAR, INTEGER, CARDINAL, etc.). Dynamically created items using ":=" would copy pointers to the actual data — undesirable when the intended effect is to make a copy of the data itself.

DisposeProc   ($\updownarrow$Item) — Defines a generic procedure type (for which an actual procedure must be provided) that will deallocate any dynamically allocated resources associated with a given instance of an Item. Use of this routine prevents the creation of dangling pointers (a.k.a. garbage) for items created using NEW or ALLOCATE when these items are released by a generic module.

NoAssignProc   Defines a procedure *constant* representing the standard Modula-2 assignment operator ":=" which cannot be used as a procedure type parameter.

NoDisposeProc Defines a procedure *constant* representing disposal of items statically allocated on the stack. This may be used for primitive data items CHAR, INTEGER, etc. It is more efficient to test for an empty disposal routine than to force the client to provide a disposal routine that does nothing.

```
--*)

TYPE AssignProc = PROCEDURE ( Item            (*-- in    *))
                            : Item            (*-- out   *);

TYPE DisposeProc = PROCEDURE (VAR Item         (*-- inout *));

CONST NoDisposeProc = VAL(DisposeProc, NIL);
CONST NoAssignProc  = VAL(AssignProc, NIL);

(*--
```

4.3.3.4 Selectors

EqualProc   (↓Item ↓Item) ↑BOOLEAN — A generic function procedure type (which requires an actual procedure) that yields semantics equivalent to the standard Modula-2 relational operators for simple data types.

NoEqualProc   Defines a procedure *constant* representing the standard Modula-2 equality operator "=" which cannot be used as a procedure type parameter.

```
--*)

TYPE EqualProc = PROCEDURE ( Item       (*-- in *),
                             Item       (*-- in *))
                           : BOOLEAN (*-- out *);
CONST NoEqualProc = VAL(EqualProc, NIL);

(*--
```

CompareProc   (↓Item ↓Item) ↑Relation — A generic function procedure type (for which an actual procedure must be provided) that yields semantics equivalent to the standard Modula-2 comparison operator establishing the ordering relationship for simple data types. This type of routine attempts to answer the question, "What is the ordering relation between the first (or left) operand and the second (or right) operand?"

RelationProc   (↓Item ↓Relation ↓Item) ↑Boolean — A generic function procedure type (for which an actual procedure must be provided) that yields semantics equivalent to the standard Modula-2 ordering relations used in comparisons to evaluate the existence of a given ordering relation between (compatible) data types. This type of routine attempts to answer the question, "Does the ordering relation between the first (or left) operand and the second (or right) operand match the given relation?"

RelOpProc   (↓Item ↓RelOp ↓Item) ↑Boolean — Same as *RelationProc* above, except that the full set of relational operators are allowed, e.g., $<$, $\leq$, $=$, $\neq$, $>$, and $\geq$.

--*)

```
TYPE CompareProc = PROCEDURE  ( Item       (*-- in *),
                                Item       (*-- in *))
                              : Relation (*-- out*);
TYPE RelationProc = PROCEDURE ( Item       (*-- in *),
                                Relation   (*-- in *),
                                Item       (*-- in *))
                              : BOOLEAN   (*-- out*);
TYPE RelOpProc = PROCEDURE     ( Item       (*-- in *),
                                RelOp      (*-- in *),
                                Item       (*-- in *))
                              : BOOLEAN   (*-- out*);

CONST NoCompareProc = VAL(CompareProc, NIL);

(*--
```

4.3.3.5 Iterators

AccessProc   (↓Item) — Defines a generic procedure type (for which an actual procedure must be provided) that permits read-only access to a generic item from within the standard iterator operation *Traverse*.

ChangeProc   (↕Item) — Defines a generic procedure type (for which an actual procedure must be provided) that permits read-write access to a generic item from within the standard iterator operation *TravChange*.

LoopAccessProc	(↓Item) ↑Continue — Defines a generic procedure type (for which an actual procedure must be provided) that permits read-only access to a generic item from within the standard iterator operation *LoopOver*. The actual routine matching this declaration may control continuation of the iteration through the function result *Continue*, where: TRUE continues the iteration FALSE terminates the iteration

These two results account for the renaming of the BOOLEAN function result, clarifying the semantic meaning of the result.

LoopChangeProc	(↕Item) ↑Continue — Defines a generic procedure type (for which an actual procedure must be provided) that permits read-write access to a generic item from within the standard iterator operation *LoopChange*. The actual routine matching this declaration may control continuation of the iteration through the function result *Continue*, where: TRUE continues the iteration FALSE terminates the iteration

These two results account for the renaming of the BOOLEAN function result, clarifying the semantic meaning of the result.

```
--*)

TYPE AccessProc     = PROCEDURE (    Item    (*-- in    *));
TYPE ChangeProc     = PROCEDURE (VAR Item    (*-- inout *));

TYPE Continue       = BOOLEAN;
TYPE LoopAccessProc = PROCEDURE ( Item       (*-- in    *))
                                 : Continue (*-- out   *);
TYPE LoopChangeProc = PROCEDURE (VAR Item.   (*-- inout *))
                                 : Continue (*-- out   *);
END Items.
```

4.3.4 Items Implementation Module

```
IMPLEMENTATION MODULE Items;
(*=============================================================
    Version  : 1.07 04 Dec. 1987 C. Lins
    Compiler : TML Modula-2 Compiler for the Apple Macintosh
    Code Size: R+ 50 bytes, R- 50 bytes
    Component: Structure - Generic Item Types
```

```
REVISION HISTORY
v1.07 04 Dec. 1987 C. Lins:
Initial TML Modula-2 implementation.

IMPLEMENTATION DESIGN NOTES
 • The actual type of the opaque type Item must be defined.
==============================================================*)


FROM SYSTEM IMPORT
 (*--Type*) ADDRESS;

TYPE Item = ADDRESS;

END Items.
```

4.3.5 Character Items Definition Module

Frequently, the generic facilities provided by the Items module will be undesirable, perhaps due to the nature of the specific application, the need to reduce the space requirements of a program, or a desire for increased efficiency. Furthermore, the basic data types, CHAR and INTEGER, especially, are used so widely, that having modules tailored to these types is very desirable. This section presents an Items module customized for CHAR items, while the next section does the same for INTEGER items.

```
DEFINITION MODULE CharItems;
(*==============================================================
   Version : 1.00 17 Dec. 1987 C. Lins
   Compiler : TML Modula-2 Compiler for the Apple Macintosh
   Component: Generic Item Structure Utility - Character Items

   INTRODUCTION
   This module provides support for generic data items, restrict-
   ed to types compatible with CHAR. Assignment, equality test-
   ing, and relational operations are all provided by the lan-
   guage.

   REVISION HISTORY
   v1.00 17 Dec. 1987 C. Lins:
       Initial TML Modula-2 implementation.
==============================================================*)

TYPE Item          = CHAR; (*-- The CHAR item data type *)
CONST NullItem      = 0C;   (*-- The 'null' value *)
```

```
TYPE AssignProc      = PROCEDURE (     Item (*-- in *))
                                     : Item (*-- out *);

TYPE EqualProc       = PROCEDURE (     Item (*-- in *),
                                       Item (*-- in *))
                                     : BOOLEAN (*-- out *);

TYPE AccessProc      = PROCEDURE (     Item (*-- in *));
TYPE ChangeProc      = PROCEDURE ( VAR Item (*-- inout *));

TYPE Continue        = BOOLEAN;
TYPE LoopAccessProc  = PROCEDURE (     Item (*-- in *))
                                     : Continue (*-- out *);

TYPE LoopChangeProc  = PROCEDURE ( VAR Item (*-- inout *))
                                     : Continue (*-- out *);

END CharItems.
```

4.3.6 Integer Items Definition Module

```
DEFINITION MODULE IntegerItems;
(*================================================================
   Version  : 1.03 23 Dec. 1987 C. Lins
   Compiler : TML Modula-2 Compiler for the Apple Macintosh
   Component: Utility - INTEGER Item Type Definitions

   INTRODUCTION
   This module provides operations supporting INTEGER Items.

   REVISION HISTORY
   v1.03 23 Dec. 1987 C. Lins:
      Initial TML Modula-2 implementation.
================================================================*)
TYPE Item         .    = INTEGER; (*-- Discrete item data type*)
CONST NullItem         = 0; (*-- An 'empty' INTEGER value *)

TYPE AssignProc      = PROCEDURE ( Item (*-- in *))
                                   : Item (*-- out *);

TYPE EqualProc       = PROCEDURE ( Item (*-- in *),
                                   Item (*-- in *))
                                 : BOOLEAN (*-- out *);

TYPE AccessProc      = PROCEDURE ( Item (*-- in *));
TYPE ChangeProc      = PROCEDURE ( VAR Item (*-- inout *));
```

```
TYPE Continue      = BOOLEAN;
TYPE LoopAccessProc = PROCEDURE ( Item (*-- in *))
                                : Continue (*-- out *);

TYPE LoopChangeProc = PROCEDURE ( VAR Item (*-- inout *))
                                : Continue (*-- out *);

END IntegerItems.
```

4.3.7 Item Operations Definition Module

```
DEFINITION MODULE ItemOperations;
(*=============================================================
    Version  : 1.01 04 Dec. 1987 C. Lins
    Compiler : TML Modula-2 Compiler for the Apple Macintosh
    Component: Structure Utility - Generic Item Operations
```

4.3.7.1 Introduction

This module provides predefined routines for the standard data types, (CHAR, IN-TEGER, etc.) compatible with procedure types exported by the *Items* module.

4.3.7.2 Constructors

AssignItem   (↓Item) ↑Item — Assignment *operator* for generic Items. The data types of both Items should be the same.

4.3.7.3 Selectors

EqualItems   (↓Item ↓Item) ↑BOOLEAN — Equality *operator* for generic Items.

Compare   (↓Item ↓Item) ↑Relation — Ordering relation *operator* for generic Items. Since opaque variables cannot be compared, other than equality, separate routines are needed for each type to be compared.

```
=============================================================*)

FROM Items IMPORT
      (*--Type*) Item;
FROM Relations IMPORT
      (*--Type*) Relation;
```

```
(*--
  -- Predefined Assignment Routine for the Standard Data
  -- Types as Generic Items.
--*)

PROCEDURE AssignItem ( source : Item      (*-- in  *))
                              : Item      (*-- out *);

(*--
  -- Predefined Equality Comparison Routine for the Standard
  -- Data Types as Generic Items.
--*)

PROCEDURE EqualItems (    left : Item     (*-- in  *);
                         right: Item      (*-- in  *))
                              : BOOLEAN    (*-- out *);

(*--
  -- Predefined Comparison Routines for the Standard Data
  -- Types as Generic Items.
--*)

PROCEDURE CharCompare       ( left : Item       (*-- in  *);
                             right: Item         (*-- in  *))
                                  : Relation     (*-- out *);

PROCEDURE IntegerCompare    ( left : Item        (*-- in  *);
                             right: Item         (*-- in  *))
                                  : Relation     (*-- out *);

PROCEDURE CardinalCompare   ( left : Item        (*-- in  *);
                             right: Item         (*-- in  *))
                                  : Relation     (*-- out *);

PROCEDURE LongIntCompare    ( left : Item        (*-- in  *);
                             right: Item         (*-- in  *))
                                  : Relation     (*-- out *);

PROCEDURE LongCardCompare   ( left : Item        (*-- in  *);
                             right: Item         (*-- in  *))
                                  : Relation     (*-- out *);

PROCEDURE RealCompare       ( left : Item        (*-- in  *);
                             right: Item         (*-- in  *))
                                  : Relation     (*-- out *);

END ItemOperations.
```

4.3.8 Item Operations Implementation Module

```
IMPLEMENTATION MODULE ItemOperations;
(*==============================================================
   Version  : 1.01 04 Dec. 1987 C. Lins
   Compiler : TML Modula-2 Compiler for the Apple Macintosh
   Code Size: R+ bytes, R- 730 bytes
   Component: Structure Utility - Generic Item Operations

   INTRODUCTION
   This module provides predefined routines for the standard
   data types, (CHAR, INTEGER, etc.), compatible with the
   procedure types exported by the "Items" module.
   ==============================================================*)

FROM Items IMPORT
   (*--Type*) Item;

FROM Relations IMPORT
   (*--Type*) Relation;
   (*-----------------------*)

PROCEDURE AssignItem ( source : Item (*-- in  *))
                            : Item (*-- out *);
BEGIN
  RETURN source;
END AssignItem;
(*---------------------------*)

PROCEDURE EqualItems ( left  : Item    (*-- in  *);
                       right : Item    (*-- in  *))
                           : BOOLEAN (*-- out *);
BEGIN
  RETURN left = right;
END EqualItems;
(*---------------------------*)

PROCEDURE CharCompare ( left : Item    (*-- in  *);
                        right: Item    (*-- in  *))
                            : Relation (*-- out *);

VAR  leftChar : CHAR;
     rightChar : CHAR;

BEGIN
  leftChar  := VAL(CHAR, left);
  rightChar := VAL(CHAR, right);
  IF (leftChar = rightChar) THEN
```

```
      RETURN equal;
  ELSIF (leftChar < rightChar) THEN
      RETURN less;
  ELSIF (leftChar > rightChar) THEN
      RETURN greater;
  END (*--if*);
  RETURN incomparable; (*-- We should NEVER get here *)
END CharCompare;
(*---------------------------*)

PROCEDURE IntegerCompare ( left : Item     (*-- in *);
                           right: Item     (*-- in *))
                                 : Relation (*-- out *);

VAR leftInt  : INTEGER;
    rightInt : INTEGER;

BEGIN
  leftInt := VAL(INTEGER, left);
  rightInt := VAL(INTEGER, right);
  IF (leftInt = rightInt) THEN
      RETURN equal;
  ELSIF (leftInt < rightInt) THEN
      RETURN less;
  ELSIF (leftInt > rightInt) THEN
      RETURN greater;
  END (*--if*);
  RETURN incomparable; (*-- We should NEVER get here *)
END IntegerCompare;
(*---------------------------*)

PROCEDURE CardinalCompare ( left : Item     (*-- in  *);
                            right: Item     (*-- in  *))
                                  : Relation (*-- out *);

VAR leftCard  : CARDINAL;
    rightCard : CARDINAL;

BEGIN
  leftCard  := VAL(CARDINAL, left);
  rightCard := VAL(CARDINAL, right);

  IF (leftCard = rightCard) THEN
      RETURN equal;
  ELSIF (leftCard < rightCard) THEN
      RETURN less;
  ELSIF (leftCard > rightCard) THEN
      RETURN greater;
      END (*--if*);
      RETURN incomparable; (*-- We should NEVER get here *)
END CardinalCompare;
(*---------------------------*)
```

```
PROCEDURE LongIntCompare ( left : Item      (*-- in *);
                           right: Item      (*-- in *))
                                 : Relation (*-- out *);
VAR    leftLongInt : LONGINT;
       rightLongInt : LONGINT;

BEGIN
  leftLongInt  := VAL(LONGINT, left);
  rightLongInt := VAL(LONGINT, right);

  IF (leftLongInt = rightLongInt) THEN
    RETURN equal;
  ELSIF (leftLongInt < rightLongInt) THEN
    RETURN less;
  ELSIF (leftLongInt > rightLongInt) THEN
    RETURN greater;
  END (*--if*);
  RETURN incomparable; (*-- We should NEVER get here *)
END LongIntCompare;
(*--------------------------*)

PROCEDURE LongCardCompare ( left : Item      (*-- in *);
                            right: Item      (*-- in *))
                                  : Relation (*-- out *);

VAR    leftLongCard : LONGCARD;
       rightLongCard : LONGCARD;

BEGIN
  leftLongCard  := VAL(LONGCARD, left);
  rightLongCard := VAL(LONGCARD, right);
  IF (leftLongCard = rightLongCard) THEN
    RETURN equal;
  ELSIF (leftLongCard < rightLongCard) THEN
    RETURN less;
  ELSIF (leftLongCard > rightLongCard) THEN
    RETURN greater;
  END (*--if*);
  RETURN incomparable; (*-- We should NEVER get here *)
END LongCardCompare;
(*--------------------------*)

PROCEDURE RealCompare ( left : Item      (*-- in  *);
                        right: Item      (*-- in  *))
                              : Relation (*-- out *);

VAR leftReal : REAL;
    rightReal : REAL;

BEGIN
  leftReal  := VAL(REAL, left);
  rightReal := VAL(REAL, right);
    IF (leftReal = rightReal) THEN
```

```
        RETURN equal;
    ELSIF (leftReal < rightReal) THEN
        RETURN less;
    ELSIF (leftReal > rightReal) THEN
        RETURN greater;
    END (*--if*);
    RETURN incomparable; (*-- We should NEVER get here *)
END RealCompare;
(*--------------------------*)


END ItemOperations.
```

4.3.9 Type Manager Definition Module

The Type Manager module provides simple facilities for defining generic item types and associating assignment, comparison and disposal routines with that type.

The constructor *Create* builds a new data type identifier associating a name (optional), assignment, comparison, and disposal procedures with the generated TypeID. *Create* ensures that NIL procedures will not be invoked by generic abstract data type modules by replacing *NoAssignProc* and *NoDisposeProc* procedure constants with *ItemOperations.AssignItem* and a *dummy* procedure that does nothing, respectively. Types are assumed to be global to the program entity, and so a *Destroy* routine is not provided.

The selectors *NameOf*, *AssignOf*, *CompareOf*, and *DisposeOf* return the individual attributes of the given TypeID; while *AttributesOf* returns all four attributes.

TypeIDs have been predefined for the standard Modula-2 data types CHAR, INTEGER, CARDINAL, LONGINT, LONGCARD, and REAL and selectors have been provided to retrieve these predefined TypeIDs (since it is not possible to have opaque constants other than NIL). Each has been defined with the appropriate routine(s) from the ItemOperations module.

Undesired Events and Exceptions:
  Overflow — Unable to allocate a new type.
  Undefined Type — Given TypeID is the *NullType*.

```
DEFINITION MODULE TypeManager;
(*===========================================================
   Version  : 1.00 28 Dec. 1987 C. Lins
   Compiler : TML Modula-2 Compiler for the Apple Macintosh
   Component: Tool - Dynamic Type Management Utility
 ===========================================================*)
```

```
FROM Items IMPORT
   (*--Type*) AssignProc, CompareProc, DisposeProc;
   (*-----------------------*)

TYPE   TypeID;
TYPE   TypeName   = ARRAY [0 .. 15] OF CHAR;
CONST  NullType   = VAL(TypeID, NIL);


   (*-----------------------*)
   (*      CONSTRUCTORS      *)

PROCEDURE Create     (     theName    : TypeName    (*-- in  *);
                           assignment : AssignProc  (*-- in  *);
                           comparison : CompareProc (*-- in  *);
                           deallocate : DisposeProc (*-- in  *))
                                      : TypeID       (*-- out *);

PROCEDURE CharTypeID    () : TypeID (*-- out *);
PROCEDURE IntegerTypeID  () : TypeID (*-- out *);
PROCEDURE CardinalTypeID () : TypeID (*-- out *);
PROCEDURE LongIntTypeID  () : TypeID (*-- out *);
PROCEDURE LongCardTypeID () : TypeID (*-- out *);
PROCEDURE RealTypeID    () : TypeID (*-- out *);


   (*-----------------------*)
   (*      SELECTORS         *)

PROCEDURE NameOf          (     theType    : TypeID      (*-- in  *);
                           VAR theName    : TypeName    (*-- out *));

PROCEDURE AssignOf        (     theType    : TypeID      (*-- in  *))
                                          : AssignProc  (*-- out *);

PROCEDURE CompareOf       (     theType    : TypeID      (*-- in  *))
                                          : CompareProc (*-- out *);

PROCEDURE DisposeOf       (     theType    : TypeID      (*-- in  *))
                                          : DisposeProc (*-- out *);

PROCEDURE AttributesOf(     theType    : TypeID      (*-- in  *);
                       VAR theName    : TypeName    (*-- out *);
                       VAR assignment: AssignProc  (*-- out *);
                       VAR comparison: CompareProc (*-- out *);
                       VAR deallocate: DisposeProc (*-- out *));

END TypeManager.
```

4.3.10 Type Manager Implementation Module

```
IMPLEMENTATION MODULE TypeManager;
(*============================================================
   Version  : 1.01 03 Jan 1988 C. Lins
   Compiler : TML Modula-2 Compiler for the Apple Macintosh
   Code Size: R- 840 bytes
   Component: Tool - Dynamic Type Management Utility

   REVISION HISTORY
   v1.01 03 Jan 1988 C. Lins:
     Initial TML Modula-2 implementation
=============================================================*)

FROM SYSTEM IMPORT
  (*--Proc*) ADR;

FROM MacSystem IMPORT
  (*--Proc*) Allocate;

FROM Items IMPORT
  (*--Type*) Item, AssignProc, CompareProc, DisposeProc;

FROM ItemOperations IMPORT
  (*--Proc*)  AssignItem, CharCompare, IntegerCompare,
              CardinalCompare, LongIntCompare, LongCardCompare,
              RealCompare;
  (*----------------------*)

TYPE TypeID   = POINTER TO TypeNode;
TYPE TypeNode = RECORD
        name    : TypeName;    (*-- Name for this type   *)
        assign  : AssignProc;  (*-- Assignment routine   *)
        compare : CompareProc; (*-- Comparison routine   *)
        dispose : DisposeProc; (*-- Item Disposal routine*)
     END (*-- TypeNode *);
  (*----------------------*)

TYPE SimpleTypes = (chars, ints, cards, longints, longcards,
                    reals);
VAR  basicTypes : ARRAY SimpleTypes OF TypeNode;
  (*----------------------*)

PROCEDURE NullDispose (VAR theItem : Item (*-- inout *));
BEGIN
END NullDispose;
  (*--------------------------*)
```

```
(*------------------------*)
(*        CONSTRUCTORS      *)

PROCEDURE Build (     theName    : TypeName    (*-- in  *);
                      assignment : AssignProc  (*-- in  *);
                      comparison : CompareProc (*-- in  *);
                      deallocate : DisposeProc (*-- in  *);
                  VAR theTypeNode: TypeNode    (*-- out *));

BEGIN
  WITH theTypeNode DO
    name     := theName;
    assign   := assignment;
    compare  := comparison;
    dispose  := deallocate;
  END (*--with*);
END Build;
(*---------------------------*)

PROCEDURE Create (    theName    : TypeName    (*-- in  *);
                      assignment : AssignProc  (*-- in  *);
                      comparison : CompareProc (*-- in  *);
                      deallocate : DisposeProc (*-- in  *))
                                 : TypeID      (*-- out *);

VAR newType : TypeID;

BEGIN
  Allocate(newType, SIZE(TypeNode));
  IF (newType ≠ NullType) THEN
    Build(theName, assignment, comparison, deallocate,
        newType^);
  END (*--if*);
  RETURN newType;
END Create;
(*---------------------------*)

PROCEDURE CharTypeID        () : TypeID (*-- out *);
BEGIN
  RETURN ADR(basicTypes[chars]);
END CharTypeID;
(*---------------------------*)

PROCEDURE IntegerTypeID     () : TypeID (*-- out *);
BEGIN
  RETURN ADR(basicTypes[ints]);
END IntegerTypeID;
(*---------------------------*)

PROCEDURE CardinalTypeID    () : TypeID (*-- out *);
BEGIN
  RETURN ADR(basicTypes[cards]);
END CardinalTypeID;
(*---------------------------*)
```

```
PROCEDURE LongIntTypeID   () : TypeID (*-- out *);
BEGIN
  RETURN ADR(basicTypes[longints]);
END LongIntTypeID;
(*---------------------------*)


PROCEDURE LongCardTypeID  () : TypeID (*-- out *);
BEGIN
  RETURN ADR(basicTypes[longcards]);
END LongCardTypeID;
(*---------------------------*)


PROCEDURE RealTypeID      () : TypeID (*-- out *);
BEGIN
  RETURN ADR(basicTypes[reals]);
END RealTypeID;
(*---------------------------*)


   (*----------------------*)
   (*        SELECTORS       *)

PROCEDURE NameOf          (   theType : TypeID     (*-- in *);
                          VAR theName : TypeName   (*-- out *));
BEGIN
  IF (theType = NullType) THEN
    theName := "";
  ELSE
    theName := theType^.name;
  END (*--if*);
END NameOf;
(*---------------------------*)


PROCEDURE AssignOf        (   theType : TypeID      (*-- in *))
                                      : AssignProc (*-- out *);
BEGIN
  IF (theType = NullType) THEN
    RETURN AssignItem;
  END (*--if*);
    RETURN theType^.assign;
END AssignOf;
(*---------------------------*)

PROCEDURE CompareOf       (   theType : TypeID       (*-- in *))
                                      : CompareProc (*-- out *);
BEGIN
  IF (theType = NullType) THEN
    RETURN NoCompareProc;
  END (*--if*);
    RETURN theType^.compare;
END CompareOf;
(*---------------------------*)


PROCEDURE DisposeOf       (   theType : TypeID       (*-- in *))
                                      : DisposeProc (*-- out *);
```

```
BEGIN
  IF (theType = NullType) THEN
    RETURN NullDispose;
  END (*--if*);
    RETURN theType^.dispose;
END DisposeOf;
(*---------------------------*)

PROCEDURE AttributesOf(     theType    : TypeID      (*-- in  *);
                       VAR theName     : TypeName    (*-- out *);
                       VAR assignment  : AssignProc  (*-- out *);
                       VAR comparison  : CompareProc (*-- out *);
                       VAR deallocate  : DisposeProc (*-- out *));

BEGIN
  IF (theType = NullType) THEN
    theName         := "";
    assignment      := AssignItem;
    comparison      := NoCompareProc;
    deallocate      := NullDispose;
  ELSE
    WITH theType^ DO
      theName    := name;
      assignment := assign;
      comparison := compare;
      deallocate := dispose;
    END (*--with*);
  END (*--if*);
END AttributesOf;
(*---------------------------*)


(*~~~~~~~~~~~~~~~~~~~~~~~~~~~~~*)
(*~~ MODULE INITIALIZATION  ~~*)

BEGIN
  Build("CHAR",      AssignItem,  CharCompare,
                     NullDispose, basicTypes[chars]);
  Build("INTEGER",   AssignItem,  IntegerCompare,
  Build("CHAR",      AssignItem,  CharCompare,
                     NullDispose, basicTypes[ints]);
  Build("CARDINAL",  AssignItem,  CardinalCompare,
  Build("CHAR",      AssignItem,  CharCompare,
                     NullDispose, basicTypes[cards]);
  Build("LONGINT",   AssignItem,   LongIntCompare,
  Build("CHAR",      AssignItem,  CharCompare,
                     NullDispose, basicTypes[longints]);
  Build("LONGCARD",  AssignItem,  LongCardCompare,
  Build("CHAR",      AssignItem,  CharCompare,
                     NullDispose, basicTypes[longcards]);
  Build("REAL",      AssignItem,  RealCompare,
  Build("CHAR",      AssignItem,  CharCompare,
                     NullDispose, basicTypes[reals]);
END TypeManager.
```

4.3.11 Error Handling Definition Module

The following is a sample definition for the error handling module used throughout this book. It is assumed that users will provide their own implementation of this module.

```
DEFINITION MODULE ErrorHandling;

FROM SYSTEM IMPORT (*--Type*) BYTE;

TYPE ModuleNo  = CARDINAL;
TYPE Operation = BYTE;
TYPE Exception = BYTE;
TYPE HandlerProc = PROCEDURE (ModuleNo, Operation, Exception);

PROCEDURE Raise (    theModule    : ModuleNo    (*-- in *);
                     theOperation : Operation   (*-- in *);
                     theException : Exception   (*-- in *);
                     theHandler   : HandlerProc (*-- in *));
END ErrorHandling.
```

References

[1] G. Booch, *Software Components With Ada Structures, Tools, and Subsystems*, Benjamin/Cummings, Menlo Park, CA, 1987.

[2] J. Bruckner and J. Harp, "Macro Modules in Modula-2," *Journal of Pascal, Ada, and Modula-2*, Vol. 6 (6), (Nov./Dec. 1987) pp. 5-10.

[3] J. Bruckner and J. Harp, "Implementing Opaque Types in Generic Data Structures in Modula-2," *Journal of Pascal, Ada, and Modula-2*, Vol. 6 (4), (Jul./Aug. 1987) pp. 14-30.

[4] P.C. Clements, S.R. Faulk, and D.L. Parnas, *Interface Specifications for the SCR (A7-E) Application Data Types Module*, (NRL Report 8734), Naval Research Laboratory, Washington, D.C., 1983.

[5] P.C. Clements, R.A. Parker, D.L. Parnas, and J. Shore, *A Standard Organization for Specifying Abstract Interfaces*, (NRL Report 8815), Naval Research Laboratory, Washington, D.C., 1984.

[6] A.L. Crawford, "An Extension to Modula-2 for Generic Types," *Journal of Pascal, Ada, and Modula-2*, Vol. 6 (6), (Nov./Dec. 1987) pp. 11-16.

[7] J. Gougen, "Parameterized Programming," *IEEE Transactions on Software Engineering*, SE-10 (5), (Sep. 1984), pg. 138.

[8] K. Gough, "Writing Generic Utilities in Modula-2," *Journal of Pascal, Ada, and Modula-2*, Vol. 5 (3), (May/Jun. 1986) pp. 53-62.

[9]   C.W. Reynolds, "On Implementing Generic Data Structures in Modula-2," *Journal of Pascal, Ada, and Modula-2*, Vol. 6 (5), (Sep./Oct. 1987) pp. 26-38.

[10] A. Wegmann, "Object Oriented Programming Using Modula-2," *Journal of Pascal, Ada, and Modula-2*, Vol. 5 (3), (Mar./Apr. 1986) pp. 5-17.

[11] R.S. Wiener and G. Ford, *Data Structures Using Modula-2*, John Wiley & Sons, New York, NY, 1985, pp. 289-317.

[12] N. Wirth, *Programming in Modula-2*, 3rd. ed., Springer-Verlag, New York, NY, 1985, pp. 128-135.

[13] N. Wirth, *Algorithms and Data Structures*, Prentice-Hall, Englewood Cliffs, NJ, 1986, pp. 49-52.

5 The Stack Abstraction

This chapter presents the specification for the Stack abstraction.

- Section 5.1 describes the concept of a stack and defines terms used to describe a stack and its state.

- Section 5.2 follows with a (selective) list of uses and applications where stack objects have been used in computer programs. Specifications for each stack operation is presented in the following order:
  - Section 5.3 Constructor operations
  - Section 5.4 Selector operations
  - Section 5.5 Iterator operations

- Section 5.6 describes the exception conditions that may occur as a result of invoking a stack operation.

- Section 5.7 concludes with a summary of stack operations and exceptions.

5.1 Stacks: Concepts and Definitions

A *stack* is a restricted form of list where addition and removal of items occur at only one end of the list, called the *top*. The number of items presently on a stack is denoted by the term, *depth*. Figure 5.1 graphically depicts these terms and their interrelationships.

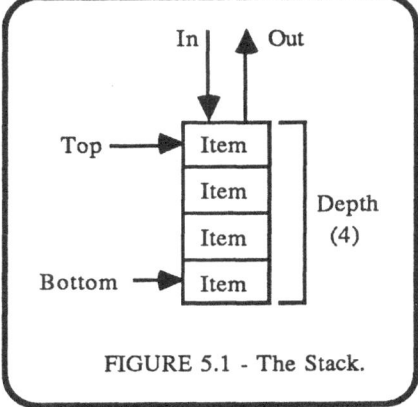

FIGURE 5.1 - The Stack.

Stack	An ordered sequence of items accessible from only one end.
Top	The end at which the stack may be accessed.
Depth	The number of items presently on a stack.
NullStack	Term used (in this publication) for the undefined stack.

5.2 Selected Summary of Stack Applications and Uses

Stacks are most useful for "processing nested structures of unpredictable depth" [Standish, pg. 20]. Some areas where stacks have been found useful include:

- the parsing of arithmetic expressions;
- conversion of an arithmetic expression between infix and postfix forms;
- evaluation of a postfix arithmetic expression;
- reversal of the items in a list;
- managing subroutine invocation and returns;
- symbol table management and syntax analysis of a blocked programming language (such as Pascal, Modula-2) by a compiler;
- processing during a goal-directed search where each goal has one or more subgoals (path-searching, tree traversal, etc.);
- in programming techniques for the removal of recursive procedure calls;
- in various garbage collection algorithms;
- maintaining a list (i.e., stack) of things to do later;
- adaptive numerical integration (see [19]).

The references, at the end of the chapter provides readers with a point of departure for their own investigations.

5.3 Stack Constructor Operations

5.3.1 Create (↑Stack)

Requires   **nothing**

Modifies   **nothing**

Effects   Generates a new (empty) stack object. After successful creation of the new object, the following operations will yield the given results:
IsDefined (Stack') = True
IsEmpty (Stack') = True
IsEqual (Stack', Stack') = True
IsEqual (Stack', OtherStack) = IsEmpty (OtherStack)
TopOf (Stack') = Underflow & NullItem
DepthOf (Stack') = 0
Pop (Stack') = Underflow
PopTopOf (Stack') = Underflow & NullItem

Signals   Overflow **when** the stack could not be created **ensuring** returns the NullStack

5.3.2 Destroy (↕Stack)

Requires   **nothing**

Modifies   **at most** Stack

Effects   Removes all items from the stack, making the stack empty, release
             the stack variable, and set the stack to the NullStack. After destroy-
             ing the given object, the following operations will yield the given
             results:
             IsDefined (Stack') = False
             IsEmpty (Stack') = Undefined & True
             IsEqual (Stack', AnyStack) = Undefined & False
             TopOf (Stack') = Undefined & NullItem
             DepthOf (Stack') = Undefined & 0
             Pop (Stack') = Undefined
             PopTopOf (Stack') = Undefined & NullItem

Signals   Undefined **when** ¬IsDefined (Stack) **ensuring modifies noth-
             ing**

5.3.3 Clear (↕Stack)

Requires   **nothing**
Modifies   **at most** Stack

Effects   Removes all items from the stack, making the stack empty. Passes
             items on the stack to the item disposal routine, if any, associated
             with the stack's data type for release of dynamically allocated re-
             sources associated with each item.
             IsEmpty (Stack') = TRUE
             DepthOf (Stack') = 0

Signals   Undefined **when** ¬IsDefined (Stack) **ensuring modifies noth-
             ing**

5.3.4 Assign(↓SourceStack ↕TargetStack)

Requires   **nothing**

Modifies   **at most** TargetStack

Effects   Creates an exact duplicate of the stack Source in the stack Target.
             The target stack is cleared, if necessary, before attempting the assign-
             ment operation. If the target stack is undefined, then it is automati-
             cally created. The AssignmentProcedure of the source stack, if any,
             is used to copy items from the source stack to the target stack.
             IsEqual (Source, Target') = TRUE

Signals   Overflow **when** insufficient memory resources available to create a
            new stack **ensuring modifies at most** TargetStack

Signals   Undefined **when** ¬IsDefined(Source) **ensuring modifies nothing**

5.3.5   Push (↕Stack ↓Item)

Requires   **nothing**

Modifies   **at most** Stack

Effects   Adds an item at the current top of the stack. Places a given item on
            the stack and the top of the stack now references this item.
            DepthOf(Stack') = DepthOf(Stack) + 1
            IsEqual(Stack , Pop(Stack')) = TRUE
            TopOf(Stack') = Item

Signals   Overflow **when** insufficient memory resources available to add item
            to the stack **ensuring modifies at most** Stack

Signals   Undefined **when** ¬IsDefined(Stack) **ensuring modifies nothing**

5.3.6   Pop (↕Stack)

Requires   **nothing**

Modifies   **at most** Stack

Effects   Removes the topmost item from the stack, but does not return it. If
            the stack has been defined with an item disposal routine, then this
            routine is used to deallocate any dynamically allocated resources as-
            sociated with the item.
            DepthOf(Stack') = DepthOf(Stack) - 1

Signals   Underflow **when** IsEmpty(Stack) **ensuring modifies nothing**

Signals   Undefined **when** ¬IsDefined(Stack) **ensuring modifies nothing**

5.3.7   PopTopOf (↕Stack) ↑Item

Requires   **nothing**

Modifies   **at most** Stack

Effects   Removes and returns the topmost item from the stack. This conven-
            ience routine combines the facilities of TopOf and Pop. Does not
            deallocate the item when removed from the stack since its value is
            returned to the caller.
            DepthOf(Stack') = DepthOf(Stack) - 1

Signals   Underflow **when** IsEmpty(Stack) **ensuring modifies nothing** and returns NullItem.

Signals   Undefined **when** ¬IsDefined(Stack) **ensuring modifies nothing** and returns NullItem.

5.4 Stack Selector Operations

5.4.1 IsDefined (↓Stack) ↑Boolean

Requires   **nothing**

Modifies   **nothing**

Effects   Returns True if the stack has been created and not yet destroyed.

Signals   **nothing**

5.4.2 IsEmpty (↓Stack) ↑Boolean

Requires   **nothing**

Modifies   **nothing**

Effects   Returns the logical value of True if the stack contains no items. DepthOf(Stack) = 0?

Signals   Undefined **when** ¬IsDefined(Stack) **ensuring** returns True

5.4.3 IsEqual (↓LeftStack ↓RightStack) ↑Boolean

Requires   **nothing**

Modifies   **nothing**

Effects   Equality test for two stacks of the same type. Returns the logical value of True if the two given stacks contain the same items. If a comparison routine has been provided when the stacks were created, this routine is used to determine the (in)equality of items instead of the standard Modula-2 equality operator.

Signals   Undefined **when** ¬IsDefined(LeftStack) **ensuring** returns False

Signals   Undefined **when** ¬IsDefined(RightStack) **ensuring** returns False

Signals   TypeError **when** TypeOf(LeftStack) ≠ TypeOf(RightStack) **ensuring** returns False

5.4.4 TopOf (↓Stack) ↑Item

Requires	**nothing**
Modifies	**nothing**
Effects	Returns the topmost item on the stack. The stack is unchanged.
Signals	Underflow **when** IsEmpty (Stack) **ensuring** returns NullItem
Signals	Undefined **when** ¬IsDefined (Stack) **ensuring** returns NullItem

5.4.5 DepthOf (↓Stack) ↑Cardinal

Requires	**nothing**
Modifies	**nothing**
Effects	Returns a count of the number of items presently in the stack. If the stack is empty then its depth is zero.
Signals	Undefined **when** ¬IsDefined (Stack) **ensuring** returns zero

5.5 Stack Iterator Operations

5.5.1 LoopOver (↓Stack ↓LoopAccessProcedure)

Requires	LoopAccessProcedure ≠ NIL
Where	LoopAccess Procedure = **procedure**(↓Item)↑Boolean
Modifies	**nothing**
Effects	Performs the given operation on one or more items of the stack from top to bottom. Passes each item on the stack to a given Loop-AccessProcedure until all items have been processed or the Loop-AccessProcedure returns False.
Signals	Undefined **when** ¬IsDefined (Stack) **ensuring modifies nothing** and the LoopAccessProcedure is not invoked

5.5.2 LoopChange (↓Stack ↓LoopChangeProcedure)

Requires	LoopChange Procedure ≠ NIL
Where	LoopChange Procedure = **procedure**(↕Item)↑Boolean
Modifies	**nothing**

Effects   Performs a given operation on one or more items of the stack from
              top to bottom. Passes each item on the stack to the given Loop-
              ChangeProcedure until all items have been processed or the Loop-
              ChangeProcedure returns False. This operation is a variation of
              LoopOver where item values may be altered from within the Loop-
              ChangeProcedure.

Signals   Undefined **when** ¬IsDefined (Stack) **ensuring modifies noth-
              ing** and the LoopChangeProcedure is not invoked

5.5.3 Traverse (↓Stack ↓AccessProcedure)

Requires   AccessProcedure ≠ NIL

Where   Access Procedure = **procedure**(↓Item)

Modifies   **nothing**

Effects   Performs a given operation for every item on the stack from top to
              bottom. Passes each item on the stack to the given AccessProcedure
              until all items have been processed.

Signals   Undefined **when** ¬IsDefined (Stack) **ensuring modifies noth-
              ing** and the AccessProcedure is not invoked

5.5.4 TraverseChange (↓Stack ↓ChangeProcedure)

Requires   ChangeProcedure ≠ NIL

Where   Change Procedure = **procedure**(↕Item)

Modifies   **nothing**

Effects   Performs the given operation for every item on the stack from top to
              bottom. Each item on the stack is passed to the given ChangeProce-
              dure until all items have been processed. This operation is a varia-
              tion of Traverse where item values may be altered from within the
              ChangeProcedure.

Signals   Undefined **when** ¬IsDefined (Stack) **ensuring modifies noth-
              ing** and the ChangeProcedure is not invoked

5.6 Stack Exceptions

5.6.1 Initialization Failed

The *initfailed* exception is raised during module initialization. It is signaled when initial data structures required by a stack module cannot be allocated. Depending on the implementation, other conditions may occur during module initialization that may cause this exception to be raised. Typically, the program is terminated as a result of this exception. This is because certain prerequisites have not been met in order to use the module.

5.6.2 Overflow

Stack overflow occurs when either of two conditions arise:

1. a stack cannot be created, and
2. attempting to add an item to a stack.

In the first case *overflow* indicates that the program is (at present) operating under severe memory limitations, for the local data of a stack variable cannot be dynamically allocated on the heap. The second situation could occur if:

1. an attempt is made of copy a stack with a large number of (small) items, or
2. the individual item itself consumes a (relatively) large amount of space, either during a push or stack copy operation.

5.6.3 Type Error

A *type error* occurs whenever an attempt is made to operate on stacks that have not been defined to be of the same type, (indicated by their TypeIDs).

5.6.4 Underflow

Stack *underflow* occurs whenever an attempt is made to access an item from an empty stack.

5.6.5 Undefined

This exception can occur when an attempt is made to access a stack variable that has not been initialized by way of the Create operation. Unfortunately, this case cannot be detected within Modula-2 without incurring a runtime penalty. The approach could be taken in all components of locally defining a list of stacks that have been created and not yet destroyed. This would permit the component to then verify that the module actually created the stack being operated on. An alternative would be to simply test for the NullStack (i.e., NIL) to avoid the consequences of system breakdown. This is a viable solution if one assumes that the module's routines will not be subjected to a malicious attack. Such an attack can be delivered in Modula-2 due to the facilities for relaxation of the normally strict type-checking. For our purposes, an undefined stack is defined by the *NullStack.*

5.7 Summary

5.7.1 Operations Summary

Constructor
Operation

Assign	Stack × Stack → Stack
Clear	Stack → Stack
Create	→ Stack
Destroy	Stack → λ
Pop	Stack → Stack
PopTopOf	Stack → Stack × Item
Push	Stack × Item → Stack

Selector
Operation

DepthOf	Stack → CARDINAL
IsDefined	Stack → BOOLEAN
IsEmpty	Stack → BOOLEAN
IsEqual	Stack × Stack → BOOLEAN
TopOf	Stack → Item

Iterator
Operation

LoopChange	Stack ×	LoopChangeProcedure
LoopOver	Stack ×	LoopAccessProcedure
Traverse	Stack ×	AccessProcedure
TraverseChange	Stack ×	ChangeProcedure

5.7.2 Exceptions Summary

Exception	*Raised By Operation*
InitFailed	Module Initialization
Overflow	Assign, Create, Push
TypeError	IsEqual
Undefined	Assign, Clear, DepthOf, Destroy, IsEmpty, IsEqual, Loop-Change, LoopOver, Pop, PopTopOf, Push, TopOf, Trav-Change, Traverse
Underflow	Pop, PopTopOf, TopOf

Operation	*Raises Exception*
Assign	Overflow, Undefined
Clear	Undefined
Create	Overflow
DepthOf	Undefined
Destroy	Undefined
Initialization	InitFailed
IsDefined	–
IsEmpty	Undefined
IsEqual	TypeError, Undefined
LoopChange	Undefined
LoopOver	Undefined
Pop	Underflow, Undefined
PopTopOf	Underflow, Undefined
Push	Overflow, Undefined
TopOf	Underflow, Undefined
TravChange	Undefined
Traverse	Undefined

References

[1] A. Aho, J. Hopcroft, and J. Ullman, *Data Structures and Algorithms*, Addison-Wesley, Reading, MA 1983, pp. 53-56, 64-69.

[2] A. Aho, R. Sethi, and J. Ullman, *Compilers: Principles, Techniques, and Tools*, Addison-Wesley, Reading, MA 1986.

[3] K. Christian, *A Guide to Modula-2*, Springer-Verlag, New York, NY 1986, pp. 328-331.

[4] P. B. Hansen, *Brinch Hansen on Pascal Compilers*, Prentice-Hall, Englewood Cliffs, NJ 1985.

[5] R. Hunter, *Compilers: Their Design and Construction Using Pascal*, John Wiley and Sons, New York, NY 1985.

[6] D. Knuth, *The Art of Computer Programming, Vol. 1, Fundamental Algorithms*, Addison-Wesley, Reading, MA 1968, pp. 240-248.

[7] J. Korsh and G. Laison, "A Multiple-Stack Manipulation Procedure," *Communications of the ACM*, Vol. 26(11), (Nov. 1983) pp. 921-923.

[8] B. Liskov and J. Guttag, *Abstraction and Specification in Program Development*, The MIT Press, Cambridge, MA 1986, pp. 72, 217-218, 250, 313-321.

[9] B. Liskov and S. N. Zilles, "Specification Techniques for Data Abstraction," *IEEE Transactions of Software Engineering*, Vol. SE-1(1), (Mar. 1975) pp. 7-19. (In *Tutorial on Software Design Techniques*, 4th ed., P. Freeman and A. I. Wasserman, (eds.), IEEE Computer Society Press, 1983.)

[10] M. Milenkovic, *Operating Systems: Concepts and Design*, McGraw-Hill, New York, NY 1987.

[11] J. Moore and K. McKay, *Modula-2 Text and Reference*, Prentice-Hall, Englewood Cliffs, NJ 1987, pp. 94-98.

[12] H. Schildt, *Modula-2 Made Easy*, Osborne McGraw-Hill, Berkeley, CA 1986, pp. 267-269.

[13] G. Silberman, "Stack Processing Techniques in Delayed-Staging Storage Hierarchies," *Communications of the ACM*, Vol. 26(11), (Nov. 1983) pp. 999-1007.

[14] T.A. Standish, *Data Structure Techniques*, Addison-Wesley, Reading, MA 1980, pp. 19-41.

[15] A. Tenenbaum and M. Augenstein, *Data Structures Using Pascal*, Prentice-Hall, Englewood Cliffs, NJ 1981.

[16] W. Waite and G. Goos, *Compiler Construction*, Springer-Verlag, New York, NY 1984.

[17] J. Welsh and A. Hay, *A Model Implementation of Standard Pascal*, Prentice-Hall International (UK) Ltd. 1986.

[18] R. Wiener and G. Ford, *Modula-2 A Software Development Approach*, John Wiley & Sons, New York, NY 1985, pp. 247-253.

[19]   R. Wiener and R. Sincovec, *Data Structures Using Modula-2*, John Wiley & Sons, New York, NY 1986, pp. 21-26, 31-35, 46-52, 59-69, 120-134.

[20]   D. Yun Yeh and T. Munakata, "Dynamic Initial Allocation and Local Reallocation Procedures for Multiple Stacks," *Communications of the ACM*, Vol. 29(2), (Feb. 1986) pp. 134-141.

6 The Bounded Stack

This chapter presents a bounded implementation of the stack abstraction described in the previous chapter. This particular form has four properties: *Sequential*, *Bounded*, *Managed* and *Iterator*, describing specific aspects of the implementation as follows:

Sequential   Can only be used in a non-tasking environment, or by only one task.

Bounded   The maximum size of a stack is given when the stack is created.

Managed   Memory space for items and objects is returned to the system when no longer needed.

Iterator   Routines for looping over each of the stack items are provided.

Section 6.1 contains the interface to the Stack Enumerations module used by the stack implementations in this and the next chapters. The bounded stack module interface follows in Section 6.2 and its implementation in Section 6.3.

6.1 Stack Enumerations Interface

This module provides centralized definitions of theoperations and exceptions for all stack modules.

```
DEFINITION MODULE StackEnum;
(*===============================================================
   Version  : 1.00 07 Jan 1988 C. Lins
   Compiler : TML Modula-2 Compiler for the Apple Macintosh
   Component: Stack Structure Utility - Enumerations

   REVISION HISTORY
   v1.00 07 Jan 1988 C. Lins:
       Initial TML Modula-2 implementation
================================================================*)

    (*--------------------*)
    (*- STACK OPERATIONS -*)

TYPE Operations = (modinit, create, destroy, clear, assign,
                   push, pop, poptopof,isdefined, isempty,
                   isequal, sizeof, typeof, topof, depthof,
```

```
                    loopover, loopchange, traverse, travchange,
                    seize, release
                  );

TYPE Constructors = Operations [ create    .. poptopof ];
TYPE Selectors    = Operations [ isdefined .. depthof ];
TYPE Iterators    = Operations [ loopover  .. travchange ];
TYPE GuardedOps   = Operations [ seize     .. release ];


    (*-------------------*)
    (*— STACK EXCEPTIONS —*)


TYPE Exceptions = (noerr,      (*— Nothing went wrong, all's
                                   well. *)
                   initfailed, (*— Module initialization
                                   failure. *)
                   overflow,   (*— Stack cannot grow big enough
                                   for the requested
                                   operation. *)
                   typeerror,  (*— TypeID mismatch between
                                   stacks *)
                   undefined,  (*— Stack has not been Created,
                                   or the stack has been
                                   Destroyed. *)
                   underflow   (*— Stack is already empty. *)
                  );

TYPE ExceptionSet = SET OF Exceptions;

END StackEnum.
```

6.2 StackSBMI Interface

The section below presents the interface to the bounded stack. The section briefly describes the purpose and implementation specifics of each routine together, mentioning the complexity measure of the actual implementation.

```
DEFINITION MODULE StackSBMI;
(*===========================================================
    Version  : 1.13 07 Jan 1988 C. Lins
    Compiler : TML Modula-2 Compiler for the Apple Macintosh
    Component: Monolithic Structures - Stack (Opaque version)
               Sequential Bounded Managed Iterator
```

```
INTRODUCTION
This module provides the definition of the bounded stack
composed of generic Items.

REVISION HISTORY
v1.13 07 Jan 1988 C. Lins:
   Initial implementation for TML Modula-2.
=========================================================*)

FROM Items IMPORT
   (*-Type*) Item, AccessProc, LoopAccessProc, ChangeProc,
             LoopChangeProc;

FROM StackEnum IMPORT
   (*-Type*) Exceptions;

FROM ErrorHandling IMPORT
   (*-Type*) HandlerProc;

FROM TypeManager IMPORT
   (*-Type*) TypeID;
   (*--------------*)

TYPE  Stack;
TYPE  SizeRange = [1..8100];

CONST NullStack = VAL(Stack, NIL);

(*
```

6.2.1 Exceptions

ModuleID   is used by the exception handling mechanism to distinguish this module from other modules.

StackError   returns the exception code from the most recent stack operation. A result of *noerr* indicates successful completion of the operation $O(1)$.

GetHandler   returns the exception handler routine associated with the given exception. The routine is a function procedure returning a procedure as its result but the *HandlerProc* may not be called from within the *GetHandler* call itself. The procedure result must be assigned to a procedure variable before invocation. Exception handlers are given an initial value of *ExitOnError* except for the handler for *noerr* which is initialized to the null exception handler $O(1)$.

SetHandler   associates an exception handler routine with the given exception and is the inverse of *GetHandler*. This routine may be used to override the default settings for the exception handlers O(1).

```
*)

CONST ModuleID = 1;

PROCEDURE StackError ()              : Exceptions  (*— out *);
PROCEDURE GetHandler ( theError      : Exceptions  (*— in  *))
                                     : HandlerProc (*— out *);
PROCEDURE SetHandler ( theError      : Exceptions  (*— in  *);
                       theHandler : HandlerProc (*— in  *));

(*
```

6.2.2 Constructors

Create   attempts to generate a new, empty stack of the given maximum size (*theSize*) and Item operations associated with the given data type identifier (*theType*).

    theSize parameter defines the maximum depth desired for the bounded form of stack. The TypeID supports Items of any data type. *Create* can use *theType* to assign one item to another and to release any dynamically allocated resources associated with an Item without knowing the Item's internal composition. In this way, one may create a stack whose items consist of other (dynamically allocated) structures, as well as stacks consisting of the basic data types.

    Create returns the new stack upon successful completion of the routine. If it is not possible to make the stack, *Create* raises the exception *overflow* and returns the constant *NullStack* O(1).

Destroy   clears the given stack of items and then destroys it. *Destroy* is the inverse of *Create*, making a stack undefined O(1).

Clear   removes all items from the given stack. It uses the stack's *theType* attribute (assigned when the stack was created) to retrieve the item deallocation routine for use with the items of the stack. Clearing the stack returns it to the empty state O(n).

Assign   attempts to duplicate the source stack (*theStack*) in the target stack (*toStack*). It automatically creates the target stack, if necessary using the size and data type attributes of the source stack. If this step is unnecessary, (the target stack has already been previously created), the target is cleared of its present contents, its data type is set to that of the source stack but the size is left unchanged O(n).

There is no guarantee that the client module would desire the target stack to be defined with the same size as the source. The target stack size must minimally be capable of storing all items present in the source stack. In some cases the target stack size should be greater than the source stack size, for example during error recovery of a bounded stack overflow caused by the stack depth encountering the stack size. The client module may attempt to increase the stack size using the assignment mechanism.

A method is provided to assign the contents of one item to another item in order to permit Items of any data type. The Type-ID of the source stack, as above for *Create*, accomplishes this.

Push   adds items to the given stack. The given item is placed on the stack top. If the depth is already at maximum size for the given stack the *overflow* exception will be raised and the stack remains unchanged O(1).

Pop   removes the topmost item from the given stack. If the given stack is empty on entry to *Pop* the *underflow* exception will be raised and the stack remains unchanged O(1).

PopTopOf   is a convenience routine that combines semantics of the constructor *Pop* and the selector *TopOf*. The only difference from Pop is that the routine returns the item's value rather than disposing of it O(1).

```
*)

PROCEDURE Create    (    theSize  : SizeRange (*— in    *);
                         theType  : TypeID    (*— in    *))
                                  : Stack     (*— out   *);

PROCEDURE Destroy   (VAR theStack : Stack     (*— inout *));

PROCEDURE Clear     (VAR theStack : Stack     (*— inout *));

PROCEDURE Assign    (    theStack : Stack     (*— in    *);
                     VAR toStack   : Stack     (*— inout *));

PROCEDURE Push      (VAR toStack   : Stack     (*— inout *);
                         theItem  : Item      (*— in    *));

PROCEDURE Pop       (VAR theStack : Stack     (*— inout *));

PROCEDURE PopTopOf  (VAR theStack : Stack     (*— inout *))
                                  : Item      (*— out   *);
```

(*

6.2.3 Selectors

IsDefined   attempts to determine whether a given stack is valid —
                     that is, has been created and not yet destroyed. This process
                     may be as simple or complicated as the implementor de-
                     sires and the requirements of the application demand O(1).

IsEmpty   returns true if the given stack contains no items — in oth-
                     er words, has a depth of zero. Undefined stacks are always
                     considered empty O(1).

IsEqual   returns true if left and right stacks have been created and
                     contain the same items of the same data type. An unde-
                     fined stack is not equal to any other stack, including itself
                     O(n).

SizeOf & TypeOf   return the values given the stack when it was created so the
                     user of the module need not maintain separate variables
                     recording this information O(1).

DepthOf   returns the number of items present on a given stack. Un-
                     defined stacks are considered to have a depth of zero O(1).

TopOf   returns the item at the current stack top. If the stack is
                     empty a stack underflow occurs and the *NullItem* is re-
                     turned (since some Item must be). Undefined stacks also
                     cause the *NullItem* to be returned O(1).
*)

```
PROCEDURE IsDefined (    theStack : Stack    (*- in  *))
                                 : BOOLEAN  (*- out *);
PROCEDURE IsEmpty    (    theStack : Stack    (*- in  *))
                                 : BOOLEAN  (*- out *);
PROCEDURE IsEqual    (    left     : Stack    (*- in  *);
                         right    : Stack    (*- in  *))
                                 : BOOLEAN  (*- out *);
PROCEDURE SizeOf     (    theStack : Stack    (*- in  *))
                                 : CARDINAL (*- out *);
PROCEDURE TypeOf     (    theStack : Stack    (*- in  *))
                                 : TypeID   (*- out *);
PROCEDURE DepthOf    (    theStack : Stack    (*- in  *))
                                 : CARDINAL (*- out *);
PROCEDURE TopOf      (    theStack : Stack    (*- in  *))
                                 : Item     (*- out *);
    (*---------------*)
```

```
(*
```

6.2.4 Iterators

The iterator routines *LoopOver* and *LoopChange* provide facilities for looping over some or all items of a stack, with read-only and read-write access to each item, respectively. *theProcess* procedure parameter to these routines returns a BOOLEAN function result. TRUE allows the iteration to proceed to the next item and FALSE terminates the iteration O(n).

Traverse and *TravChange* iterators provide facilities for looping over all items of a stack, with read-only and read-write access to each item, respectively O(n).

All four iterators traverse the given stack from the topmost item towards the bottom of the stack. Obviously, if given an empty stack the processing procedure will not be invoked.

```
*)

PROCEDURE LoopOver    ( theStack  : Stack          (*— in *);
                         theProcess: LoopAccessProc (*— in *));
PROCEDURE LoopChange (  theStack  : Stack          (*— in *);
                         theProcess: LoopChangeProc (*— in *));

PROCEDURE Traverse    ( theStack  : Stack          (*— in *);
                         theProcess: AccessProc     (*— in *));
PROCEDURE TravChange (  theStack  : Stack          (*— in *);
                         theProcess: ChangeProc     (*— in *));

END StackSBMI.
```

6.3 StackSBMI Implementation

This module provides the implementation of the bounded stack composed of generic Items.

```
IMPLEMENTATION MODULE StackSBMI;
(*===============================================================
    Version  : 1.13 07 Jan 1988 C. Lins
    Compiler : TML Modula-2 Compiler for the Apple Macintosh
    Code Size: R- 2348 bytes
    Component: Monolithic Structures - Stack (Opaque)
               Sequential Bounded Managed Iterator
```

```
REVISION HISTORY
v1.13 07 Jan 1988 C. Lins
    Initial implementation for TML Modula-2.
============================================================*)

FROM MacSystem IMPORT
  (*-Proc*) Allocate, Deallocate;

FROM Items IMPORT
  (*-Cons*) NullItem, NoDisposeProc,
  (*-Type*) Item, AssignProc, DisposeProc, AccessProc,
            ChangeProc, LoopAccessProc, LoopChangeProc;

FROM ErrorHandling IMPORT
  (*-Type*) HandlerProc,
  (*-Proc*) NullHandler, ExitOnError, Raise;

FROM StackEnum IMPORT
  (*-Type*) Exceptions, Operations;

FROM TypeManager IMPORT
  (*-Cons*) NullType,
  (*-Type*) TypeID,
  (*-Proc*) AssignOf, DisposeOf;

(*
```

6.3.1 Internal Representation

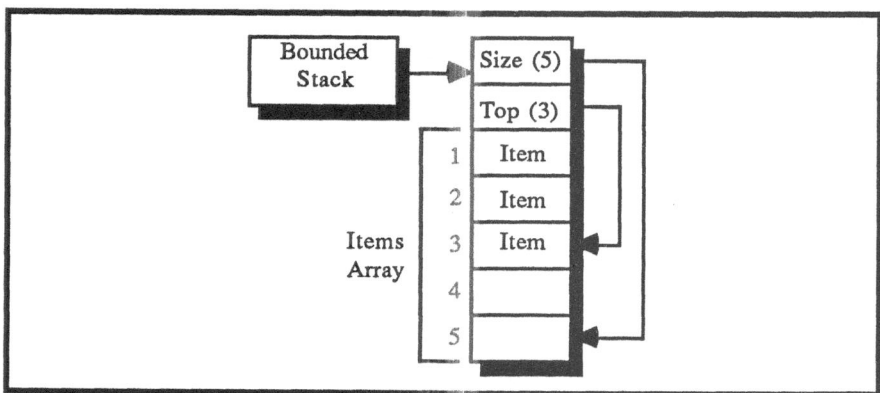

Figure 6.1 The Bounded Stack

The internal representation of a bounded stack dynamically allocates a record on the heap. This record will be made just large enough to hold the declared maximum size of the stack. The items array type declaration covers the maximum allowable size range of a bounded stack, but actually allocates only size entries. This technique permits great savings in the amount of space actually used for each bounded stack.

When a stack is created *top* is initialized to zero and this value is used to represent an empty stack. Furthermore, *top* may never exceed the value of *size*. Encountering this condition indicates a stack overflow.
```
*)

TYPE ItemsArray = ARRAY SizeRange OF Item;

TYPE BoundedStack = RECORD
        dataID: TypeID;     (*— Defined data type for this stack*)
        size  : SizeRange;  (*— Maximum # items on this stack *)
        top   : CARDINAL;   (*— Current stack top := 0 *)
        items : ItemsArray; (*— Dynamic array [1..size] of item *)
     END (*— BoundedStack *);

TYPE Stack = POINTER TO BoundedStack;


(*
```

6.3.2 Exceptions

Two variables support the exception handling mechanism. The first, *stackError*, is used to record the exception code from each operation; while *handlers* is an array of exception handling procedures indexed by the exception code.

The routines *StackError*, *GetHandler*, and *SetHandler* have been previously described in the definition module, and their operation should be readily apparent.

RaiseErrIn is a local routine used to set the *stackError* variable and invoke the *Raise* routine of the ErrorHandling module.
```
*)

VAR stackError : Exceptions;
VAR handlers   : ARRAY Exceptions OF HandlerProc;

   (*--------------*)

PROCEDURE StackError ()              : Exceptions  (*— out *);
BEGIN
   RETURN stackError;
END StackError;
   (*--------------*)
```

```
PROCEDURE GetHandler ( theError    : Exceptions (*- in  *))
                                    : HandlerProc (*- out *);
BEGIN
  RETURN handlers[theError];
END GetHandler;
(*--------------*)

PROCEDURE SetHandler ( theError    : Exceptions  (*- in  *);
                       theHandler : HandlerProc (*- in  *));
BEGIN
  handlers[theError] := theHandler;
END SetHandler;
(*--------------*)

PROCEDURE RaiseErrIn ( theRoutine : Operations  (*- in  *);
                       theError   : Exceptions  (*- in  *));
BEGIN
  stackError := theError;
  Raise(ModuleID, theRoutine, theError, handlers[theError]);
END RaiseErrIn;
(*--------------*)

(*
```

6.3.3 Constructors

Create begins by clearing the *stackError* field under the assumption of a successful result.

The header for the stack must then be allocated in a local variable since the function result cannot be manipulated but only returned. The key to this allocation step is the calculation of the number of bytes necessary based on the size of an individual item and the number of items requested. We must not forget the space for storing *theSize*, *theType*, and the stack *top*. The constant *minStackSize* accomplishes this regardless of the number and size of these "static" fields. The calculation is unaffected by changes in the number or size of these fields that may come about due to future maintenance. If the bounded stack could not be allocated, the overflow exception must be raised, and the NullStack returned.

At this point, all possibility of failure has been avoided and the bounded stack header can be initialized to its empty state (top set to zero), and the size limit and data type ID can be stored for this bounded stack. Lastly, the new stack can be returned to the caller.
```
*)
```

```
PROCEDURE Create (     theSize : SizeRange (*- in  *);
                       theType : TypeID    (*- in  *))
                               : Stack     (*- out *);

CONST minStackSize = SIZE(BoundedStack) - SIZE(ItemsArray);
VAR newStack : Stack;

BEGIN
  stackError := noerr;
  Allocate(newStack, minStackSize + SIZE(Item) * VAL(INTEGER,
      theSize));
    IF (newStack ≠ NIL) THEN
      WITH newStack^ DO
      dataID := theType;
      size   := theSize;
      top    := 0;
    END (*-with*);
    RETURN newStack;
  END (*-if*);
  RaiseErrIn(create, overflow);
  RETURN NullStack;
END Create;

(*--------------*)
```

```
(*
```
Destroy takes advantage of *Clear* setting *stackError* to *noerr* and raising the *undefined* stack exception. If it succeeds, *Destroy* releases the allocated stack header.
```
*)
```

```
PROCEDURE Destroy (VAR theStack : Stack (*- inout *));
BEGIN
  Clear(theStack);
  IF (stackError = noerr) THEN
    Deallocate(theStack);
  END (*-if*);
END Destroy;
(*--------------*)
```

```
(*
```
After initializing *stackError* and verifying that the given stack is a valid object, *Clear* retrieves the item disposal routine associated with the stack's data type from the TypeManager module. Though that module ensures that the disposal routine is not a NIL procedure, it would be inefficient to repeatedly invoke a procedure that did nothing (most compilers are not smart enough to avoid calling an NIL procedure or one that does not contain any executable statements). So to clear the stack of items it may be necessary to dispose of the individual items followed by setting *top* to zero.
```
*)
```

```
PROCEDURE Clear   (VAR theStack : Stack   (*- inout *));

VAR itemIndex : CARDINAL;      (*- loop index over items *)
    freeItem  : DisposeProc;   (*- item disposal routine *)

BEGIN
  stackError := noerr;
  IF (theStack ≠ NIL) THEN
    WITH theStack^ DO
      freeItem := DisposeOf(dataID);
      IF (freeItem ≠ NoDisposeProc) THEN
        FOR itemIndex := MIN(SizeRange) TO top DO
          freeItem(items[itemIndex]);
        END (*-for*);
      END (*-if*);
      top := 0;
    END (*-with*);
  ELSE
    RaiseErrIn(clear, undefined);
  END (*-if*);
END Clear;
(*-------------*)


(*
```

Assignment for bounded objects is simpler to implement than their unbounded counterparts since the opportunity for overflow is restricted to when the target object is (re-)created. If the target object exists and is capable of holding all of the source object's items the target can be safely cleared and its data type updated appropriately. Otherwise, the overflow exception is raised and the assignment operation is aborted. When the target object is undefined it must be created using the data type and size attributes of the source object. If overflow does not occur, the actual assignment can commence, otherwise its suffices to exit (*Create* has already raised the exception).

The assignment operator cannot be used to copy the whole items array as only a slice of the array's index range was actually allocated and who knows what other dynamically allocated objects follow it in memory. Nor can assignment be used to copy individual items as the data type of those items is unknown; using assignment for dynamically allocated items would cause structural sharing of items, which is not desired.
```
*)

PROCEDURE Assign  ( theStack   : Stack (*- in    *);
                    VAR toStack : Stack (*- inout *));

VAR itemIndex : CARDINAL;     (*- loop index over items   *)
    assignItem: AssignProc;   (*- item assignment routine *)
```

```
BEGIN
  stackError := noerr;
  IF (theStack ≠ NIL) THEN
    IF (toStack ≠ NIL) THEN
      IF (theStack^.top ≤ toStack^.size) THEN
        Clear(toStack);
        toStack^.dataID := theStack^.dataID;
      ELSE
        RaiseErrIn(assign, overflow);
      END (*-if*);
    ELSE
      WITH theStack^ DO
        toStack := Create(size, dataID);
      END (*-with*);
    END (*-if*);
    IF (stackError ≠ noerr) THEN
      RETURN;
    END (*-if*);

    WITH theStack^ DO
      assignItem := AssignOf(dataID);
      FOR itemIndex := MIN(SizeRange) TO top DO
        toStack^.items[itemIndex] := assignItem(items
            [itemIndex]);
      END (*-for*);
      toStack^.top := top;
    END (*-with*);
  ELSE
    RaiseErrIn(assign, undefined);
  END (*-if*);
END Assign;
(*--------------*)


(*
```

Push is simple to implement: if the stack is not already full, the array index to the stack top is advanced and *theItem* is stored there; otherwise the *overflow* exception is raised. Of course, the *undefined* exception is raised if the source stack is NIL.

```
*)

PROCEDURE Push (VAR toStack : Stack (*- inout *);
                    theItem : Item  (*- in     *));
BEGIN
  stackError := noerr;
  IF (toStack ≠ NIL) THEN
    WITH toStack^ DO
      IF (top < size) THEN
        INC(top);
```

```
              items[top] := theItem;
          ELSE
              RaiseErrIn(push, overflow);
          END (*—if*);
      END (*—with*);
  ELSE
      RaiseErrIn(push, undefined);
  END (*—if*);
END Push;
(*-------------*)
```

(*
Pop is the inverse of Push, requiring a test for stack underflow, deallocation of the item, and decrementing the stack top.

  PopTopOf is similar to *Pop* except the item is not deallocated, but instead is returned to the caller.
*)

```
PROCEDURE Pop (VAR theStack : Stack (*— inout *));

VAR freeItem : DisposeProc; (*— item disposal routine *)

BEGIN
  stackError := noerr;
  IF (theStack ≠ NIL) THEN
     WITH theStack^ DO
        IF (top ≠ 0) THEN
           freeItem := DisposeOf(dataID);
           freeItem(items[top]);
           DEC(top);
        ELSE
           RaiseErrIn(pop, underflow);
        END (*—if *);
     END (*—with *);
  ELSE
     RaiseErrIn(pop, undefined);
  END (*—if*);
END Pop;
(*-------------*)

PROCEDURE PopTopOf (VAR theStack : Stack (*— inout *))
                                  : Item  (*— out    *);

VAR theItem : Item; (*— item to be returned *)

BEGIN
  stackError := noerr;
```

```
    IF (theStack ≠ NIL) THEN
      WITH theStack^ DO
        IF (top ≠ 0) THEN
          theItem := items[top];
          DEC(top);
          RETURN theItem;
        END (*—if*);
      END (*—with*);
      RaiseErrIn(poptopof, underflow);
    ELSE
      RaiseErrIn(poptopof, undefined);
    END (*—if*);

    (*— Return the empty item if an exception occurred. *)

    RETURN NullItem;
END PopTopOf;
(*--------------*)


(*
```

6.3.4 Selectors

IsDefined checks that the given stack object has been bound to a dynamic entity
by testing for a non-NIL pointer.
```
*)

PROCEDURE IsDefined ( theStack : Stack    (*— in  *))
                                : BOOLEAN (*— out *);
BEGIN
  RETURN (theStack ≠ NIL);
END IsDefined;
(*--------------*)


(*
```
IsEmpty simply tests the index to the stack top being equal to zero, returning
the appropriate logical value. As mentioned in the interface, an undefined stack is
considered empty.
```
*)

PROCEDURE IsEmpty ( theStack : Stack    (*— in  *))
                             : BOOLEAN (*— out *);

BEGIN
  stackError := noerr;
  IF (theStack ≠ NIL) THEN
```

```
      RETURN theStack^.top = 0;
    END (*—if*);
    RaiseErrIn(isempty, undefined);
    RETURN TRUE;
END IsEmpty;
(*--------------*)
```

(*

IsEqual essentially scans both stacks looking for the first mismatch (inequality)
which indicates the stacks are unequal, otherwise if the FOR loop completes the
stacks must be equal. This assumes that the stacks have been defined, have been
given the same data type ID, and have the same depth. The first two of these assumptions, if unfounded, raise the exceptions *undefined* and *typeerror*, respectively. If the stacks do not have the same depth then at least one item differs between
them, and therefore they are unequal.
*)

```
PROCEDURE IsEqual ( left  : Stack    (*— in  *);
                    right : Stack    (*— in  *))
                          : BOOLEAN  (*— out *);

VAR index : CARDINAL; (*— loop index over items *)

BEGIN
   stackError := noerr;
   IF (left ≠ NIL) & (right ≠ NIL) THEN
     IF (left^.dataID = right^.dataID) THEN
       IF (left^.top = right^.top) THEN

         FOR index := MIN(SizeRange) TO left^.top DO
           IF (left^.items[index] ≠ right^.items[index]) THEN
             RETURN FALSE;
           END (*—if*);
         END (*—for*);
         RETURN TRUE;

       END (*—if*);
     ELSE
       RaiseErrIn(isequal, typeerror);
     END (*—if*);
   ELSE
     RaiseErrIn(isequal, undefined);
   END (*—if*);
   RETURN FALSE;
END IsEqual;
(*--------------*)
```

```
(*
```

Both *SizeOf* and *TypeOf* return the current values of *size* and *dataID*, respectively, for the given stack. Undefined stacks raise an exception and return so-called
"null" values. *DepthOf* returns the number of items on the stack, or zero for undefined stacks.

```
*)

PROCEDURE SizeOf ( theStack : Stack    (*- in  *))
                            : CARDINAL (*- out *);
BEGIN
  stackError := noerr;
  IF (theStack ≠ NIL) THEN
    RETURN theStack^.size;
  END (*-if*);
  RaiseErrIn(sizeof, undefined);
  RETURN 0;
END SizeOf;
(*--------------*)

PROCEDURE TypeOf ( theStack : Stack   (*- in  *))
                            : TypeID  (*- out *);
BEGIN
  stackError := noerr;
  IF (theStack ≠ NIL) THEN
    RETURN theStack^.dataID;
  END (*-if*);
  RaiseErrIn(typeof, undefined);
  RETURN NullType;
END TypeOf;
(*--------------*)

PROCEDURE DepthOf ( theStack : Stack    (*- in  *))
                             : CARDINAL (*- out *);
BEGIN
  stackError := noerr;
  IF (theStack ≠ NIL) THEN
    RETURN theStack^.top;
  END (*-if*);
  RaiseErrIn(depthof, undefined);
  RETURN 0;
END DepthOf;
(*--------------*)

PROCEDURE TopOf ( theStack   : Stack    (*- in  *))
                             : Item     (*- out *);
BEGIN
  stackError := noerr;
  IF (theStack ≠ NIL) THEN
```

```
    WITH theStack^ DO
      IF (top ≠ 0) THEN
        RETURN items[top];
      END (*-if*);
    END (*-with*);
    RaiseErrIn(topof, underflow);
  ELSE
    RaiseErrIn(topof, undefined);
  END (*-if*);

  (*- Return the empty item if an exception occurred *)
  RETURN NullItem;
END TopOf;
(*--------------*)


(*
```

6.3.5 Iterators

The two looping iterator routines, *LoopOver* and *LoopChange*, utilize the same algorithm; the essential difference is the type of procedure parameter that is invoked for each item processed. A similar statement can be made about the two traversal routines, *Traverse* and *TravChange*. In all cases, the iteration begins with the top stack item and ends with the bottom stack item.
```
*)

PROCEDURE LoopOver ( theStack  : Stack          (*- in *);
                     theProcess: LoopAccessProc (*- in *));

VAR index : CARDINAL; (*- loop index over items *)

BEGIN
  stackError := noerr;
  IF (theStack ≠ NIL) THEN
    WITH theStack^ DO
      FOR index := top TO MIN(SizeRange) BY -1 DO
        IF ¬theProcess(items[index]) THEN
          RETURN;
        END (*-if*);
      END (*-for*);
    END (*-with*);
  ELSE
    RaiseErrIn(loopover, undefined);
  END (*-if*);
END LoopOver;

(*--------------*)
```

```
PROCEDURE LoopChange    ( theStack  : Stack            (*- in *);
                          theProcess: LoopChangeProc (*- in *));

VAR index : CARDINAL; (*- loop index over items *)

BEGIN
  stackError := noerr;
  IF (theStack ≠ NIL) THEN
    WITH theStack^ DO
      FOR index := top TO MIN(SizeRange) BY -1 DO
        IF ¬theProcess(items[index]) THEN
          RETURN;
        END (*-if*);
      END (*-for*);
    END (*-with*);
  ELSE
    RaiseErrIn(loopchange, undefined);
  END (*-if*);
END LoopChange;
(*-------------*)


PROCEDURE Traverse ( theStack  : Stack       (*- in *);
                     theProcess: AccessProc (*- in *));

VAR index : CARDINAL; (*- loop index over items *)

BEGIN
  stackError := noerr;
  IF (theStack ≠ NIL) THEN
    WITH theStack^ DO
      FOR index := top TO MIN(SizeRange) BY -1 DO
        theProcess(items[index]);
      END (*-for*);
    END (*-with*);
  ELSE
    RaiseErrIn(traverse, undefined);
  END (*-if*);
END Traverse;
(*-------------*)


PROCEDURE TravChange ( theStack  : Stack       (*- in *);
                       theProcess: ChangeProc (*- in *));

VAR index : CARDINAL; (*- loop index over items *)

BEGIN
  stackError := noerr;
  IF (theStack ≠ NIL) THEN
    WITH theStack^ DO
```

```
      FOR index := top TO MIN(SizeRange) BY -1 DO
        theProcess(items[index]);
      END (*-for*);
    END (*-with*);
  ELSE
    RaiseErrIn(traverse, undefined);
  END (*-if*);
END TravChange;
(*-------------*)


(*
```

6.3.6 Module Initialization

In the module initialization the local exception handlers array variables are set to
default handlers (*ExitOnError*) except for the *noerr* handler which is given the
null handler. *stackError* is given the value *noerr* avoiding an undefined state.
```
*)

BEGIN
  FOR stackError := initfailed TO MAX(Exceptions) DO
    SetHandler(stackError, ExitOnError);
  END (*-for*);
  SetHandler(noerr, NullHandler);
  stackError := noerr;
END StackSBMI.
```

References

[1] A. Aho, J. Hopcroft, and J. Ullman, *Data Structures and Algorithms*, Addi-
     son-Wesley, Reading, MA 1983, pp. 37-53.

[2] G. Booch, *Software Components With Ada Structures, Tools, and Subsys-
     tems*, Benjamin/Cummings, Menlo Park, CA 1987.

[3] D. Knuth, *The Art of Computer Programming, Vol. 1, Fundamental Algo-
     rithms*, Addison-Wesley, Reading, MA 1973.

[4] R. Wiener and R. Sincovec, *Data Structures Using Modula-2*, John Wiley &
     Sons, New York, NY 1986.

[5] N. Wirth, *Algorithms and Data Structures*, Prentice-Hall, Englewood Cliffs,
     NJ 1986, pp. 180-195.

[6] N. Wirth, *Algorithms + Data Structures = Programs*, Prentice-Hall, Engle-
     wood Cliffs, NJ 1976.

[7] N. Wirth, *Programming in Modula-2*, Springer-Verlag, New York, NY 1983.

7 The Unbounded Stack

This chapter presents an implementation of the stack abstraction described in Chapter 5. This form has the properties Sequential, Unbounded, Managed, and Iterator which describe specific aspects of the implementation as follows:

Sequential   Can only be used in a non-tasking environment, or by only one task.

Unbounded   The stack size varies dynamically as items are added and removed.

Managed   Memory space for items and objects is returned to the system when no longer needed.

Iterator   Routines are provided for looping over each of stack item.

Section 7.1 contains the interface to the Unbounded Stack module followed by its implementation in Section 7.2.

7.1 StackSUMI Interface

The interface to the unbounded stack is presented below. The purpose and implementation specifics of each routine is briefly described along with mention of the complexity measure of the actual implementation.

```
DEFINITION MODULE StackSUMI;
(*===============================================================
    Version  : 1.13 07 Jan 1988 C. Lins
    Compiler : TML Modula-2 Compiler for the Apple Macintosh
    Component: Monolithic Structures - Stack (Opaque version)
               Sequential Unbounded Managed Iterator

    INTRODUCTION
    This module provides the stack ADT composed of generic Items.

    REVISION HISTORY
    v1.13 07 Jan 1988 C. Lins:
        Initial implementation for TML Modula-2.
===============================================================*)

FROM Items IMPORT
    (*--Type*) Item, AccessProc, LoopAccessProc, ChangeProc,
        LoopChangeProc;
```

```
FROM StackEnum  IMPORT
  (*--Type*) Exceptions;

FROM ErrorHandling IMPORT
  (*--Type*) HandlerProc;

FROM TypeManager IMPORT
  (*--Type*) TypeID;
(*----------------------*)

TYPE  Stack;
CONST NullStack = VAL(Stack, NIL);

(*
```

7.1.1 Exceptions

ModuleID   is used by the exception handling mechanism to distinguish this
              module from other modules.

StackError returns the exception code from the most recent stack operation.
              A *noerr* result indicates successful completion of the operation O
              (1).

GetHandler returns the exception handler routine associated with a given ex-
              ception. The routine is a function procedure returning a procedure
              as its result but the *HandlerProc* may not be called from within
              the *GetHandler* call itself. Before invocation the procedure result
              must be first assigned to a procedure variable. Exception handlers
              are given an initial value of *ExitOnError* except for the handler
              for *noerr* which is initialized to the null exception handler O(1).

SetHandler associates an exception handler routine with the given exception
              and is the inverse of *GetHandler*. This routine may be used to
              override the default settings for the exception handlers O(1).

```
*)

CONST ModuleID = 2;

PROCEDURE StackError ()              : Exceptions  (*-- out *);

PROCEDURE GetHandler ( theError    : Exceptions  (*-- in  *))
                                    : HandlerProc (*-- out *);
PROCEDURE SetHandler ( theError    : Exceptions  (*-- in  *);
                       theHandler : HandlerProc (*-- in  *);
```

(*

7.1.2 Constructors

Create   attempts to generate a new, empty stack associated with the given
data type identifier (*theType*) and Item operations. The *TypeID* is
used to support Items of any data type. The component can use
theType to assign one item to another and to release dynamically
allocated resources associated with an Item without knowledge of
the Item's internal composition. In this way, one may create a
stack whose items consist of other (dynamically allocated) structures, as well as stacks consisting of the basic data types. Create
returns the new stack upon successful completion of the routine. If
the stack cannot be created, the modula raises the overflow exception and returns the constant *NullStack* O(1).

Destroy   clears the given stack of any items and then destroys the stack itself. Where Create makes a defined stack, Destroy makes the stack
undefined O(n).

Clear   removes from the given stack of all items and uses *theType* attribute of the stack (assigned when the stack was created) to retrieve
the item deallocation routine for items of the stack. Clearing the
stack returns it to the empty state O(n).

Assign   attempts to generate a duplicate of the source stack (*theStack*) in
the target stack (*toStack*). It automatically creates the target stack
using the data type attribute of the source stack, if necessary. If
this step is unnecessary (the target stack having been previously
created), the target is cleared of its present contents, and its data
type is set to that of the source stack O(n).

To accommodate Items of any data type, the *TypeID* of the source
stack is used to assign the contents of one item to another item.
This employs the assignment routine for the given *TypeID*.

Push   adds items to the given stack. A given item is placed on the stack
top. If the stack cannot be expanded for *theItem*, the module raises
the *overflow* exception and the stack remains unchanged O(1).

Pop   removes the topmost item from the given stack. If the given stack
is empty on entry to *Pop*, the module raises the *underflow* exception and the stack remains unchanged O(1).

PopTopOf   is a convenience routine combining semantics of the constructor
Pop and the selector *TopOf*. It differs from Pop in that the item's
value is returned rather than disposed of O(1).

*)

```
PROCEDURE Create    (     theType  : TypeID (*-- in    *))
                          : Stack  (*-- out   *);

PROCEDURE Destroy (VAR theStack  : Stack  (*-- inout *));

PROCEDURE Clear   (VAR theStack  : Stack  (*-- inout *));

PROCEDURE Assign    (     theStack : Stack  (*-- in    *);
                    VAR toStack    : Stack  (*-- inout *));

PROCEDURE Push    (VAR toStack    : Stack  (*-- inout *);
                        theItem    : Item   (*-- in    *));

PROCEDURE Pop     (VAR theStack  : Stack  (*-- inout *));

PROCEDURE PopTopOf (VAR theStack  : Stack  (*-- inout *))
                          : Item   (*-- out   *);

(*
```

7.1.3 Selectors

IsDefined attempts to determine whether a given stack is valid — that is, the stack has been created and not yet destroyed. This procedure may be as simple or complicated as the implementor desires and the requirements of the application demands O(1).

IsEmpty returns true if a given stack contains no items; in other words, its depth is zero. Undefined stacks are always considered empty O(1).

IsEqual returns true if the left and right stacks contain the same items in the same order. Obviously, both must also have the same data type and have been created. An undefined stack is not equal to any other stack, including itself O(n).

TypeOf returns the *typeID* value given to the stack when it was created or used as the target of an assignment operation. It is provided so that the user of the module need not maintain a separate variable recording this information O(1).

DepthOf returns the number of items present on the given stack. Undefined stacks are considered to have a depth of zero O(1).

TopOf returns the item currently at the top of the stack. If the stack is empty a stack underflow occurs and the *NullItem* is returned (since the procedure must return *some* Item). Undefined stacks also cause the *NullItem* to be returned O(1).

```
*)
```

```
PROCEDURE IsDefined (    theStack : Stack     (*-- in  *))
                                  : BOOLEAN   (*-- out *);

PROCEDURE IsEmpty    (    theStack : Stack     (*-- in  *))
                                  : BOOLEAN   (*-- out *);

PROCEDURE IsEqual    (    left     : Stack     (*-- in  *);
                          right    : Stack     (*-- in  *))
                                  : BOOLEAN   (*-- out *);

PROCEDURE TypeOf     (    theStack : Stack     (*-- in  *))
                                  : TypeID    (*-- out *);

PROCEDURE DepthOf    (    theStack : Stack     (*-- in  *))
                                  : CARDINAL  (*-- out *);

PROCEDURE TopOf      (    theStack : Stack     (*-- in  *))
                                  : Item      (*-- out *);

(*
```

7.1.4 Iterators

The iterator routines *LoopOver* and *LoopChange* provide facilities for looping over some or all items of a stack, and providing read-only and read-write access to each item, respectively. *theProcess* procedure parameter to these routines returns a BOOLEAN function result where TRUE allows the iteration to proceed to the next item and FALSE causes the iteration to be terminated. O(n).

Traverse and *TravChange* iterators provide facilities for looping over all items of a stack, with read-only and read-write access to each item, respectively. O(n).

All four iterators traverse the given stack from the topmost item towards the bottom of the stack. Obviously, if given an empty stack the processing procedure will not be invoked.
*)

```
PROCEDURE LoopOver   ( theStack    : Stack          (*-- in *);
                       theProcess  : LoopAccessProc (*-- in *));

PROCEDURE LoopChange ( theStack    : Stack          (*-- in *);
                       theProcess  : LoopChangeProc (*-- in *));

PROCEDURE Traverse   ( theStack    : Stack          (*-- in *);
                       theProcess  : AccessProc     (*-- in *));
```

```
PROCEDURE TravChange ( theStack    : Stack        (*-- in *);
                       theProcess  : ChangeProc   (*-- in *));

END StackSUMI.

(*
```

7.2   StackSUMI Implementation

This module provides the implementation for the operations of the unbounded
stack abstract data type.

```
IMPLEMENTATION MODULE StackSUMI;

(*===============================================================
   Version  : 1.13 07 Jan 1988 C. Lins
   Compiler : TML Modula-2 Compiler for the Apple Macintosh
   Code Size: R- 2452 bytes
   Component: Monolithic Structures - Stack (Opaque)
              Sequential Unbounded Managed Iterator

   REVISION HISTORY
   v1.13 07 Jan 1988 C. Lins:
     Initial implementation for TML Modula-2.
===============================================================*)

FROM MacSystem IMPORT
   (*--Proc*) Allocate, Deallocate;

FROM Items IMPORT
   (*--Cons*) NullItem, NoDisposeProc,
   (*--Type*) Item, AssignProc, DisposeProc, AccessProc,
             ChangeProc, LoopAccessProc, LoopChangeProc;

FROM ErrorHandling IMPORT
   (*--Type*) HandlerProc,
   (*--Proc*) NullHandler, ExitOnError, Raise;

FROM StackEnum IMPORT
   (*--Type*) Exceptions, Operations;
```

```
FROM TypeManager IMPORT
  (*--Cons*) NullType,
  (*--Type*) TypeID,
  (*--Proc*) AssignOf, DisposeOf;
  (*-------------------*)

(*
```

7.2.1 Internal Unbounded Stack Representation

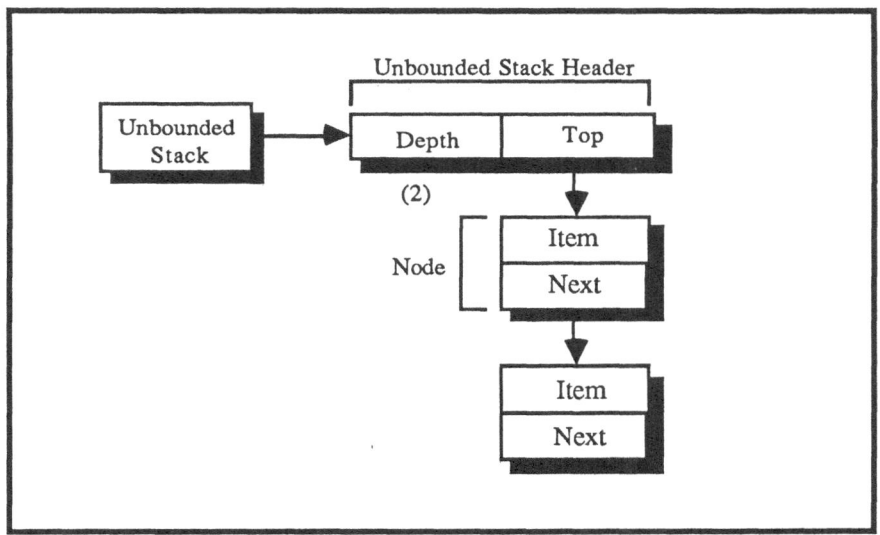

Figure 7.1 The Unbounded Stack

7.2.1.1 Stack Header

The internal representation of an unbounded stack uses a singly linked list of nodes, with a header node, called *UnboundedStack*. This header contains a pointer to the topmost node on the stack, a count of the current stack depth, and the data *typeID* of the stack. An empty stack is represented by an *UnboundedStack* with a *Top* pointer of NIL and a *Depth* of zero. A NIL value for the Stack will be accepted as a legal value for an empty stack when this will not disrupt the semantics of the invoked operation.

7.2.1.2 Node

Each node in the list of stack items contains the Item stored on the stack and
a link to the node immediately beneath it. The link for the bottommost node
on the stack contains a value of NIL to represent the end of the stack.

7.2.1.3   Management of Free Stack Nodes

A separate list of free nodes is kept global for all items popped from the
stack. The FreeList is effectively a FreeStack due to the LIFO management
scheme employed. This technique minimizes calls to Allocate and Deallocate
system routines, since both (especially Allocate) involve a large overhead
compared to the bounded form.

7.2.1.4   Stack – Representation of Depth

The cost to maintain the depth of each stack is relatively small, consisting of
a field to store the depth (a CARDINAL) and the execution cost to maintain
this field whenever an item is pushed or popped from the stack. The alternative would be to iterate over every item in the stack to calculate the depth
whenever this operation was requested. The implementation used yields an algorithm of O(1) time complexity for determination of the stack's depth as op-
posed to an O(n) algorithm. This is purchased at the expense of a small increase in space complexity and a small increase in the proportionality
constants for the time complexity of Push and Pop.

7.2.1.5   Stack – Representation of an Empty Stack

Representation of an opaque type is restricted to POINTER types [Wirth85,
pg. 169]. An alternative representation for an empty stack would use a value
of NIL for the Stack. This would simplify testing for an empty stack but
would complicate primitive operations such as Pop and Clear, which would
then require the Free operation as a parameter.

7.2.2 Efficiency of Operations

We violate the abstraction within the implementation of a component by examining the internal components of the data structure. Repetitive invocations of procedures supporting the abstraction may be replaced with the 'inline' equivalent of the operation. This is most commonly done when testing for the empty stack condition and in copying items.
*)

```
TYPE NodePtr = POINTER TO Node;

TYPE Node   = RECORD (*-- a stack node *)
        item : Item;      (*-- generic data item *)
        next : NodePtr;   (*-- next node beneath this one *)
      END (*-- Node *);

TYPE UnboundedStack = RECORD
        dataID: TypeID;   (*-- Defined data type*)
        depth : CARDINAL; (*-- current stack depth, := 0 *)
          top : NodePtr;  (*-- current stack top := NIL *)
        END (*-- UnboundedStack *);

TYPE Stack = POINTER TO UnboundedStack;

(*----------------------*)

(*
```

7.2.3 Exceptions

Two variables are required to support the exception handling mechanism. The first, *stackError*, is used to record the exception code from each operation; while *handlers* is an array of exception handling procedures indexed by the exception code.

The definition module described the routines *StackError*, *GetHandler* and *SetHandler* and their operation should be readily apparent. *RaiseErrIn* is a local routine used to set *stackError* and to invoke the *Raise* routine of the ErrorHandling module.
*)

```
VAR stackError : Exceptions;
VAR handlers : ARRAY Exceptions OF HandlerProc;

   (*--------------------*)
```

```
PROCEDURE StackError ()              : Exceptions  (*-- out *);
BEGIN
  RETURN stackError;
END StackError;
(*---------------------------*)


PROCEDURE GetHandler ( theError   : Exceptions  (*-- in  *))
                                  : HandlerProc (*-- out *);
BEGIN
  RETURN handlers[theError];
END GetHandler;
(*---------------------------*)


PROCEDURE SetHandler ( theError  : Exceptions  (*-- in *);
                       theHandler: HandlerProc (*-- in *));
BEGIN
  handlers[theError] := theHandler;
END SetHandler;
(*---------------------------*)


PROCEDURE RaiseErrIn ( theRoutine: Operations  (*-- in *);
                       theError   : Exceptions  (*-- in *));
BEGIN
  stackError := theError;
  Raise(ModuleID, theRoutine, theError, handlers[theError]);
END RaiseErrIn;
(*---------------------------*)


(*─────────────────────────────────────────────────
↓ Local  ↓  Local  ↓  Local  ↓  Local  ↓  Local  ↓  Local  ↓
─────────────────────────────────────────────────*)

    MODULE FreeListMgr;
    (*-- This local module controls access to the Available node
    list.
      -- Version 1.00 07 Jun. 1987 C. Lins *)

    IMPORT Node, NodePtr, Allocate, Deallocate;
    EXPORT FreeNode, GetNode;

    VAR FreeList : NodePtr; (*-- Free list of available stack
    nodes *)

    (*---------------------------*)
```

(*

FreeNode adds a given node to the front of the free list. *theNode's next* field is linked to the front of the free list and the node becomes the new front of the free list.
*)

```
PROCEDURE FreeNode (VAR theNode: NodePtr);
BEGIN
   theNode^.next := FreeList;
   FreeList      := theNode;
END FreeNode;
(*---------------------------*)
```

(*
GetNode attempts to generate a new stack node. If the free list is empty, it attempts to allocate an entirely new node. If the allocation attempt fails, return False and exit, otherwise return a function result of True to the new node and exit. If the free list is not empty, remove the first available node from the free list and return the used node to the caller along with a function result of True.
*)

```
PROCEDURE GetNode (VAR theNode: NodePtr (*--out *)): BOOLEAN;
BEGIN
   IF (FreeList = NIL) THEN
     Allocate(theNode, SIZE(Node));
     IF (theNode = NIL) THEN
       RETURN FALSE;
     END (*--if*);
   ELSE
     theNode := FreeList;
     FreeList := FreeList^.next;
   END (*--if*);
   RETURN TRUE;
END GetNode;
(*-------------------------*)

(* ~~~~~~~~~~~~~~~~~~~~~~~~~~~~~~~~~~~~~~~~~~~~ *)
(* ~~~~~  Local Module Initialization  ~~~~~ *)

BEGIN
   FreeList := NIL; (*-- Initialize the free list to empty. *)
END FreeListMgr;
```

```
(*---------------------------------------------------------
↑  Local  ↑  Local  ↑  Local  ↑  Local  ↑  Local  ↑  Local  ↑
---------------------------------------------------------*)
```

(*

7.2.4 Constructors

Create begins by clearing the *stackError* field under the assumption of a successful result.

Create then allocates the stack header in a local variable, since the function result can only be returned, not manipulated. If the unbounded stack could not be allocated, *Create* must raise the *overflow* exception and return the *NullStack*.

At this point, all possibility of failure has been avoided and the unbounded stack header can be initialized to its empty state (*top* is set to NIL, *depth* set to zero), and the data type ID can be stored for this unbounded stack. Lastly, the new stack is returned to the caller.
*)

```
PROCEDURE Create (    theType : TypeID (*-- in *))
                            : Stack  (*-- out *);

VAR newStack : Stack;

BEGIN
  stackError := noerr;
  Allocate(newStack, SIZE(UnboundedStack));
  IF (newStack ≠ NIL) THEN
    WITH newStack^ DO
      dataID := theType;
      depth := 0;
      top := NIL;
    END (*--with*);
    RETURN newStack;
  END (*--if*);
  RaiseErrIn(create, overflow);
  RETURN NullStack;
END Create;
(*---------------------------*)


(*
```

Destroy takes advantage of the fact that *Clear* sets *stackError* to *noerr* and raises the *undefined* stack exception. So if Clear succeeds, Destroy simply releases the allocated stack header.
*)

```
PROCEDURE Destroy (VAR theStack : Stack (*-- inout *));
BEGIN
  Clear(theStack);
  IF (stackError = noerr) THEN
    Deallocate(theStack);
  END (*--if*);
END Destroy;
(*---------------------------*)
```

(*

After initializing *stackError* and verifying that a given stack is a valid object, *Clear* retrieves the item disposal routine associated with the stack's data type from the TypeManager module. Each item on the stack is then deallocated followed by its stack node. To do this safely a local variable, *nodeToFree*, is used to hold each node. The loop invariant takes advantage of the fact that the bottommost stack node contains a *next* field of NIL and this will automatically cause *top* to contain that value once all stack nodes have been cleared. The last step is to reset *depth* to zero.
*)

```
PROCEDURE Clear (VAR theStack : Stack (*-- inout *));

VAR nodeToFree : NodePtr;    (*-- node to deallocate *)
    freeItem   : DisposeProc; (*-- item disposal routine *)

BEGIN
   stackError := noerr;
   IF (theStack ≠ NIL) THEN
     WITH theStack^ DO
       freeItem := DisposeOf(dataID);
       WHILE (top ≠ NIL) DO
         nodeToFree := top;
         top := top^.next;
         freeItem(nodeToFree^.item);
         FreeNode(nodeToFree);
       END (*--while*);
       depth := 0;
     END (*--with*);
   ELSE
     RaiseErrIn(clear, undefined);
   END (*--if*);
END Clear;
(*--------------------------*)
```

(*

A complication is raised by assignment for unbounded objects — overflow may occur while adding individual stack nodes. An undefined target stack object must be created using the data type attribute of the source object. The actual assignment can commence if overflow does not occur, otherwise the program exits. (*Create* has already raised the exception.) When the target object is defined upon entry to the *Assign* operation, it is sufficient to *Clear* the existing contents and update the data type with that of the source stack. If the source stack is empty, the routine may simply exit. Otherwise it copies the top node from the source to the target followed by a loop over any remaining items.

Two node pointers are necessary in order to properly copy the source stack: one, to loop through each of the source nodes, and a second to keep track of the last node added to the target stack.

The assignment operator cannot be used to copy individual items since the data type of those items is unknown. Using assignment for dynamically allocated items would cause an undesirable structural sharing of items.
*)

```
PROCEDURE Assign (    theStack : Stack (*-- in      *);
                  VAR toStack  : Stack (*-- inout *));

VAR fromIndex : NodePtr;   (*-- node to add from source stack *)
    toIndex   : NodePtr;   (*-- last node added to targ stack *)
    assignItem: AssignProc;(*-- item assignment routine *)

BEGIN
  IF (theStack ≠ NIL) THEN
    IF (toStack ≠ NIL) THEN
      Clear(toStack);
      toStack^.dataID := theStack^.dataID;
    ELSE
      toStack := Create(theStack^.dataID);
    END (*--if*);

    IF (stackError ≠ noerr) OR (theStack^.top = NIL) THEN
      RETURN;
    END (*--if*);

    assignItem := AssignOf(theStack^.dataID);
    IF GetNode(toStack^.top) THEN
      WITH toStack^.top^ DO
        item := assignItem(theStack^.top^.item);
        next := NIL;
      END (*--with*);
      fromIndex := theStack^.top;
      toIndex   := toStack^.top;
      INC(toStack^.depth);
    ELSE
      RaiseErrIn(assign, overflow);
    END (*--if*);

    WHILE (stackError = noerr) & (fromIndex^.next ≠ NIL) DO
      fromIndex := fromIndex^.next;
      IF GetNode(toIndex^.next) THEN
        toIndex := toIndex^.next;
        WITH toIndex^ DO
          item := assignItem(fromIndex^.item);
```

```
                next := NIL;
            END (*--with*);
            INC(toStack^.depth);
          ELSE
            RaiseErrIn(assign, overflow);
          END (*--if*);
      END (*--while*);
    ELSE
      RaiseErrIn(assign, undefined);
    END (*--if*);
END Assign;
(*---------------------------*)
```

```
(*
```
Push attempts to retrieve a stack node for the new item, which if successful permits storing the data for new stack top and a link to the current stack top. Then *Push* can update the stack top to point to the new node and the depth can be updated. If a stack node cannot be allocated, the *overflow* exception is raised and the stack is left unchanged.
```
*)
```

```
PROCEDURE Push (VAR toStack : Stack (*-- inout *);
                    theItem : Item  (*-- in    *));

VAR newNode: NodePtr;

BEGIN
  stackError := noerr;
  IF (toStack ≠ NIL) THEN
    IF GetNode(newNode) THEN
      WITH toStack^ DO
        newNode^.item := theItem;
        newNode^.next := top;
        top := newNode;
        INC(depth);
      END (*--with*);
    ELSE
      RaiseErrIn(push, overflow);
    END (*--if*);
  ELSE
    RaiseErrIn(push, undefined);
  END (*--if*);
END Push;
(*---------------------------*)
```

```
(*
```
Pop is the inverse of *Push*, requiring a test for stack underflow, before effectively undoing what was done in order to place a node on the stack.

PopTopOf is similar to *Pop* except it returns the item to the caller rather than deallocating it.
```
*)

PROCEDURE Pop (VAR theStack : Stack (*-- inout *));

VAR nodeToPop: NodePtr;
    freeItem : DisposeProc; (*-- item disposal routine *)

BEGIN
   stackError := noerr;
   IF (theStack ≠ NIL) THEN
     WITH theStack^ DO
       IF (top ≠ NIL) THEN         (*--Check for stack underflow *)
          nodeToPop := top;        (*-- Remember current top of
                                           stack *)

          top := top^.next;        (*-- Update the top of stack *)

          DEC(depth);              (*-- Maintain correct depth
                                           count*)
          freeItem := DisposeOf(dataID);
          freeItem(nodeToPop^.item); (*-- Safely recover the item
                                           space *)
          FreeNode(nodeToPop);     (*-- Recover the node space *)
       ELSE
          RaiseErrIn(pop, underflow);
       END (*--if*);
     END (*--with*);
   ELSE
     RaiseErrIn(pop, undefined);
   END (*--if*);
END Pop;
(*--------------------------*)


PROCEDURE PopTopOf (VAR theStack : Stack   (*-- inout *))
                                  : Item    (*-- out   *);

VAR  oldTop  : NodePtr; (*original top stack node *)
     topItem : Item;     (*item to be returned *)

BEGIN
   stackError := noerr;
   IF (theStack ≠ NIL) THEN
     WITH theStack^ DO
```

```
      IF (top ≠ NIL) THEN      (*-- Check for stack underflow *)
         oldTop := top;        (*-- Remember current top of stack*)
         topItem:= top^.item; (*-- Remember current item at stack
                                        top *)
         top      := top^.next; (*-- Update stack top *)
         DEC(depth);           (*-- Maintain correct depth count *)
         FreeNode(oldTop);     (*-- Recover node space *)
         RETURN topItem;       (*-- Return data item *)
      END (*--if*);
   END (*--with*);
   RaiseErrIn(poptopof, underflow);
 ELSE
   RaiseErrIn(poptopof, undefined);
 END (*--if*);
 RETURN NullItem;
END PopTopOf;
(*---------------------------*)


(*
```

7.2.5 Selectors

IsDefined is a simple test for a defined stack object, simply testing for the stack top being not NIL and returning true or false as appropriate
```
*)

PROCEDURE IsDefined ( theStack : Stack    (*-- in  *))
                                 : BOOLEAN (*-- out *);

BEGIN
  RETURN (theStack ≠ NIL);
END IsDefined;
(*---------------------------*)


(*
```
IsEmpty simply tests the link to the stack top being NIL, returning the appropriate logical value. As mentioned in the interface, an undefined stack is considered empty.
```
*)

PROCEDURE IsEmpty ( theStack : Stack    (*-- in  *))
                               : BOOLEAN (*-- out *);

BEGIN
  stackError := noerr;
  IF (theStack ≠ NIL) THEN
```

```
      RETURN theStack^.top = NIL;
    END (*--if*);

    RaiseErrIn(isempty, undefined);
    RETURN TRUE;
  END IsEmpty;
  (*--------------------------*)
```

(*

IsEqual scans both stacks looking for the first inequality between items which indicates the stacks are unequal. If the loop completes the stacks must be equal. This assumes that both stacks:

        1. have been defined,
        2. have been given the same data type ID, and
        3. have the same depth.

The first two of these assumptions, if unfounded, raise the exceptions, *undefined* and *typeerror*, respectively. Invariably, since the stacks have the same depth, when *leftIndex* is NIL, by definition *rightIndex* will also be NIL.
*)

```
PROCEDURE IsEqual (    left  : Stack   (*-- in  *);
                       right : Stack   (*-- in  *))
                             : BOOLEAN (*-- out *);

VAR leftIndex : NodePtr;
    rightIndex: NodePtr;

BEGIN
  stackError := noerr;
  IF (left ≠ NIL) & (right ≠ NIL) THEN
    IF (left^.dataID = right^.dataID) THEN
      IF (left^.depth = right^.depth) THEN
        leftIndex := left^.top;
        rightIndex:= right^.top;
        WHILE (leftIndex ≠ NIL) &
            (leftIndex^.item = rightIndex^.item) DO
          leftIndex := leftIndex^.next;
          rightIndex:= rightIndex^.next;
        END (*--while*);
        RETURN (leftIndex = NIL);
      END (*--if*);
    ELSE
      RaiseErrIn(isequal, typeerror);
    END (*--if*);
  ELSE
    RaiseErrIn(isequal, undefined);
```

```
  END (*--if*);
  RETURN FALSE;
END IsEqual;
(*---------------------------*)

PROCEDURE TypeOf (    theStack : Stack    (*-- in  *))
                              : TypeID (*-- out *);
BEGIN
  stackError := noerr;
  IF (theStack ≠ NIL) THEN
    RETURN theStack^.dataID;
  END (*--if*);
  RaiseErrIn(typeof, undefined);
  RETURN NullType;
END TypeOf;
(*---------------------------*)

PROCEDURE DepthOf (    theStack : Stack      (*-- in  *))
                              : CARDINAL (*-- out *);
BEGIN
  stackError := noerr;
  IF (theStack ≠ NIL) THEN
    RETURN theStack^.depth;
  END (*--if*);
  RaiseErrIn(depthof, undefined);
  RETURN 0;
END DepthOf;
(*---------------------------*)

PROCEDURE TopOf (    theStack : Stack (*-- in  *))
                            : Item  (*-- out *);
BEGIN
  stackError := noerr;
  IF (theStack ≠ NIL) THEN
    WITH theStack^ DO
      IF (top ≠ NIL) THEN
        RETURN top^.item;
      END (*--if*);
    END (*--with*);
    RaiseErrIn(topof, underflow);
  ELSE
    RaiseErrIn(topof, undefined);
  END (*--if*);

  RETURN NullItem;
END TopOf;
(*---------------------------*)
```

```
(*
```

7.2.6 Iterators

The two "looping" iterator routines, *LoopOver* and *LoopChange*, utilize the
same algorithm; the essential difference is the type of procedure parameter invoked for each item processed. The situation is similar with the two traversal
routines *Traverse* and *TravChange*. In all cases, the iteration begins with the top
stack item and ends with the bottom stack item.

```
*)

PROCEDURE LoopOver ( theStack : Stack          (*-- in *);
                     theProcess: LoopAccessProc (*-- in *));

VAR index : NodePtr;

BEGIN
  stackError := noerr;
  IF (theStack ≠ NIL) THEN
    index := theStack^.top;
    WHILE (index ≠ NIL) & theProcess(index^.item) DO
      index := index^.next;
    END (*--while*);
  ELSE
    RaiseErrIn(loopover, undefined);
  END (*--if*);
END LoopOver;
(*---------------------------*)

PROCEDURE LoopChange ( theStack  : Stack          (*-- in *);
                       theProcess: LoopChangeProc (*-- in *));

VAR index : NodePtr;

BEGIN
  stackError := noerr;
  IF (theStack ≠ NIL) THEN
    index := theStack^.top;
    WHILE (index ≠ NIL) & theProcess(index^.item) DO
      index := index^.next;
    END (*--while*);
  ELSE
    RaiseErrIn(loopchange, undefined);
  END (*--if*);
END LoopChange;
(*-------------------------*)
```

```
PROCEDURE Traverse ( theStack  : Stack       (*-- in *);
                     theProcess: AccessProc (*-- in *));

VAR index : NodePtr;

BEGIN
  stackError := noerr;
  IF (theStack ≠ NIL) THEN
    index := theStack^.top;
    WHILE (index ≠ NIL) DO
      theProcess(index^.item);
      index := index^.next;
    END (*--while*);
  ELSE
    RaiseErrIn(traverse, undefined);
  END (*--if*);
END Traverse;
(*--------------------------*)

PROCEDURE TravChange ( theStack  : Stack       (*-- in *);
                       theProcess: ChangeProc (*-- in *));

VAR index : NodePtr;

BEGIN
  stackError := noerr;
  IF (theStack ≠ NIL) THEN
    index := theStack^.top;
    WHILE (index ≠ NIL) DO
      theProcess(index^.item);
      index := index^.next;
    END (*--while*);
  ELSE
    RaiseErrIn(travchange, undefined);
  END (*--if*);
END TravChange;
(*--------------------------*)
```

(*

7.2.7 Module Initialization

Module initialization sets the local exception handlers array variables to default handlers (*ExitOnError*) except for the *noerr* handler which is given the null handler. *stackError* is given the value *noerr* avoiding an undefined state.
*)

```
BEGIN
  FOR stackError := initfailed TO MAX(Exceptions) DO
    SetHandler(stackError, ExitOnError);
  END (*--for*);
  SetHandler(noerr, NullHandler);
  stackError := noerr;
END StackSUMI.
```

References

[1] A. Aho, J. Hopcroft, and J. Ullman, *Data Structures and Algorithms*, Addison-Wesley, Reading, MA 1983, pp. 37-53.

[2] G. Booch, *Software Components With Ada Structures, Tools, and Subsystems*, Benjamin/Cummings, Menlo Park, CA 1987.

[3] D. Knuth, *The Art of Computer Programming, Vol. 1, Fundamental Algorithms*, Addison-Wesley, Reading, MA 1973.

[4] R. Wiener and R. Sincovec, *Data Structures Using Modula-2*, John Wiley & Sons, New York, NY 1986.

[5] N. Wirth, *Algorithms and Data Structures*, Prentice-Hall, Englewood Cliffs, NJ 1986.

[6] N. Wirth, *Algorithms + Data Structures = Programs*, Prentice-Hall, Englewood Cliffs, NJ 1976.

[7] N. Wirth, *Programming in Modula-2*, Springer-Verlag, New York, NY 1983.

8 The String Abstraction

This chapter presents the specification for the String abstraction.

- Section 8.1 describes the concept of a String and defines terms used to describe a String and its state.

- Section 8.2 lists some uses and applications of String objects in computer programs.

- Section 8.3 Constructor operations for String operation.

- Section 8.4 Selector operations for String operation.

- Section 8.5 Iterator operations for String operation.

- Section 8.6 discusses the exception conditions that may occur as a result of invoking a String operation

- Section 8.7 summarizes String operations and exceptions.

8.1 Strings: Concepts and Definitions

A *string* is an ordered sequence of items permitting addition and removal of items at any position in the sequence. *Length* denotes the number of items presently in a string. Each item is referenced by its *position* within the string, where 0 < position ≤ Length(String). Figure 8.1 depicts these terms and their interrelationships.

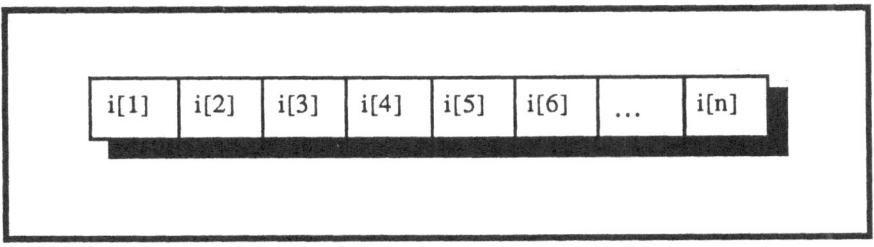

Figure 8.1 The String Abstraction

String   An ordered sequence of *n* items, where $n \geq 0$. Items of a string may be added, deleted, or replaced at any position within the string.

Length   The number of items presently in a string.

Position   A reference to the location of an item within a string, measured from the front of the string. The numbering of positions will follow the convention of starting with one.

Substring   A "contiguous sequence of items" of a string.

NullString Term used (in this publication) for the undefined string.

8.2 Selected Summary of String Applications and Uses

The string abstraction is most commonly applied as a string of character items. Computer languages commonly provide this as a predefined type, though only rarely will all of the operations applicable to the string abstraction be provided as a part of the language. Modula-2 has been justifiably criticized for the weakness of its string processing capabilities. Obviously, many applications require character strings for such diverse tasks as compiling and assembling of human-readable text, text editing, formatting, spell checking, indexing, cross-reference generators, file compression and cryptography. The man-machine interface must be tailored towards human beings who must be able to read the machine's messages and output.

As far as Modula-2 is concerned, *numbers* are strings of numeric digits, *arrays* are (bounded) strings of some given base type. A Modula-2 string is an ordered sequence of items (like other list structures) with a rich set of operations that permit manipulation of items within the string at any position. Compilers view a source program as a string of symbols, such as identifiers, operators, etc. Compiler theory evaluates lexical and syntactic structure in terms of strings.

This chapter examines the string in its most general form, providing a specification for the string abstract data type with a powerful set of operations.

8.3 String Constructor Operations

8.3.1 Create () ↑String

Requires	**nothing**
Modifies	**nothing**
Effects	Generates a new (empty) string object
	IsDefined (String') = True
	IsEmpty (String') = True
	IsEqual (String', String') = True
	IsEqual (String', OtherString) = IsEmpty (OtherString)
	LengthOf (String') = 0
Signals	Overflow **when** the string could not be created **ensuring** returns the NullString

8.3.2 Destroy (↕String)

Requires	**nothing**
Modifies	**at most** String
Effects	Removes all items from the string making the string empty, release the string variable, and set the string to the NullString
	IsDefined (String') = False
	IsEmpty (String') = Undefined & True
	IsEqual (String', AnyString) = Undefined & False
	LengthOf (String') = Undefined & 0
Signals	Undefined **when** ¬IsDefined (String) **ensuring modifies nothing**

8.3.3 Clear (↕String)

Requires	**nothing**
Modifies	**at most** String
Effects	Removes all items from the string, making the string empty
	e.g., IsEmpty(String') = TRUE
Signals	Undefined **when** ¬IsDefined (String) **ensuring modifies nothing**

8.3.4 Assign (↓Source ↕Target)

Requires	**nothing**
Modifies	**at most** Target
Effects	Creates an exact duplicate of the string Source in the string Target. The target string is cleared, if necessary, before attempting the assignment operation. An undefined target string is automatically created. An Assignment routine, (if provided at creation for the source string) is used to copy items from the source string to the target string. For example, Assign('xyz','123') results in the target string containing the string 'xyz'.

IsEqual (Source, Target') = TRUE

Signals	Overflow **when** insufficient memory resources available to create a new string **ensuring modifies at most** Target
Signals	Undefined **when** ¬IsDefined (Source) **ensuring modifies nothing**

8.3.5 Prepend (↓SourceString ↕TargetString)

Requires	**nothing**
Modifies	**at most** TargetString
Effects	Adds a string to the front of an existing string. The resulting target string consists of the source string followed by the original target string.
Signals	Overflow **when** TargetString is too small for the result **ensuring modifies at most** TargetString
Signals	Undefined **when** ¬IsDefined (SourceString)	¬IsDefined (TargetString) **ensuring modifies nothing**

8.3.6 Append (↓SourceString ↕TargetString)

Requires	**nothing**
Modifies	**at most** TargetString
Effects	Adds a string to the end of an existing string. The resulting target string consists of the original target string followed by the source string.
Signals	Overflow **when** TargetString is too small for the result **ensuring modifies at most** TargetString
Signals	Undefined **when** ¬IsDefined (SourceString)	¬IsDefined (TargetString) **ensuring modifies nothing**

8.3.7 Insert (↓SourceString ↕TargetString ↓Position)

Requires	**nothing**
Modifies	**at most** TargetString
Effects	Adds a string to an existing string at a given position.

TargetString' = TargetString[1..Position-1] + SourceString + TargetString[Position..LengthOf(TargetString)];

> e.g., Insert('123','xyz',1) = '123xyz' equivalent to Prepend ('123','xyz')
> e.g., Insert('123','xyz',2) = 'x123yz'
> e.g., Insert('123','xyz',3) = 'xy123z'
> e.g., Insert('123','xyz',4) = 'xyz123' equivalent to Append ('123','xyz')

Signals	Overflow **when** TargetString is too small for the result **ensuring modifies at most** TargetString
Signals	PositionError **when** ¬(1 ≤ Position ≤ LengthOf(TargetString)+1) **ensuring modifies nothing**
Signals	Undefined **when** ¬IsDefined (SourceString)	¬IsDefined (TargetString) **ensuring modifies nothing**

8.3.8 Delete (↕SourceString ↓FromPosition ↓ToPosition)

Requires	**nothing**
Modifies	**at most** SourceString
Effects	Removes the items from an existing string between the given positions, inclusive. String' = String[1..FromPosition-1] + String[ToPosition+1..LengthOf(String)]
Signals	PositionError **when** ¬(1 ≤ FromPosition ≤ ToPosition ≤ LengthOf (SourceString)) **ensuring modifies nothing**
Signals	Undefined **when** ¬IsDefined (SourceString) **ensuring modifies nothing**

8.3.9 Replace (↕TargetString ↓Position ↓ReplacementString)

Requires	**nothing**
Modifies	**at most** TargetString

Effects	Replaces the items of an existing string with the items of another string starting at the given position. TargetString' = TargetString[1..Position-1] + ReplacementString; e.g., Replace('xyz',1,'123') = '123' equivalent to Assign ('123','xyz') e.g., Replace('xyz',2,'123') = 'x123' e.g., Replace('xyz',2,'1') = 'x1' ·
Signals	Overflow **when** the target string is too small for the result **ensuring modifies at most** TargetString
Signals	PositionError **when** ¬(1 ≤ Position ≤ LengthOf(TargetString)) **ensuring modifies nothing**
Signals	Undefined **when** ¬IsDefined (TargetString) I ¬IsDefined (ReplacementString) **ensuring modifies nothing** `

8.3.10 SetItem (↕String ↓Position ↓Item)

Requires	**nothing**
Modifies	**at most** String
Effects	Replaces a single item of an existing string at the given position. ItemOf(String', Position) = Item, formally, String' = String [1..Position-1] + Item + String[Position+1..LengthOf(String)]
Signals	PositionError **when** ¬(1 ≤ Position ≤ LengthOf(String)) **ensuring modifies nothing**
Signals	Undefined **when** ¬IsDefined (String) **ensuring modifies nothing**

8.4 String Selector Operations

8.4.1 IsDefined (↓String) ↑Boolean

Requires	**nothing**
Modifies	**nothing**
Effects	Returns True if the string has been created and not yet destroyed.
Signals	**nothing**

8.4.2 IsEmpty (↓String) ↑Boolean

Requires	**nothing**
Modifies	**nothing**
Effects	Returns the logical value of True if the string contains no items. LengthOf(String) = 0?
Signals	Undefined **when** ¬IsDefined (String) **ensuring** returns True

8.4.3 IsEqual (↓LeftString ↓RightString) ↑Boolean

Requires	**nothing**
Modifies	**nothing**
Effects	Equality test for two strings of the same type, returning the logical value of True if two given strings contain the same items with same positions in each string. A comparison/equality routine (if provided at string creation) is used to determine the (in)equality of items in lieu of the standard Modula-2 (in)equality operator.
Signals	Undefined **when** ¬IsDefined (LeftString) **ensuring** returns False
Signals	Undefined **when** ¬IsDefined (RightString) **ensuring** returns False
Signals	TypeError **when** LeftString.TypeID ≠ RightString.TypeID **ensuring** returns False

8.4.4 LengthOf (↓String) ↑Cardinal

Requires	**nothing**
Modifies	**nothing**
Effects	Returns a count of the number of items presently in a string. If the string is empty then the length returned will be zero.
Signals	Undefined **when** ¬IsDefined (String) **ensuring** returns zero

8.4.5 IsLessThan (↓LeftString ↓RightString) ↑Boolean

Requires	**nothing**
Modifies	**nothing**
Effects	Returns the logical value of True if the first string is less than the second string. For example, LeftString < RightString.

Signals	Undefined **when** ¬IsDefined (LeftString)	¬IsDefined (RightString) **ensuring** returns False
Signals	TypeError **when** LeftString.TypeID ≠ RightString.TypeID **ensuring** returns False

8.4.6 IsGtrThan (↓LeftString ↓RightString) ↑Boolean

Requires	**nothing**
Modifies	**nothing**
Effects	Returns the logical value of True if the first string is greater than the second string. For example, LeftString > RightString
Signals	Undefined **when** ¬IsDefined(LeftString)	¬IsDefined(RightString) **ensuring** returns False
Signals	TypeError **when** LeftString.TypeID ≠ RightString.TypeID **ensuring** returns False

8.4.7 Compare (↓LeftString ↓RightString) ↑Relation

Requires	**nothing**
Modifies	**nothing**
Effects	Returns the ordering relation between the left and right strings. r = LeftString ? RightString
Signals	Undefined **when** ¬IsDefined(LeftString)	¬IsDefined(RightString) **ensuring** returns Incomparable
Signals	TypeError **when** LeftString.TypeID ≠ RightString.TypeID **ensuring** returns Incomparable

8.4.8 ItemOf (↓String ↓Position) ↑Item

Requires	**nothing**
Modifies	**nothing**
Effects	Returns a single item of an existing string from the given position. Item = String[Position]
Signals	PositionError **when** ¬(1 ≤ Position ≤ Length Of(String)) **ensuring** returns NullItem
Signals	Undefined **when** ¬IsDefined (String) **ensuring** returns NullItem

8.4.9 SubstringOf (↓String ↑Substring)

Requires	**nothing**
Modifies	**nothing**
Effects	Returns a string as a substring. Substring = String[1..LengthOf (String)]
Signals	Overflow **when** SizeOf(Substring) < LengthOf(String) **ensuring** returns NullSubstring
Signals	Undefined **when** ¬IsDefined (String) **ensuring** returns NullSubstring

8.4.10 SliceOf (↓String ↓FromPosition ↓ToPosition ↑Substring)

Requires	**nothing**
Modifies	**nothing**
Effects	Returns a slice of the source string between the *from position* and the *to position* as a substring. Substring = String[FromPosition..ToPosition]
Signals	Overflow **when** SizeOf(Substring) < ToPosition - FromPosition + 1 **ensuring** returns NullSubstring
Signals	PositionError **when** ¬(FromPosition ≤ ToSubstring ≤ LengthOf (String)) **ensuring** returns NullSubstring
Signals	Undefined **when** ¬IsDefined (String) **ensuring** returns NullSubstring

8.5 String Iterator Operations

8.5.1 LoopOver (↓String ↓LoopAccessProcedure)

Requires	LoopAccessProcedure ≠ NIL
Where	LoopAccessProcedure = **procedure** (↓Item) ↑Continue [Boolean]
Modifies	**nothing**
Effects	Performs the given operation on one or more items of a string from the first position through the *Length* of the string. Passes each item in the string to the given *LoopAccessProcedure* until all items have been processed or *LoopAccessProcedure* returns False.

Signals   Undefined **when** ¬IsDefined (String) **ensuring modifies nothing** and the LoopAccessProcedure is not invoked.

8.5.2 LoopChange (↓String ↓LoopChangeProcedure)

Requires   LoopChangeProcedure ≠ NIL

Where   LoopChangeProcedure = **procedure** (↕Item) ↑Continue [Boolean]

Modifies   **nothing**

Effects   Performs the given operation on one or more items of the string from the first position through the Length of the string. Passes each item in the string to the given LoopChangeProcedure until all items have been processed or the LoopChangeProcedure returns False.

Signals   Undefined **when** ¬IsDefined (String) **ensuring modifies nothing** and the LoopChangeProcedure is not invoked.

8.5.3 Traverse (↓String ↓AccessProcedure)

Requires   AccessProcedure ≠ NIL

Where   AccessProcedure = **procedure** (↓Item)

Modifies   **nothing**

Effects   Performs the given operation for every item in the string from the first position through the Length of the string. Passes each item in the string to the given AccessProcedure until all items have been processed.

Signals   Undefined **when** ¬IsDefined (String) **ensuring modifies nothing** and the AccessProcedure is not invoked.

8.5.4 TraverseChange (↓String ↓ChangeProcedure)

Requires   ChangeProcedure ≠ NIL

Where   ChangeProcedure = **procedure** (↕Item)

Modifies   **nothing**

Effects   Performs the given operation for every item in the string from the first position through the Length of the string. Passes each item in the string to the given ChangeProcedure until all items have been processed.

Signals Undefined **when** ¬IsDefined (String) **ensuring modifies nothing** and the ChangeProcedure is not invoked.

8.6 String Exceptions

8.6.1 InitFailed

Module initialization raises the *initfailed* exception. It is signaled when initial data structures required by a string module cannot be allocated. Depending on the implementation, other conditions may occur during module initialization that may raise this exception. *InitFailed* typically terminates a program because certain prerequisites for using the module have not been met.

8.6.2 Overflow

String *overflow* occurs when either of two conditions arise:

1. a string cannot be created, and
2. attempting to add one or more items to a string.

The first case indicates that the program is (at present) operating under severe memory limitations since the local data of a string variable cannot be dynamically allocated on the heap. The second situation could occur if:

1. an attempt is made to copy a string with a large number of (small) items, or
2. the individual item itself consumes a (relatively) large amount of space, which cannot be copied to the target string, or
3. an attempt is made to extend a string with the contents of another string.

8.6.3 Position Error

Position error can occur in several instances and indicates an invalid position or position range. Conditions that raise this exception are:

- the position is greater than the length of the string, or
- in a range of positions, the *from position* exceeds the value of the *to position*.

8.6.4 TypeError

Type error occurs when an attempt is made to operate on two strings whose TypeIDs, (provided when the strings were created), do not match.

8.6.5 Undefined

Undefined occurs when an attempt is made to access a string variable that the *Create* operation has not initialized. Unfortunately, Modula-2 cannot detect this without incurring a runtime penalty. All components could define a list of strings that have been created and not yet destroyed. This would permit the component to verify that the module has actually created the string being operated on. The alternative, used here, is to simply test for the NullString (i.e., NIL) to avoid the consequences of system breakdown. This is a viable solution assuming that the modules routines will not be subjected to a malicious attack. Such an attack can be delivered in Modula-2 due to the facilities for relaxation of the normally strict type-checking.

8.7 Summary

8.7.1 Operations Summary

Constructor

Operation

Append	String × String → String
Assign	String × String → String
Clear	String → String
Create	→ String
Delete	String × Position × Position → String

Destroy	String	→	λ

Insert	String × String × Position → String
Prepend	String × String → String
Replace	String × Position × String → String
SetItem	String × Position × Item → String

Selector
Operation

Compare	String × String → Relation
IsDefined	String → BOOLEAN
IsEmpty	String → BOOLEAN
IsEqual	String × String → BOOLEAN
IsGtrThan	String × String → BOOLEAN
IsLessThan	String × String → BOOLEAN
ItemOf	String × Position → Item
LengthOf	String → CARDINAL
SliceOf	String × Position × Position → Substring
SubstringOf	String → Substring

Iterator
Operation

LoopChange	String × LoopChangeProcedure
LoopOver	String × LoopAccessProcedure
Traverse	String × AccessProcedure
TraverseChange	String × ChangeProcedure

8.7.2 Exceptions Summary

Exception	Raised By Operation
InitFailed	Module Initialization
Overflow	Append, Assign, Create, Insert, Prepend, SliceOf, Substring-Of
PositionError	Delete, Insert, ItemOf, Replace, SetItem, SliceOf
TypeError	Append, Compare, Insert, IsEqual, IsGtrThan, IsLessThan, Prepend, Replace
Undefined	Append, Assign, Clear, Compare, Delete, Destroy, Insert, ItemOf, IsEmpty, IsEqual, IsGtrThan, IsLessThan, Length-Of, LoopOver, Prepend, Replace, SetItem, SliceOf, SubstringOf, Traverse

Operation	Exceptions Raised
Append	Overflow, TypeError, Undefined
Assign	Overflow, Undefined
Clear	Undefined
Compare	TypeError, Undefined
Create	Overflow
Insert	Overflow, PositionError, TypeError, Undefined
ItemOf	PositionError, Undefined
IsEmpty	Undefined
IsEqual	TypeError, Undefined
IsGtrThan	TypeError, Undefined
IsLessThan	TypeError, Undefined
LengthOf	Undefined
LoopChange	Undefined
LoopOver	Undefined
Prepend	Overflow, TypeError, Undefined
Replace	Overflow, PositionError, TypeError, Undefined
SetItem	PositionError, Undefined
SliceOf	Overflow, PositionError, Undefined
SubstringOf	Overflow, Undefined
Traverse	Undefined
TraverseChange	Undefined

References

[1] A. Aho, J. Hopcroft, and J. Ullman, *Data Structures and Algorithms*, Addison-Wesley, Reading, MA 1983, pp. 53-56, 64-69.

[2] G. Booch, *Software Components with Ada Data Structures, Tools, and Subsystems*, Benjamin/Cummings, CA 1987.

[3] R. Wiener and R. Sincovec, *Data Structures Using Modula-2*, John Wiley & Sons, New York, NY 1986.

[4] N. Wirth, *Programming in Modula-2*, 3rd. ed., Springer-Verlag, New York, NY 1985.

9 The Bounded Character String

This chapter presents a bounded implementation of the String abstraction, described in the previous chapter. This particular form has the properties Sequential, Bounded, Managed and Iterator. These describe specific aspects of the implementation as follows:

Sequential Can only be used in a non-tasking environment or by a single task.

Bounded The maximum size of a string is given when the string is created.

Managed Memory space for items and objects is returned to the system when no longer needed.

Iterator Routines are provided for looping over each of the string items.

As noted in the last chapter, strings are often formed of characters or items that can be represented by characters. For this reason both bounded and unbounded string modules will use the Character Items module instead of the more generic Items module.

Section 9.1 contains the interface to the String Enumerations module used by the string implementations of this, and the next, chapter. The bounded string module interface follows in Section 9.2 and its implementation in Section 9.3.

9.1 String Enumerations Interface

```
DEFINITION MODULE StringEnum;
(*=============================================================
    Version  : 1.01 10 Jan 1988 C. Lins
    Compiler : TML Modula-2 Compiler for the Apple Macintosh
    Component: Tool - String Enumerations Utility

    THE ABSTRACTION
    This module provides enumeration definitions for string
    operations and exceptions.

    REVISION HISTORY
    v1.01 10 Jan 1988 C. Lins:
        Initial TML Modula-2 implementation.
=============================================================*)
```

```
TYPE Operations    = (modinit,
                       create, destroy, clear, assign,
                       prepend, append, insert, delete,
                       replace, setitem, construct,
                       isdefined, isempty, lengthof, sizeof,
                       typeof, compare, isequal, itemof,
                       substringof, sliceof,
                       loopover, loopchange, traverse, travchange,
                       seize, release
                      );

TYPE Constructors = Operations [create .. construct ];
TYPE Selectors    = Operations [isdefined .. sliceof];
TYPE Iterators    = Operations [loopover .. travchange];
TYPE GuardedOps   = Operations [seize .. release];

TYPE Exceptions    = (noerr,
                       initfailed,
                       overflow,
                       positionerr,
                       typeerror,
                       undefined
                      );

TYPE ExceptionSet = SET OF Exceptions;

END StringEnum.
```

9.2 StringCSBMI Interface

The interface to the bounded string is presented below. The purpose and implementation specifics of each routine is briefly described along with mention of the
complexity measure of the actual implementation.

```
DEFINITION MODULE StringCSBMI;
(*=============================================================
    Version   : 1.01 10 Jan 1988 C. Lins
    Compiler  : TML Modula-2 Compiler for the Apple Macintosh
    Component : Monolithic Structure String (Opaque version)
                Character Sequential Bounded Managed Iterator

    THE ABSTRACTION
    This module provides the String data type localized for
    CHAR items.
```

```
REVISION HISTORY
v1.01 10 Jan 1988 C. Lins:
    Initial TML Modula-2 implementation.
=========================================================*)

FROM ErrorHandling IMPORT
  (*--Type*) HandlerProc;

FROM CharItems IMPORT
  (*--Type*) Item, AccessProc, ChangeProc, LoopAccessProc,
             LoopChangeProc;

FROM Relations IMPORT
  (*--Type*) Relation;

FROM StringEnum IMPORT
  (*--Type*) Exceptions;
  (*----------------------*)

TYPE String;
TYPE StringSize  = [ 1 .. 32000 ];
TYPE Position    = StringSize;
CONST NullString = VAL(String, NIL);

(*
```

9.2.1 Exceptions

ModuleID   is used by the exception handling mechanism to distinguish this module from all other modules.

StringError   returns the exception code from the most recent string operation. A result of *noerr* indicates successful completion of the operation O(1).

GetHandler   returns the exception handler routine associated with the given exception. The routine is a function procedure returning a procedure as its result but the *HandlerProc* may not be called from within the *GetHandler* call itself. Before invocation the procedure result must first be assigned to a procedure variable. Exception handlers are given an initial value of *ExitOnError* except for the handler for *noerr* which is initialized to the null exception handler O(1).

SetHandler   associates an exception handler routine with the given exception and is the inverse of *GetHandler*. This routine may be used to override the default settings for the exception handlers O(1).

```
*)
```

```
CONST ModuleID = 108;

PROCEDURE StringError ()                 : Exceptions  (*-- out *);

PROCEDURE GetHandler  ( theError   : Exceptions  (*-- in  *))
                                    : HandlerProc (*-- out *);

PROCEDURE SetHandler  ( theError   : Exceptions  (*-- in  *);
                        theHandler : HandlerProc (*-- in  *));

(*
```

9.2.2 Constructors

Create   attempts to generate a new, empty string of the given maximum
size (*theSize*), which defines the desired maximum string length.
This module uses character items so all the standard operations
(such as assignment and comparison) can be applied directly and
therefore a TypeID and associated user-defined routines are unnecessary. Upon successful completion the create routine returns the
new string. If it is not possible to create the string, *Create* raises
the *overflow* exception and returns the constant *NullString* O(1).

Destroy   takes the given string, clears it of any items, and then destroys the
string itself. Where *Create* defines a string, *Destroy* makes the
string undefined O(1).

Clear   removes all items from a given string. Clearing the string returns
it to the empty state O(1).

Assign   attempts to generate a duplicate of the source string (*theString*) in
the target string (*toString*). *Assign* automatically creates the target
string, if necessary using the size attribute of the source string. If
this step is unnecessary (because the target string has been previously created), *Assign* clears the target of its present contents but
leaves the size unchanged. There is no guarantee that the client
module would wish to define the target string with the same size
as the source. At minimum the target string size must be capable
of storing all items present in the source string. It may be desirable that the target string size be greater than the source string size.
Such a situation could occur during error recovery of a bounded
string overflow caused by the string length encountering the string
size. Also, the client module may effectively attempt to increase
the string size using the assignment mechanism O(m+n).

Prepend   adds the first string to the beginning of the second string O(m+n).

Append   adds the first string to the end of the second string O(m+n).

Insert   adds the first string to the second string at the given string index position O(m+n).

Delete   removes characters from the given string between given index positions, inclusive O(n).

Replace   removes characters from a string from a given index position to the end of the string and then inserts the replacement string at the end of the given source string. The length of the source string may grow due to the effects of the replacement O(m+n).

SetItem   changes a single character of the source string at the specified index position O(1).

Construct   permits building a dynamic string from the usual Modula-2 form of string O(n).

```
*)

PROCEDURE Create     (    theSize    : StringSize  (*--in    *))
                                     : String      (*--out   *);

PROCEDURE Destroy    (VAR theString  : String      (*--inout*));

PROCEDURE Clear      (VAR theString  : String      (*--inout*));

PROCEDURE Assign     (    theString  : String      (*--in    *);
                      VAR toString   : String      (*--inout*));

PROCEDURE Prepend    (    theString  : String      (*--in    *);
                      VAR toString   : String      (*--inout*));

PROCEDURE Append     (    theString  : String      (*--in    *);
                      VAR toString   : String      (*--inout*));

PROCEDURE Insert     (    theString  : String      (*--in    *);
                      VAR toString   : String      (*--inout*);
                          theIndex   : Position     (*--in    *));

PROCEDURE Delete     (VAR theString  : String      (*--inout*);
                          fromIndex  : Position     (*--in    *);
                          toIndex    : Position     (*--in    *));

PROCEDURE Replace    (VAR theString  : String      (*--inout*);
                          theIndex   : Position     (*--in    *);
                          withString : String      (*--in    *));
```

```
PROCEDURE SetItem    (VAR theString  : String      (*--inout*);
                          theIndex    : Position    (*--in  *);
                          theItem     : Item        (*--in  *));

PROCEDURE Construct (VAR theString   : String       (*--inout*);
                         theSubstring: ARRAY OF Item(*--in
*));

(*
```

9.2.3 Selectors

IsDefined   attempts to determine whether the given string is valid — it has
               been created and not yet destroyed. How this is accomplished may
               be as simple or complicated as the implementor desires and the re-
               quirements of the application demand O(1).

IsEmpty   returns true if the given string contains no items, otherwise false.
               Undefined strings are considered empty O(1).

SizeOf   returns the maximum possible size (and therefore, position) for the
               given string O(1).

LengthOf   returns the number of characters present in the string O(1). The
               function result from both routines are declared CARDINAL (in-
               stead of StringSize or Position) as undefined strings return zero.

Compare   establishes the ordering relation between two strings.

IsEqual   returns true if two strings contain the same items O(Min(m,n)) in
               the same positions.

ItemOf   retrieves a single item at the given index position from the string
               O(1).

SliceOf   returns a contiguous sequence of characters from a string between
               two index positions.

SubstringOf returns the whole string as a contiguous sequence of characters.
               Both *SliceOf* and *SubstringOf* terminate their results with 0C if
               necessary by the rules of Modula-2.
*)

```
PROCEDURE IsDefined ( theString  : String      (*-- in  *))
                                 : BOOLEAN     (*-- out *);

PROCEDURE IsEmpty   ( theString  : String      (*-- in  *))
                                 : BOOLEAN     (*-- out *);
```

```
PROCEDURE SizeOf      ( theString  : String       (*-- in  *))
                                   : CARDINAL     (*-- out *);

PROCEDURE LengthOf    ( theString  : String       (*-- in  *))
                                   : CARDINAL     (*-- out *);

PROCEDURE Compare     ( left       : String       (*-- in  *);
                        right      : String       (*-- in  *))
                                   : Relation     (*-- out *);

PROCEDURE IsEqual     ( left       : String       (*-- in  *);
                        right      : String       (*-- in  *))
                                   : BOOLEAN      (*-- out *);

PROCEDURE ItemOf      ( theString  : String       (*-- in  *);
                        theIndex   : Position     (*-- in  *))
                                   : Item         (*-- out *);

PROCEDURE SliceOf     ( theString  : String       (*-- in  *);
                        fromIndex  : Position     (*-- in  *);
                        toIndex    : Position     (*-- in  *);
                  VAR theSlice     : ARRAY OF Item (*-- out *));

PROCEDURE SubstringOf( theString   : String       (*-- in  *);
                  VAR toSubstring: ARRAY OF Item (*-- out *));

(*
```

9.2.4 Iterators

The iterator routines *LoopOver* and *LoopChange* provide facilities for looping over some or all items of a string, with read-only and read-write access to each item, respectively. *theProcess* procedure parameter to these routines returns a BOOLEAN function result where TRUE permits the iteration to proceed to the next item and FALSE terminates the iteration O(n).

Traverse and *TravChange* iterators provide facilities for looping over all items of a string, with read-only and read-write access to each item, respectively O(n).

All four iterators traverse the given string from the item at the first position towards items at greater positions within the string. Obviously, the processing procedure will not be invoked if given an empty string.
```
*)
```

```
PROCEDURE LoopOver    ( theString : String        (*-- in *);
                        theProcess: LoopAccessProc (*-- in *));

PROCEDURE LoopChange ( theString : String        (*-- in *);
                        theProcess: LoopChangeProc (*-- in *));

PROCEDURE Traverse    ( theString : String        (*-- in *);
                        theProcess: AccessProc    (*-- in *));

PROCEDURE TravChange ( theString : String        (*-- in *);
                        theProcess: ChangeProc    (*-- in *));

END StringCSBMI.
```

9.3 StringCSBMI Implementation

```
IMPLEMENTATION MODULE StringCSBMI;
(*=============================================================
   Version  : 1.01 10 Jan 1988 C. Lins
   Compiler : TML Modula-2 Compiler for the Apple Macintosh
   Code Size: R- 3370 bytes
   Component: Monolithic Structure String (Opaque version)
             Character Sequential Bounded Managed Iterator

   REVISION HISTORY
   v1.01 10 Jan 1988 C. Lins:
       Initial TML Modula-2 implementation.
=============================================================*)

FROM MacSystem IMPORT
   (*--Proc*) Allocate, Deallocate;

FROM ErrorHandling IMPORT
   (*--Type*) HandlerProc,
   (*--Proc*) NullHandler, ExitOnError, Raise;

FROM CharItems IMPORT
   (*--Cons*) NullItem,
   (*--Type*) Item, AccessProc, ChangeProc,
             LoopAccessProc, LoopChangeProc;

FROM Relations IMPORT
   (*--Type*) Relation;

FROM StringEnum IMPORT
```

```
(*--Type*) Exceptions, Operations;

   (*----------------------*)

(*
```

9.3.1 Internal Bounded String Representation

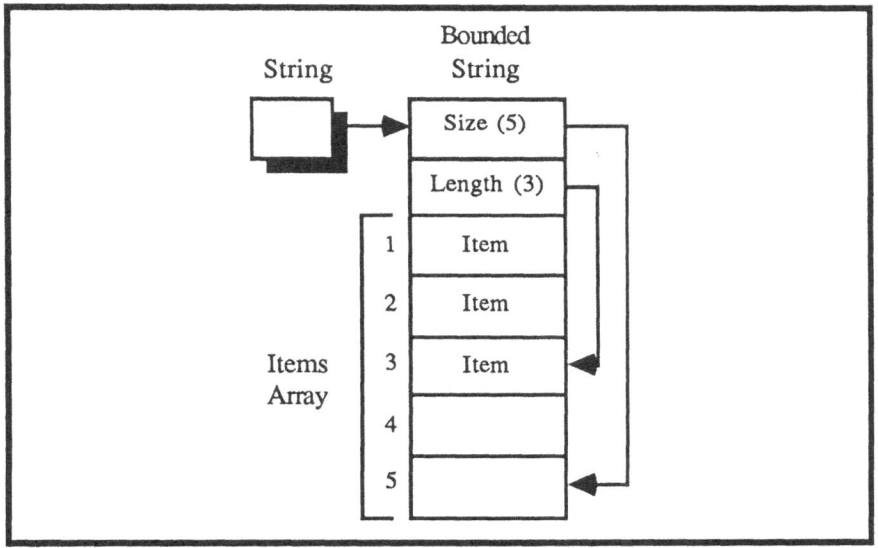

Figure 9.1 The Bounded String

As with the internal representation for a bounded stack, representation for the bounded string is a record dynamically allocated on the heap. This record will be just large enough to hold the declared maximum size of the string. Though the *items* array type declaration covers the maximum allowed size range of a bounded string, only *size* entries are actually allocated. This technique permits great savings in the amount of space actually used for each bounded string.

length is initialized to zero when a string is created and this value represents an empty string. Furthermore, *length* may never exceed the value of *size*. This condition indicates string overflow.

Representation Invariants include:
- MIN(SizeRange) ≤ size ≤ MAX(SizeRange)
- MIN(SizeRange) ≤ length ≤ size
*)

```
TYPE Substring = ARRAY StringSize OF Item;

TYPE BoundedString = RECORD
        size   : StringSize; (*-- Maximum String Size *)
        length : CARDINAL;   (*-- Current String Length *)
        items  : Substring;  (*-- ARRAY[1..size] of Items *)
     END (*-- BoundedString *);

TYPE String = POINTER TO BoundedString;

(*
```

9.3.2 Exceptions

The exception handling mechanism requires two variables. The first, *stringErrc* records the exception code from each operation; while *handler* is an array of e ception handling procedures indexed by the exception code.

The definition module routines *StringError*, *GetHandler* and *SetHandler* ha been previously described in the definition module and their operation should l readily apparent. The local routine *RaiseErrIn* sets the stringError variable and i vokes the *Raise* routine of the ErrorHandling module.
*)

```
VAR stringError : Exceptions;
VAR handler     : ARRAY Exceptions OF HandlerProc;

    (*-----------------------*)

PROCEDURE StringError ()             : Exceptions (*-- out  *);
BEGIN
  RETURN stringError;
END StringError;
(*--------------------------*)

PROCEDURE GetHandler ( theError   : Exceptions  (*-- in  *))
                                   : HandlerProc (*-- out *);
BEGIN
  RETURN handler[theError];
END GetHandler;

(*--------------------------*)
```

```
PROCEDURE SetHandler ( theError   : Exceptions  (*-- in *);
                       theHandler : HandlerProc (*-- in *));

BEGIN
  handler[theError] := theHandler;
END SetHandler;
(*---------------------------*)


PROCEDURE RaiseErrIn ( theRoutine : Operations (*-- in *);
                       theError   : Exceptions (*-- in *));
BEGIN
  stringError := theError;
  Raise(ModuleID, theRoutine, theError, handler[theError]);
END RaiseErrIn;
(*---------------------------*)


(*
```

9.3.3 Local Routines

Two routines local to the string module are used by exported routines. They are declared here following the convention of having routines declared prior to their use. Modula-2 (unlike Pascal) does not require this but some single-pass compilers impose restrictions in this regard. This technique facilitates porting the software to such compilers.

LengthSubstr determines the length of a *substring* which is a standard Modula-2 string. The substring parameter being tested is declared *call-by-reference* to avoid the overhead involved in copying the open array implicit in *call-by-value* parameters. Note that *LengthSubstr* must first explicitly check for the special case of an empty string, "", which is represented as a string containing only the string terminator character.

The second routine, *FromToOK*, checks whether the following precondition holds:

$$\text{fromIndex} \leq \text{toIndex} \leq \text{stringLength}$$

which is required for routines such as Delete and SliceOf. The routine takes advantage of the fact that if *toIndex* is less than or equal to the *stringLength* and the *fromIndex* is less than or equal to the *toIndex*, then the *fromIndex* must also be less than or equal to the *stringLength*.
```
*)
```

```
PROCEDURE LengthSubstr (VAR theSubstring : ARRAY OF Item (*-- in
                                            *))
                                          : CARDINAL (*-- out *);
BEGIN
  IF (HIGH(theSubstring) = 0) & (theSubstring[0] = NullItem)
    THEN
    RETURN 0;
  END (*--if*);
  RETURN HIGH(theSubstring) + 1;
END LengthSubstr;
(*--------------------------*)


PROCEDURE FromToOK ( fromIndex    : Position (*-- in *);
                     toIndex      : Position (*-- in *);
                     stringLength : CARDINAL (*-- in *))
                                  : BOOLEAN  (*-- out *);
BEGIN
  RETURN (toIndex ≤ stringLength) & (fromIndex ≤ toIndex);
END FromToOK;
(*--------------------------*)


(*
```

9.3.4 Constructors

Create begins by clearing the *stringError* field under the assumption of a success-ful result.

Create then allocates the header for the string in a local variable since the function result cannot be manipulated but only returned. The key to this alloca-tion step is the calculation of the number of bytes necessary based on the size of an individual item and the number of items requested. The constant expression *staticSize* allocates space for storing *theSize* and the string length regardless of the number and size of these "static" fields and is unaffected by changes due to future maintenance. If the bounded string could not be allocated, *Create* raises the overflow exception and returns the *NullString*.

At this point, all possibility of failure has been avoided and the bounded string header can be initialized to its empty state (length set to zero) and the size limit stored for this bounded string. Lastly, the new string can be returned to the caller.

```
*)
```

```
PROCEDURE Create ( theSize : StringSize (*-- in  *))
                           : String      (*-- out *);

CONST staticSize = SIZE(BoundedString) - SIZE(Substring);
CONST itemSize   = SIZE(Item);
VAR   newString  : String;

BEGIN
  stringError := noerr;
  Allocate(newString, staticSize + itemSize * VAL(INTEGER,
        theSize));
  IF (newString ≠ NIL) THEN
    WITH newString^ DO
      size   := theSize;
      length := 0;
    END (*--with*);
    RETURN newString;
  END (*--if*);
  RaiseErrIn(create, overflow);
  RETURN NullString;
END Create;
(*---------------------------*)
```

(*
Destroy deallocates the bounded string header which automatically sets *theString*
to the *NullString*.
*)

```
PROCEDURE Destroy (VAR theString : String (*-- inout *));
BEGIN
  stringError := noerr;
  IF (theString ≠ NIL) THEN
    Deallocate(theString);
  ELSE
    RaiseErrIn(destroy, undefined);
  END (*--if*);
END Destroy;
(*---------------------------*)
```

(*
Clear simply sets the string length to zero, effectively removing all of its items.
*)

```
PROCEDURE Clear (VAR theString : String (*-- inout *));
BEGIN
  stringError := noerr;
  IF (theString ≠ NIL) THEN
    theString^.length := 0;
```

```
      ELSE
         RaiseErrIn(clear, undefined);
      END (*--if*);
   END Clear;
   (*--------------------------*)
```

(*
Assignment for bounded objects is simpler to implement than their unbounded counterparts since the opportunity for overflow is restricted to the moment when the target object is (re-)created. The source string must be defined, otherwise *Assign* raises the *undefined* exception.

The assignment can be safely accomplished if three things are true:
- the target string exists,
- the source and target strings represent different string objects (since assignment of a string to itself is a useless operation), and
- the target string is capable of holding all of the source string's items.

Otherwise, *Assign* raises the overflow exception and aborts the operation. An undefined target object must be created using the size attribute of the source. If overflow does not occur the actual assignment can commence, otherwise it exits. (*Create* has already raised the exception).

The *Assign* operator cannot copy the whole items array since only a slice of the array's index range is actually allocated and *Assign* cannot determine the presence and size of subsequent dynamically allocated objects. Since the strings are formed from the basic data type CHAR, the assignment operator can copy individual items from one string to another with no chance for structural sharing to occur. This is accomplished through a simple loop over each of the items of the source. The target string's length can then be updated to match that of the source string.
*)

```
PROCEDURE Assign (     theString : String (*-- in    *);
                   VAR toString  : String (*-- inout *));

VAR index : CARDINAL; (*-- loop index over items *)

BEGIN
   stringError := noerr;
   IF (theString ≠ NIL) THEN
     IF (theString ≠ toString) THEN
       IF (toString ≠ NIL) THEN
         IF (theString^.length > toString^.size) THEN
           RaiseErrIn(assign, overflow);
         END (*--if*);
```

```
      ELSE
        toString := Create(theString^.size);
      END (*--if*);
      IF (stringError ≠ noerr) THEN
        RETURN;
      END (*--if*);
      WITH theString^ DO
        FOR index := MIN(StringSize) TO length DO
          toString^.items[index] := items[index];
        END (*--for*);
        toString^.length := length;
      END (*--with*);
    END (*--if*);
  ELSE
    RaiseErrIn(assign, undefined);
  END (*--if*);
END Assign;
(*---------------------------*)
```

```
(*
```
Prepend and *Append* simply make use of the *Insert* routine to add items to the
front or the back of the target string, respectively.
```
*)
```

```
PROCEDURE Prepend (     theString    : String (*-- in     *);
                    VAR toString     : String (*-- inout  *));
BEGIN
  Insert(theString, toString, 1);
END Prepend;
(*---------------------------*)
```

```
PROCEDURE Append  (     theString    : String (*-- in     *);
                    VAR toString     : String (*-- inout  *));
BEGIN
  Insert(theString, toString, LengthOf(toString) + 1);
END Append;
(*---------------------------*)
```

```
(*
```
Insert adds the items of one string to an existing string at a given index position.
The routine makes room for new string items by shifting items to the right of
the insertion index by the number of items being inserted. It then proceeds to insert the new string items into the vacated positions. The modified string's length
is then updated to reflect the newly inserted items.
```
*)
```

```
PROCEDURE Insert (     theString : String    (*-- in     *);
                   VAR toString  : String    (*-- inout *);
                       theIndex  : Position  (*-- in     *));
```

```
VAR newLength : CARDINAL;
    index     : CARDINAL; (*-- loop index over items *)

BEGIN
  stringError := noerr;
  IF (theString # NIL) & (toString # NIL) THEN
    WITH toString^ DO
      newLength := theString^.length + length;
      IF (theIndex > length + 1) THEN
        RaiseErrIn(insert, positionerr);
      ELSIF (newLength > size) THEN
        RaiseErrIn(insert, overflow);
      ELSE
        FOR index := length TO theIndex BY -1 DO
          items[index + theString^.length]:= items[index];
        END (*--for*);
        FOR index := MIN(StringSize) TO theString^.length DO
          items[theIndex + index - 1] := theString^.items
          [index];
        END (*--for*);
        length := newLength;
      END (*--if*);
    END (*--with*);
  ELSE
    RaiseErrIn(insert, undefined);
  END (*--if*);
END Insert;
(*-------------------------*)
```

(*
Delete removes items from an existing string between the given index positions,
inclusive. Invalid index positions raise *positionerr* and abort the operation. The
algorithm shifts items above the *toIndex* down in the string into positions beginning with *fromIndex*. It calculates the amount of this shift, called the *offset*,
loops through string items above *toIndex*, shifting each item into its new location. After moving the items the string's *length* is updated.
*)

```
PROCEDURE Delete (VAR theString : String    (*-- inout *);
                      fromIndex : Position (*-- in     *);
                      toIndex   : Position (*-- in     *));

VAR index : CARDINAL; (*-- loop index over items *)
    offset : CARDINAL; (*-- distance to move items down *)

BEGIN
  stringError := noerr;
  IF (theString # NIL) THEN
    WITH theString^ DO
```

```
      IF FromToOK(fromIndex, toIndex, length) THEN
        offset := toIndex - fromIndex + 1;
        FOR index := toIndex + 1 TO length DO
          items[index - offset] := items[index];
        END (*--for*);
        DEC(length, offset);
      ELSE
        RaiseErrIn(delete, positionerr);
      END (*--if*);
    END (*--with*);
  ELSE
    RaiseErrIn(delete, undefined);
  END (*--if*);
END Delete;
(*--------------------------*)


(*
```
Replace deletes all items of the source string from the given index to the end of
the string and then inserts the replacement string at the end of the source. If the
replacement process expands *theString*, the string *length* is adjusted accordingly.
```
*)

PROCEDURE Replace (VAR theString  : String   (*-- inout *);
                       theIndex   : Position (*-- in    *);
                       withString : String   (*-- in    *));

VAR endPosition : CARDINAL; (*-- new length of theString *)
         index : CARDINAL; (*-- loop index over items    *)

BEGIN
  stringError := noerr;
  IF (theString ≠ NIL) & (withString ≠ NIL) THEN
    endPosition := theIndex + withString^.length - 1;
    WITH theString^ DO
      IF (theIndex ≤ length) & (endPosition ≤ size) THEN
        FOR index := MIN(StringSize) TO withString^.length DO
          items[theIndex + index - 1] :=
          withString^.items[index];
        END (*--for*);
        IF (endPosition > length) THEN
          length := endPosition;
        END (*--if*);
      ELSE
        RaiseErrIn(replace, positionerr);
      END (*--if*);
    END (*--with*);
  ELSE
    RaiseErrIn(replace, undefined);
  END (*--if*);
END Replace;
(*--------------------------*)
```

```
(*
```
SetItem attempts to assign the given item to the string at the given index position. The index must be within the string's current length otherwise *SetItem*
raises the *positionerr* exception, avoiding assignment outside the string's current
bounds.
```
*)

PROCEDURE SetItem (VAR theString : String   (*-- inout *);
                       theIndex  : Position (*-- in    *);
                       theItem   : Item     (*-- in    *));

BEGIN
   stringError := noerr;
   IF (theString ≠ NIL) THEN
     WITH theString^ DO
       IF (theIndex ≤ length) THEN
         items[theIndex] := theItem;
       ELSE
         RaiseErrIn(setitem, positionerr);
       END (*--if*);
     END (*--with*);
   ELSE
     RaiseErrIn(setitem, undefined);
   END (*--if*);
END SetItem;

(*--------------------------*)


(*
```
Construct forms a bounded string from a standard Modula-2 string. If *theString*
has not yet been created then *theSubstring* must not be empty since it is meaningless to create a string with a maximum size of zero items. If *theString* does
exist, and *theSubstring* is empty, construct clears *theString*. Otherwise the routine simply loops through *theSubstring*, copying items from there to the target
string and when done updating the string's length.
```
*)

PROCEDURE Construct (VAR theString : String       (*-- inout*);
                         theSubstring: ARRAY OF Item(*-- in   *));

VAR index     : CARDINAL; (*-- loop index over items   *)
    lenSubstr : CARDINAL; (*-- # of chars in substring *)
    newString : String;

BEGIN
   stringError := noerr;
   lenSubstr := LengthSubstr(theSubstring);
   IF (theString ≠ NIL) THEN
```

```
         IF (lenSubstr = 0) THEN
           Clear(theString);
           RETURN;
         END (*--if*);
      ELSIF (lenSubstr = 0) THEN
        RaiseErrIn(construct, positionerr);
        RETURN;
      ELSE
        newString := Create(lenSubstr);
        IF (stringError = noerr) THEN
          theString := newString;
        ELSE
          RETURN;
        END (*--if*);
      END (*--if*);
      WITH theString^ DO
        (*-- The minimum lenSubstr is one (1). *)
        index := MIN(Position);
        WHILE (index ≤ lenSubstr) & (theSubstring[index - 1] ≠
            NullItem) DO
          items[index] := theSubstring[index - 1];
          INC(index);
        END (*--while*);
        length := index - 1;
      END (*--with*);
END Construct;
(*---------------------------*)

(*
```

9.3.5 Selectors

IsDefined returns true if the given string is not NIL, otherwise it returns false.
```
*)

PROCEDURE IsDefined ( theString : String  (*-- in  *))
                                : BOOLEAN (*-- out *);
BEGIN
  RETURN (theString ≠ NIL);
END IsDefined;
(*---------------------------*)

(*
```
IsEmpty simply tests for a string length of zero, returning the appropriate logical value. As mentioned in the interface, an undefined string is considered empty.
```
*)
```

```
PROCEDURE IsEmpty ( theString : String  (*-- in  *))
                                : BOOLEAN (*-- out *);
BEGIN
  stringError := noerr;
  IF (theString ≠ NIL) THEN
    RETURN theString^.length = 0;
  END (*--if*);
  RaiseErrIn(isempty, undefined);
  RETURN TRUE;
END IsEmpty;
(*---------------------------*)
```

(*
SizeOf returns the size value for the given string. An undefined string raises the
exception of the same name and returns a size of zero.
*)

```
PROCEDURE SizeOf ( theString : String   (*-- in  *))
                             : CARDINAL (*-- out *);
BEGIN
  stringError := noerr;
  IF (theString ≠ NIL) THEN
    RETURN theString^.size;
  END (*--if*);
  RaiseErrIn(sizeof, undefined);
  RETURN 0;
END SizeOf;
(*---------------------------*)
```

(*
LengthOf returns the string's current length, which is the number of items in the
string. An undefined string raises the exception of the same name and returns a
length of zero.
*)

```
PROCEDURE LengthOf ( theString : String   (*-- in  *))
                               : CARDINAL (*-- out *);
BEGIN
  stringError := noerr;
  IF (theString ≠ NIL) THEN
    RETURN theString^.length;
  END (*--if*);
  RaiseErrIn(lengthof, undefined);
  RETURN 0;
END LengthOf;
(*---------------------------*)
```

(*
Compare returns the ordering relation between two strings so that "left Relation right" is True. If either or both strings are undefined then *Compare* returns the *incomparable* relation.

Initially *Compare* sets up *minLength* with the smaller of the two string lengths, since reaching the end of a string is one condition that terminates the comparison. *Compare* also presets *relOrder* to the correct result based on length — since, other things being equal, the smaller string is less than the other.

Once this initialization is carried out, the algorithm loops through the strings from the beginning, examining each character item for the relation between them. The loop continues as long as the strings are equal or until the end of the smaller string is reached. The instant that the left item at the current index is less than its counterpart in the right string, the loop is terminated and the relation *less* is returned. Likewise when the left item is greater than the right item the relation *greater* is returned. The index is incremented for equal items advancing the algorithm towards the terminating condition, the end of the smaller string.
*)

```
PROCEDURE Compare (left  : String   (*-- in  *);
                   right : String   (*-- in  *))
                         : Relation (*-- out *);

VAR  index      : CARDINAL; (*-- Index into items arrays *)
     minLength  : CARDINAL; (*-- Smaller of the two string
                                 lengths *)
     relOrder   : Relation; (*-- Most recent comparison result *)

BEGIN
  stringError := noerr;
  relOrder := incomparable;
  IF (left ≠ NIL) & (right ≠ NIL) THEN
    WITH left^ DO
      IF (length = right^.length) THEN
        relOrder  := equal;
        minLength := length;
      ELSIF (length < right^.length) THEN
        relOrder  := less;
        minLength := length;
      ELSE
        relOrder  := greater;
        minLength := right^.length;
      END (*--if*);
    END (*--with*);
    index := MIN(StringSize);
    LOOP
      IF (index > minLength) THEN
```

```
      EXIT (*--loop*);
    END (*--if*);
    IF (left^.items[index] < right^.items[index]) THEN
      relOrder := less;
      EXIT (*--loop*);
    ELSIF (left^.items[index] > right^.items[index]) THEN
      relOrder := greater;
      EXIT (*--loop*);
    END (*--if*);
    INC(index);
  END (*--loop*);
ELSE
  RaiseErrIn(compare, undefined);
END (*--if*);
RETURN relOrder;
END Compare;
(*---------------------------*)
```

```
(*
```

IsEqual scans both strings looking for the first mismatch (inequality) which indicates the strings are unequal. If the FOR loop completes the strings must be equal. This assumes that:

1. the strings have been defined, and
2. have the same length.

The first of these assumptions, if unfounded, raises the undefined exception; while the second simply determines inequality.
```
*)
```

```
PROCEDURE IsEqual (    left  : String  (*-- in  *);
                       right : String  (*-- in  *))
                             : BOOLEAN (*-- out *);

VAR index : CARDINAL; (*-- loop index over items *)

BEGIN
  stringError := noerr;
  IF (left # NIL) & (right # NIL) THEN
    WITH left^ DO
      IF (length = right^.length) THEN
        FOR index := MIN(StringSize) TO length DO
          IF (items[index] # right^.items[index]) THEN
            RETURN FALSE;
          END (*--if*);
        END (*--for*);
        RETURN TRUE;
      END (*--if*);
```

```
      END (*--with*);
  ELSE
      RaiseErrIn(isequal, undefined);
  END (*--if*);
  RETURN FALSE;
END IsEqual;
(*---------------------------*)
```

(*

ItemOf attempts to return the item of the string at a given index position. The *positionerr* exception is raised if *theIndex* exceeds the length of the string. This exception and also an undefined string return the *NullItem* (0C).
*)

```
PROCEDURE ItemOf (     theString : String  (*-- in  *);
                       theIndex  : Position (*-- in  *))
                                 : Item     (*-- out *);
BEGIN
  stringError := noerr;
  IF (theString ≠ NIL) THEN
    WITH theString^ DO
      IF (theIndex ≤ length) THEN
        RETURN items[theIndex];
      END (*--if*);
    END (*--with*);
    RaiseErrIn(itemof, positionerr);
  ELSE
    RaiseErrIn(itemof, undefined);
  END (*--if*);
  RETURN NullItem;
END ItemOf;
(*---------------------------*)
```

(*

SliceOf extracts a portion of a given string returning the sequence of characters as a standard Modula-2 string. The range of index positions within the string *fromIndex* and *toIndex* specifies the portion of the string to be extracted. The routine must take care to index the target slice from zero and so must shift items from their positions within the source string into appropriate positions in the target slice. The preconditions:

1. fromIndex ≤ toIndex ≤ source string length, and
2. number of items between the from and to indices, inclusive, ≤ target slice size, must both be met.

If not, then the routine raises the *positionerr* and *overflow* exceptions, respectively. If necessary, the string terminator is added to the end of the slice.
*)

```
PROCEDURE SliceOf (    theString : String         (*-- in  *);
                       fromIndex : Position        (*-- in  *);
                       toIndex   : Position        (*-- in  *);
                   VAR theSlice  : ARRAY OF Item (*-- out *));

VAR index     : CARDINAL; (*-- loop index over items *)
    sliceSize : CARDINAL; (*-- # items between from and to
                              indexes *)

BEGIN
  stringError := noerr;
  IF (theString ≠ NIL) THEN
    WITH theString^ DO
      IF FromToOK(fromIndex, toIndex, length) THEN
        sliceSize := toIndex - fromIndex;
        IF (sliceSize ≤ VAL(CARDINAL, HIGH(theSlice)))
            THEN
          FOR index := fromIndex TO toIndex DO
            theSlice[index - fromIndex] := items
                     [index];
          END (*--for*);
          IF (sliceSize < VAL(CARDINAL, HIGH
             (theSlice))) THEN
            theSlice[sliceSize + 1] := NullItem;
          END (*--if*);
        ELSE
          RaiseErrIn(sliceof, overflow);
        END (*--if*);
      ELSE
        RaiseErrIn(sliceof, positionerr);
      END (*--if*);
    END (*--with*);
  ELSE
    RaiseErrIn(sliceof, undefined);
  END (*--if*);
END SliceOf;
(*---------------------------*)
```

(*
SubstringOf is similar to *SliceOf* above except that it returns the entire string.
When the Target substring is too small for all items in the Source string, *SubstringOf* raises the overflow and fills the target with as many items as will fit.
*)

```
PROCEDURE SubstringOf(  theString  : String         (*-- in  *);
                    VAR toSubstring: ARRAY OF Item (*-- out *));

VAR index      : CARDINAL; (*-- loop index over items *)
    copyLength : CARDINAL; (*-- # items to copy to substring *)
```

```
BEGIN
  stringError := noerr;
  IF (theString ≠ NIL) THEN
    WITH theString^ DO
      IF (length > VAL(CARDINAL, HIGH(toSubstring)) + 1)
        THEN
        RaiseErrIn(substringof, overflow);
        copyLength := HIGH(toSubstring) + 1;
      ELSE
        copyLength := length;
      END (*--if*);
      FOR index := MIN(StringSize) TO copyLength DO
        toSubstring[index - 1] := items[index];
      END (*--for*);
      IF (copyLength < VAL(CARDINAL, HIGH(toSubstring)))
        THEN
        toSubstring[copyLength + 1] := NullItem;
      END (*--if*);
    END (*--with*);
  ELSE
    RaiseErrIn(substringof, undefined);
  END (*--if*);
END SubstringOf;
(*--------------------------*)


(*
```

9.3.6 Iterators

The bounded string iterators *LoopOver* and *LoopChange* use the same algorithm, which is almost identical to that used with the bounded stack. The iterators reset the *stringError* state to *noerr* and tests for the undefined string, raising the *undefined* exception if such is the case. Then a simple loop is made through each item of the string — passing it to the given procedure for processing until the end of the string is reached or the visiting process returns False indicating that the iteration be terminated.

The bounded string iterators *Traverse* and *TravChange* share the same algorithm, which is almost identical to that used with the bounded stack. The *stringError* state is reset to *noerr* and a test made for the undefined string, raising the *undefined* exception if such is the case. Then a simply loop is made through each item of the string — passing it to the given procedure for processing.
```
*)

PROCEDURE LoopOver ( theString : String       (*-- in *);
                     theProcess: LoopAccessProc (*-- in *));
```

```
VAR index : CARDINAL; (*-- loop index over items *)

BEGIN
  stringError := noerr;
  IF (theString ≠ NIL) THEN
    WITH theString^ DO
      FOR index := MIN(StringSize) TO length DO
        IF ¬theProcess(items[index]) THEN
          RETURN;
        END (*--if*);
      END (*--for*);
    END (*--with*);
  ELSE
    RaiseErrIn(loopover, undefined);
  END (*--if*);
END LoopOver;
(*---------------------------*)

PROCEDURE LoopChange  ( theString : String         (*-- in *);
                        theProcess: LoopChangeProc (*-- in *));

VAR index : CARDINAL; (*-- loop index over items *)

BEGIN
  stringError := noerr;
  IF (theString ≠ NIL) THEN
    WITH theString^ DO
      FOR index := MIN(StringSize) TO length DO
        IF ¬theProcess(items[index]) THEN
          RETURN;
        END (*--if*);
      END (*--for*);
    END (*--with*);
  ELSE
    RaiseErrIn(loopchange, undefined);
  END (*--if*);
END LoopChange;
(*---------------------------*)

PROCEDURE Traverse ( theString : String     (*-- in *);
                     theProcess: AccessProc (*-- in *));

VAR index : CARDINAL; (*-- loop index over items *)

BEGIN
  stringError := noerr;
  IF (theString ≠ NIL) THEN
    WITH theString^ DO
      FOR index := MIN(StringSize) TO length DO
```

```
          theProcess(items[index]);
        END (*--for*);
      END (*--with*);
   ELSE
      RaiseErrIn(traverse, undefined);
   END (*--if*);
END Traverse;
(*--------------------------*)


PROCEDURE TravChange ( theString : String      (*-- in *);
                       theProcess: ChangeProc  (*-- in *));

VAR index : CARDINAL; (*-- loop index over items *)

BEGIN
   stringError := noerr;
   IF (theString ≠ NIL) THEN
      WITH theString^ DO
        FOR index := MIN(StringSize) TO length DO
            theProcess(items[index]);
        END (*--for*);
      END (*--with*);
   ELSE
      RaiseErrIn(travchange, undefined);
   END (*--if*);
END TravChange;
(*--------------------------*)


(*
```

9.3.7 Module Initialization

The module initialization sets the local exception handlers array variables to default handlers (*ExitOnError*), except for the *noerr* handler which is given the null handler. *stringError* is given the value *noerr* avoiding an undefined state.
```
*)

BEGIN
   FOR stringError := initfailed TO MAX(Exceptions) DO
      SetHandler(stringError, ExitOnError);
   END (*--for*);
   SetHandler(noerr, NullHandler);
   stringError := noerr;
END StringCSBMI.
```

References

[1]   G. Booch, *Software Components With Ada Structures, Tools, and Subsystems*, Benjamin/Cummings, Menlo Park, CA, 1987, pp. 104-141.

[2]   D. Knuth, *The Art of Computer Programming, Vol. 1, Fundamental Algorithms*, Addison-Wesley, Reading, MA 1973.

[3]   R. Sedgewick, *Algorithms*, Addison-Wesley, Reading, MA 1983.

[4]   R. Wiener and R. Sincovec, *Data Structures Using Modula-2*, John Wiley & Sons, New York, NY 1986, pp. 461-469.

10 The Unbounded Character String

This chapter presents an unbounded implementation of the String abstraction, described in Chapter 8. This particular form has the properties: Sequential, Unbounded, Managed, and Iterator, describing specific aspects of the implementation as follows:

Sequential   Can only be used in a non-tasking environment, or by only one task.

Unbounded   The size of a string varies dynamically as items are inserted and removed from the string.

Managed   Memory space for items and objects is returned to the system when no longer needed.

Iterator   Routines for looping over each of the string items are provided.

As noted in the previous chapter on the bounded string form, strings are nearly always formed of characters, or items that can be represented using characters, we use the Character Items module instead of the more generic Items module.

One limitation in the implementation is presented here: strings are limited to a maximum length of 32,000 characters. This is primarily due to the TML Modula-2 compiler excluding LONGINT and LONGCARD as array index types.

Section 10.1 contains the interface to the unbounded string module while the implementation follows in Section 10.2.

10.1 StringCSUMI Interface

```
DEFINITION MODULE StringCSUMI;
(*================================================================
    Version  : 1.01  10 Jan 1988  C. Lins
    Compiler : TML Modula-2 Compiler for the Apple Macintosh
    Component: Monolithic Structure - String
               Character Sequential Unbounded Managed Iterator


    THE ABSTRACTION
    This module provides a String abstraction limited to CHARs


    REVISION HISTORY
    v1.01  10 Jan 1988  C. Lins:
        Initial TML Modula-2 implementation.
================================================================*)
```

```
FROM ErrorHandling IMPORT
   (*--Type*) HandlerProc;

FROM CharItems IMPORT
   (*--Type*) Item, AccessProc, ChangeProc,
              LoopAccessProc, LoopChangeProc;

FROM Relations IMPORT
   (*--Type*) Relation;

FROM StringEnum IMPORT
   (*--Type*) Exceptions;
   (*----------------------*)

TYPE  String;
TYPE  Position   = [ 1 .. 32000 ];
CONST NullString = VAL(String, NIL);

(*
```

10.1.1 Exceptions

The exception handling mechanism uses *ModuleID* to distinguish this module from all others.

StringError   returns the exception code from the most recent string operation. A result of *noerr* indicates successful completion of the operation O(1).

GetHandler   returns the exception handler routine associated with the given exception. The routine is a function procedure returning a procedure as its result but the *HandlerProc* may not be called from within the *GetHandler* call itself. The procedure result must be first assigned to a procedure variable before invocation. Modula-2 provides exception handlers with an initial value of *ExitOnError* except for the handler for *noerr* which it initializes to the null exception handler O(1).

SetHandler   the inverse of *GetHandler*, associates an exception handler routine with the given exception. The routine may override default settings for the exception handlers O(1).

```
*)

CONST ModuleID = 109;

PROCEDURE StringError ()            : Exceptions  (*-- out   *);
```

```
PROCEDURE GetHandler  (  ofError    : Exceptions  (*-- in   *))
                                     : HandlerProc (*-- out  *);

PROCEDURE SetHandler  (  ofError    : Exceptions  (*-- in   *);
                         toHandler  : HandlerProc (*-- in   *));

(*
```

10.1.2 Constructors

Create	attempts to generate new, empty, unbounded strings. The module uses character items so all standard operations (such as assignment and comparison) can be done directly; user-defined routines are not needed. *Create* returns the new string upon successful completion of the routine. If it not possible for the string to be created, the constant *NullString* is returned instead.
Destroy	clears a given string of items and then destroys the string itself. *Destroy* is the inverse of *Create*, since *Create* defines a string and *Destroy* makes the string undefined.
Clear	removes a given string of its items, returning the string to the empty state.
Assign	attempts to generate a duplicate of the source string (*theString*) in the target string (*toString*). *Assign* automatically creates the target string, if necessary, otherwise it simply clears the target of its present contents.
Prepend	adds the first string to the beginning of the second string.
Append	adds the first string to the end of the second string.
Insert	adds the first string to the second string at the given string index position.
Delete	removes characters from the given string between the given index positions, inclusive.
Replace	removes characters from the given string beginning with the given index position to the end of the string and then inserts the replacement string at the end of the given source string. The length of the source string may grow due to the effects of the replacement.
SetItem	changes a single character of the source string at the specified index position.
Construct	permits building a dynamic string from the usual Modula-2 string form.

```
*)
```

```
PROCEDURE Create     ()                    : String    (*-- out   *);

PROCEDURE Destroy    (VAR theString : String    (*-- inout *));

PROCEDURE Clear      (VAR theString : String    (*-- inout *));

PROCEDURE Assign     (    theString : String    (*-- in    *);
                     VAR toString   : String    (*-- inout *));

PROCEDURE Prepend    (    theString : String    (*-- in    *);
                     VAR toString   : String    (*-- inout *));

PROCEDURE Append     (    theString : String    (*-- in    *);
                     VAR toString   : String    (*-- inout *));

PROCEDURE Insert     (    theString : String    (*-- in    *);
                     VAR toString   : String    (*-- inout *);
                         theIndex   : Position  (*-- in    *));

PROCEDURE Delete     (VAR theString : String    (*-- inout *);
                         fromIndex  : Position  (*-- in    *);
                         toIndex    : Position  (*-- in    *));

PROCEDURE Replace    (VAR theString : String    (*-- inout *);
                         theIndex   : Position  (*-- in    *);
                         withString : String    (*-- in    *));

PROCEDURE SetItem    (VAR theString : String    (*-- inout *);
                         theIndex   : Position  (*-- in    *);
                         theItem    : Item      (*-- in    *));

PROCEDURE Construct  (VAR theString : String    (*-- inout *);
                         theSubstring: ARRAY OF Item (*-- in    *));

(*
```

10.1.3 Selectors

IsDefined attempts to determine whether the given string is valid, has been
created and not yet destroyed. How this is accomplished may be as
simple or complicated as the implementor desires and the requirements of the application.

IsEmpty returns true if the given string contains no items, and false otherwise. Undefined strings are considered empty.

LengthOf	returns the number of characters present in the string. The function result is declared CARDINAL (instead of Position) as an undefined string returns zero.
Compare	establishes the ordering relation between two strings. *IsEqual* returns true if two strings contain the same items.
ItemOf	retrieves a single item at the given index position from the string.
SliceOf	returns a contiguous sequence of characters from a string between two index positions.
SubstringOf	returns the whole string as a contiguous sequence of characters. Both *SliceOf* and *SubstringOf* terminate their results with 0C if necessary by the rules of Modula-2.

```
*)

PROCEDURE IsDefined  (  theString  : String        (*-- in    *))
                                    : BOOLEAN       (*-- out   *);

PROCEDURE IsEmpty    (  theString  : String        (*-- in    *))
                                    : BOOLEAN       (*-- out   *);

PROCEDURE LengthOf   (  theString  : String        (*-- in    *))
                                    : CARDINAL      (*-- out   *);

PROCEDURE Compare    (  left       : String        (*-- in    *);
                        right      : String        (*-- in    *))
                                   : Relation       (*-- out   *);

PROCEDURE IsEqual    (  left       : String        (*-- in    *);
                        right      : String        (*-- in    *))
                                   : BOOLEAN        (*-- out   *);

PROCEDURE ItemOf     (  theString  : String        (*-- in    *);
                        theIndex   : Position       (*-- in    *))
                                   : Item           (*-- out   *);

PROCEDURE SliceOf    (  theString  : String        (*-- in    *);
                        fromIndex  : Position       (*-- in    *);
                        toIndex    : Position       (*-- in    *);
                    VAR theSlice   : ARRAY OF Item  (*-- out   *));

PROCEDURE SubstringOf(  theString  : String        (*-- in    *);
                    VAR toSubstring: ARRAY OF Item  (*-- out   *));
```

```
(*
```

10.1.4 Iterators

The iterator routines *LoopOver* and *LoopChange* provide facilities for looping over some or all items of a string, with read-only and read-write access to each item, respectively. A procedure parameter to these routines, *theProcess,* returns a BOOLEAN function result where TRUE allows the iteration to proceed to the next item and FALSE terminates the iteration.

Traverse and *TravChange* iterators provide facilities for looping over all items of a string, with read-only and read-write access to each item, respectively.

All four iterators traverse the given string from the item at the first position towards items at greater positions within the string. Obviously, if given an empty string the processing procedure will not be invoked.

```
*)
PROCEDURE LoopOver    ( theString : String       (*-- in   *);
                        theProcess: LoopAccessProc (*-- in   *));

PROCEDURE LoopChange ( theString : String       (*-- in   *);
                        theProcess: LoopChangeProc (*-- in   *));

PROCEDURE Traverse    ( theString : String       (*-- in   *);
                        theProcess: AccessProc    (*-- in   *));

PROCEDURE TravChange ( theString : String       (*-- in   *);
                        theProcess: ChangeProc    (*-- in   *));

END StringCSUMI.
```

10.2 StringCSUMI Implementation

```
IMPLEMENTATION MODULE StringCSUMI;
(*==============================================================
     Version  : 1.01  10 Jan 1988  C. Lins
     Compiler : TML Modula-2 Compiler for the Apple Macintosh
     Code Size: R- 3584 bytes
     Component: Monolithic Structure String (Opaque version)
               Character Sequential Bounded Managed Iterator
```

```
REVISION HISTORY
    v1.01  10 Jan 1988  C. Lins:
        Initial TML Modula-2 implementation.
========================================================*)

FROM MacSystem IMPORT
    (*--Proc*) Allocate, Deallocate;

FROM ErrorHandling IMPORT
    (*--Type*) HandlerProc,
    (*--Proc*) NullHandler, ExitOnError, Raise;

FROM CharItems IMPORT
    (*--Cons*) NullItem,
    (*--Type*) Item, AccessProc, ChangeProc,
               LoopAccessProc, LoopChangeProc;

FROM Relations IMPORT
    (*--Type*) Relation;

FROM StringEnum IMPORT
    (*--Type*) Exceptions, Operations;

    (*-----------------------*)

(*
```

10.2.1 Internal Unbounded String Representation

The unbounded string needs an internal representation that does not require a size specification when the string is created and allows the string length to vary dynamically as items are inserted and removed. An examination of the literature (Standish [4] or Wiener and Sincovec [5], for example) reveals numerous possible representations having a variety of space and time efficiency. Booch [1] demonstrates an elegant solution that may be readily derived from the bounded string form, where one maintains in the string header a pointer to the dynamically allocated array of items. Supporting this alternate structure requires an additional local routine responsible for adjusting the size of this array. Then only cosmetic changes are needed throughout the remainder of the module. This routine has been named *SetSize* in this module. The material below describes the implementation and details about it.

Like the internal representation for an unbounded stack, the representation for the unbounded string begins with a header record dynamically allocated on the heap. This header is used to store two fields:

1. the current string length, and
2. a pointer to a dynamically allocated array of items large enough to hold the current length of the string.

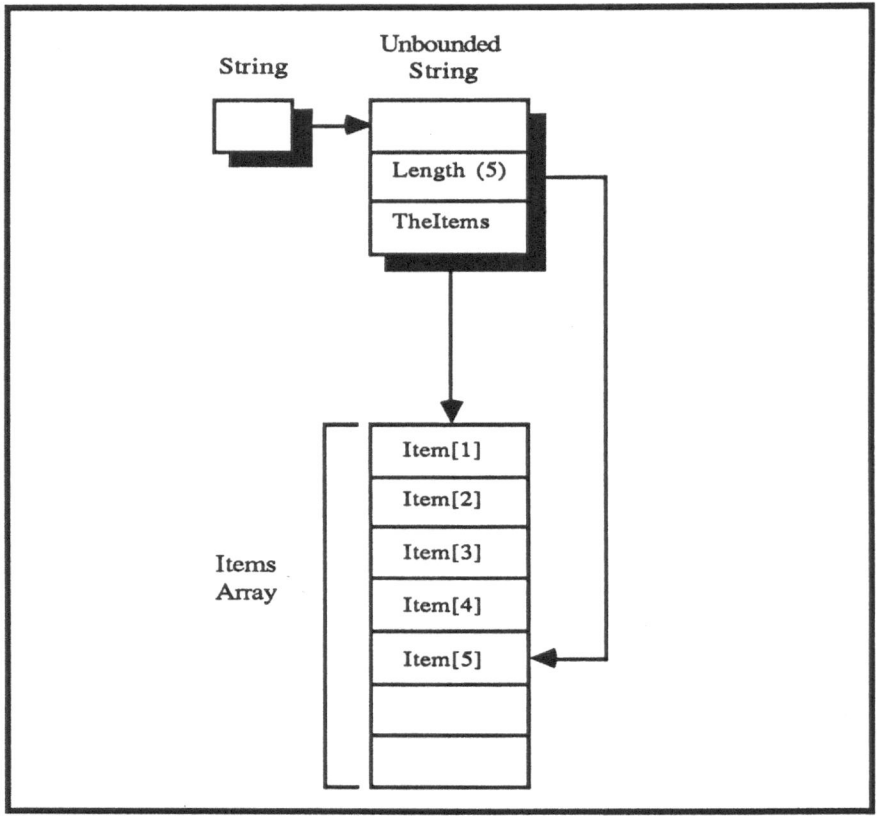

Figure 10.1 The Unbounded Character String

The implementation initializes *length* to zero when a string is created, and this value represents an empty string. Furthermore, *items* is set to NIL when the length is zero.
*)

```
TYPE  Substring  = POINTER TO ARRAY Position OF Item;

TYPE  UnboundedString = RECORD
        length : CARDINAL;  (*-- Current String Length & Size *)
        items  : Substring; (*-- ARRAY[1..length] of Items *)
      END (*-- UnboundedString *);

TYPE  String = POINTER TO UnboundedString;
```

```
(*
```

10.2.2 Exceptions

Two variables are needed to support the exception handling mechanism. The first, *stringError*, records the exception code from each operation; the second, *handler*, is an array of exception handling procedures indexed by the exception code.

The definition module has described the *StringError*, *GetHandler*, and *SetHandler* routines and their operation should be readily apparent. *RaiseErrIn* is a local routine used to set the stringError variable and invoke the *Raise* routine of the ErrorHandling module.

```
*)

VAR    stringError : Exceptions;
VAR    handler     : ARRAY Exceptions OF HandlerProc;
    (*-----------------------*)

PROCEDURE StringError ()              : Exceptions  (*-- out   *);

BEGIN
  RETURN stringError;
END StringError;
    (*-------------------------*)

PROCEDURE GetHandler  (  theError  : Exceptions (*-- in  *))
                                      : HandlerProc (*-- out  *);
BEGIN
  RETURN handler[theError];
END GetHandler;
    (*-------------------------*)

PROCEDURE SetHandler  (  theError  : Exceptions (*-- in  *);
                         theHandler : HandlerProc (*-- in  *));

BEGIN
  handler[theError] := theHandler;
END SetHandler;
    (*-------------------------*)

PROCEDURE RaiseErrIn  (  theRoutine : Operations (*-- in  *);
                         theError  : Exceptions (*-- in  *));
```

```
BEGIN
  stringError := theError;
  Raise(ModuleID, theRoutine, theError, handler[theError]);
END RaiseErrIn;
(*---------------------------*)


(*
```

10.2.3 Local Routines

Two routines local to the string module are used by other exported routines. They are declared here following convention of having routines declared prior to their use. This is not required by Modula-2 (as it was for Pascal) but some single-pass compilers impose restrictions in this regard and the technique facilitates porting the software to such compilers.

LengthSubstr determines that length of a *substring* which for our purposes is a standard Modula-2 string. The substring parameter being tested is declared call-by-reference to avoid the overhead involved in copying the open array implicit in call-by-value parameters. Note that we must first explicitly check for the special case of an empty string, "", which is represented as a string containing only the string terminator character.

The second routine, *FromToOK*, checks whether the following precondition holds:

$$\text{fromIndex} \leq \text{toIndex} \leq \text{stringLength}$$

This is required for routines such as *Delete* and *SliceOf*. The routine takes advantage of the fact that if *toIndex* is less than or equal to the *stringLength* and *fromIndex* is less than or equal to the *toIndex*, then *fromIndex* must also be less than or equal to the stringLength.
```
*)
```

```
PROCEDURE LengthSubstr  (VAR theSubstring : ARRAY OF Item (*--
                                            in    *))
                        : CARDINAL      (*--
                                            out   *);

BEGIN
  IF (HIGH(theSubstring) = 0) & (theSubstring[0] = NullItem)
    THEN
    RETURN 0;
  END (*--if*);
  RETURN HIGH(theSubstring) + 1;
END LengthSubstr;
(*---------------------------*)
```

```
PROCEDURE FromToOK    ( fromIndex     : Position    (*-- in     *);
                        toIndex       : Position    (*-- in     *);
                        stringLength  : CARDINAL    (*-- in     *))
                                      : BOOLEAN     (*-- out    *);

BEGIN
   RETURN (toIndex ≤ stringLength) & (fromIndex ≤ toIndex);
END FromToOK;
(*--------------------------*)

(*
```

10.2.4 SetSize

The *SetSize* routine changes the length of and the pointer to the dynamic array of items for an unbounded string. The input parameters are (1) the header record of the string being changed, (2) the desired new length, and (3) whether the current item values should be kept with the new item array. SetSize must correctly account for the following situations based on the desired and current lengths (using a decision table format, where an X indicates a "don't care" value):

The table indicates that decreasing the length of the string leaves the string unchanged because the implementation takes advantage of the semantics of the

Desired Length	Current Length	Preserve Value?	Action
0	X	X	Deallocate existing items array
X	0	X	Allocate new items array
Greater than current		Yes	Allocate new items array and copy item values
Greater than current		No	Allocate new items array and don't copy items values
Less than current		X	Do nothing

Deallocate operation which automatically releases the correct amount of space that was originally allocated and sets the pointer to NIL. We waste some space by not changing the items array's physical length through reallocation of the array but save the processing time spent for this operation.

The local variable *setSizeOK*, when false, indicates failure of the reallocation step. In all other cases *setSizeOK* will be true (failure cannot occur when we deallocate an items array). The value for *setSizeOK* does not always have meaning as some states never fail so it is better to use a local variable that can be checked when necessary instead of returning a function result that would have to be processed by the caller in every case.

We will examine each case from the decision table in further detail. When the new size is zero we must effectively clear the items array. This is done by simply deallocating the array and setting the string length to the desired value.

When the new size is non-zero and the string is already empty it is necessary to allocate a new items array. As there are no items to be preserved from an empty state we ignore the *valueOption* parameter. If this allocation fails, *setSizeOK* is set to false, and *SetSize* is aborted leaving the string unchanged.

Expansion of the items array occurs when the desired size is greater than the current length. A new items array is first allocated since it may be necessary to preserve the items from the current items array. If this allocation fails, *setSize-OK* is set to false, and *SetSize* is aborted leaving the string unchanged. Otherwise, if the *valueOption* has been set to *preservevalue* the individual items are copied to the new structure. Once the value has been preserved the current items array can be safely deallocated, if necessary, and the pointer to the new items array stored in its place. Lastly, the string length field can be updated.
```
*)

TYPE  SetOptions = (preservevalue, trashvalue);
VAR   setSizeOK  : BOOLEAN;

PROCEDURE SetSize (VAR theString: UnboundedString(*-- inout *);
                       totheSize    : CARDINAL       (*-- in    *);
                       valueOption  : SetOptions     (*-- in    *));

CONST itemSize = VAL(CARDINAL, SIZE(Item));
VAR   newItems : Substring;
      index    : CARDINAL; (*-- loop index over items *)

BEGIN
  setSizeOK := TRUE;
  WITH theString DO
    IF (totheSize = 0) THEN
      Deallocate(items);
    ELSIF (items = NIL) THEN
      Allocate(items, itemSize * totheSize);
      IF (items = NIL) THEN
        setSizeOK := FALSE;
        RETURN;
```

```
      END (*--if*);
   ELSIF (totheSize > length) THEN
      Allocate(newItems, itemSize * totheSize);
      IF (newItems = NIL) THEN
        setSizeOK := FALSE;
        RETURN;
      END (*--if*);
      IF (valueOption = preservevalue) THEN
         FOR index := MIN(Position) TO length DO
           newItems^[index] := items^[index];
         END (*--for*);
      END (*--if*);
      Deallocate(items);
      items := newItems;
   END (*--if*);
   length := totheSize;
  END (*--with*);
END SetSize;
(*-------------------------------*)


(*
```

10.2.5 Constructors

Create begins by clearing the *stringError* field under the assumption of a success-ful result.

The header for the string must then be allocated in a local variable since the function result cannot be manipulated but only returned. The key to this alloca-tion step is the calculation of the number of bytes necessary based on the size of an individual item and the number of items requested. We must not forget the space for storing the *Items* pointer and the string *length*. The constant expression *staticSize* accomplishes this regardless of the number and size of these "static" fields and is unaffected by changes that may come about due to future mainte-nance. If the unbounded string could not be allocated, the *overflow* exception must be raised, and the *NullString* returned.

At this point, all possibility of failure has been avoided and the bounded string header can be initialized to its empty state (*length* set to zero, *items* set to NIL). Lastly, the new string can be returned to the caller.

```
*)

PROCEDURE Create  ()  : String      (*-- out   *);

VAR   newString : String;
```

```
BEGIN
  stringError := noerr;
  Allocate(newString, SIZE(UnboundedString));
  IF (newString ≠ NIL) THEN
    WITH newString^ DO
      length := 0;
      items  := NIL;
    END (*--with*);
    RETURN newString;
  END (*--if*);
  RaiseErrIn(create, overflow);
  RETURN NullString;
END Create;
(*---------------------------*)
```

(*
Destroy simply needs to call the *SetSize* routine to deallocate the items array itself followed by deallocation of the bounded string header which automatically
sets theString to the *NullString*.
*)

```
PROCEDURE Destroy    (VAR theString  : String      (*-- inout *));
BEGIN
  stringError := noerr;
  IF (theString ≠ NIL) THEN
    SetSize(theString^, 0, trashvalue);
    Deallocate(theString);
  ELSE
    RaiseErrIn(destroy, undefined);
  END (*--if*);
END Destroy;
(*---------------------------*)
```

(*
Clear simply needs to call the *SetSize* routine to deallocate the items array itself
and set the length to zero, removing all of its items using the *trashvalue* com-
mand.
*)

```
PROCEDURE Clear      (VAR theString  : String      (*-- inout *));
BEGIN
  stringError := noerr;
  IF (theString ≠ NIL) THEN
    SetSize(theString^, 0, trashvalue);
  ELSE
    RaiseErrIn(clear, undefined);
  END (*--if*);
END Clear;
(*---------------------------*)
```

(*
The assignment for this implementation of unbounded string objects is simpler
to implement than other unbounded objects due to the opportunity for restricting
overflow to when the target object is (re-)created. This is done by the *SetSize*
routine described above, Section 10.2.4. If the target object exists and is capable
of holding all the source object's items, the target can be safely cleared and its
data type updated appropriately. Otherwise, it raises the *overflow* exception and
aborts the assignment operation. When the target object is in an undefined state,
it must be created. If overflow does not occur, the actual assignment can commence, otherwise its suffices to exit (*Create* has already raised the exception).

The assignment operator cannot be used to copy the whole items array since
only a slice of the array's index range was actually allocated and an unknown
number of other dynamically allocated objects follow it in memory. *Assignment*
can copy individual items since the data type of those items is known.
*)

```
PROCEDURE Assign     (    theString  : String      (*-- in    *);
                       VAR toString   : String      (*-- inout *));

VAR   index : CARDINAL; (*-- loop index over items *)

BEGIN
  stringError := noerr;
  IF (theString ≠ NIL) THEN
    IF (theString ≠ toString) THEN
      IF (toString ≠ NIL) THEN
        SetSize(toString^, theString^.length, trashvalue);
        IF ¬setSizeOK THEN
          RaiseErrIn(assign, overflow);
          RETURN;
        END (*--if*);
      ELSE
        toString := Create();
        IF (stringError ≠ noerr) THEN
          RETURN;
        END (*--if*);
      END (*--if*);
      WITH theString^ DO
        FOR index := MIN(Position) TO length DO
          toString^.items^[index] := items^[index];
        END (*--for*);
      END (*--with*);
    END (*--if*);
  ELSE
    RaiseErrIn(assign, undefined);
  END (*--if*);
END Assign;
(*-------------------------*)
```

```
(*
```
Prepend and *Append* make use of the *Insert* routine to add items to the front or
the back of the target string, respectively.
```
*)

PROCEDURE Prepend    (    theString  : String     (*-- in    *);
                     VAR toString   : String     (*-- inout *));
BEGIN
  Insert(theString, toString, 1);
END Prepend;
  (*---------------------------*)
PROCEDURE Append     (    theString  : String     (*-- in    *);
                     VAR toString   : String     (*-- inout *));
BEGIN
  Insert(theString, toString, LengthOf(toString) + 1);
END Append;
  (*---------------------------*)


(*
```
Insert adds the items of one string to an existing string at the given index posi-
tion. It first expands the target string to hold the new items using the *SetSize*
routine with the new length, preserving the current items. When the items array
of the string has been made large enough, room is made for new string items by
shifting items from the insertion index to the right by the number of items being inserted. Then we insert the new string items into the vacated positions. The
modified string's length is updated to reflect the newly inserted items by *SetSize*.
```
*)

PROCEDURE Insert     (    theString  : String     (*-- in    *);
                     VAR toString   : String     (*-- inout *);
                         theIndex   : Position   (*-- in    *));

VAR    oldLength : CARDINAL;
       newLength : CARDINAL;
       index     : CARDINAL; (*-- loop index over items *)

BEGIN
  stringError := noerr;
  IF (toString ≠ NIL) & (theString ≠ NIL) THEN
    WITH toString^ DO
      oldLength := length;
      newLength := theString^.length + length;
      IF (theIndex > oldLength + 1) THEN
        RaiseErrIn(insert, positionerr);
      ELSE
        SetSize(toString^, newLength, preservevalue);
        IF setSizeOK THEN
          FOR index := oldLength TO theIndex BY -1 DO
```

```
              items^[index + theString^.length] :=
                 items^[index];
           END (*--for*);
           FOR index := MIN(Position) TO
                   theString^.length DO
              items^[theIndex + index - 1] :=
                   theString^.items^[index];
           END (*--for*);
         ELSE
            RaiseErrIn(insert, overflow);
         END (*--if*);
       END (*--if*);
     END (*--with*);
   ELSE
      RaiseErrIn(insert, undefined);
   END (*--if*);
END Insert;
(*--------------------------*)
```

```
(*
```
Delete removes items from an existing string between the given index positions,
inclusive. Invalid index positions raise *positionerr* and abort the operation. The
algorithm shifts items above the *toIndex* down in the string into positions beginning with the *fromIndex*. It calculates the amount of this shift, called the *offset*, loops through string items above *toIndex*, shifting each item into its new
location. After moving, the items the string's length is updated.
```
*)
```

```
PROCEDURE Delete     (VAR theString : String     (*-- inout *);
                          fromIndex : Position    (*-- in    *);
                          toIndex   : Position    (*-- in    *));

VAR    index  : CARDINAL; (*-- loop index over items *)
       offset : CARDINAL; (*-- distance to move items *)

BEGIN
   stringError := noerr;
   IF (theString ≠ NIL) THEN
     WITH theString^ DO
       IF FromToOK(fromIndex, toIndex, length) THEN
         offset := toIndex - fromIndex + 1;
         FOR index := toIndex + 1 TO length DO
           items^[index - offset] := items^[index];
         END (*--for*);
         SetSize(theString^, length - offset,
                 preservevalue);
       ELSE
         RaiseErrIn(delete, positionerr);
```

```
        END (*--if*);
      END (*--with*);
    ELSE
      RaiseErrIn(delete, undefined);
    END (*--if*);
END Delete;
(*--------------------------*)
```

(*
Replace deletes all items of the source string from the given index to the end of
the string and then inserts the replacement string at the end of the source. If
theString was expanded by the replacement process, the string length is adjusted
accordingly.
*)

```
PROCEDURE Replace     (VAR theString : String     (*-- inout *);
                           theIndex   : Position   (*-- in    *);
                           withString : String     (*-- in    *));

VAR    endIndex : CARDINAL;
       index    : CARDINAL; (*-- loop index over items *)

BEGIN
  stringError := noerr;
  IF (theString ≠ NIL) & (withString ≠ NIL) THEN
    WITH theString^ DO
      IF (theIndex <= length) THEN
        endIndex := theIndex + withString^.length - 1;
        IF (endIndex > length) THEN
          SetSize(theString^, endIndex, preservevalue);
          IF ¬setSizeOK THEN
            RaiseErrIn(replace, overflow);
            RETURN;
          END (*--if*);
        END (*--if*);
        FOR index := MIN(Position) TO withString^.length DO
          items^[theIndex + index - 1] := withString^.items^
              [index];
        END (*--for*);
      ELSE
          RaiseErrIn(replace, positionerr);
      END (*--if*);
    END (*--with*);
  ELSE
    RaiseErrIn(replace, undefined);
  END (*--if*);
END Replace;

(*--------------------------*)
```

(*

SetItem attempts to assign a given item to the string at the given index position. The index must be within the string's current length otherwise the *positionerr* exception is raised avoiding assignment outside the string's current bounds.
*)

```
PROCEDURE SetItem    (VAR theString  : String    (*-- inout *);
                          theIndex    : Position  (*-- in    *);
                          theItem     : Item      (*-- in    *));

BEGIN
  stringError := noerr;
  IF (theString ≠ NIL) THEN
    WITH theString^ DO
      IF (theIndex ≤ length) THEN
        items^[theIndex] := theItem;
      ELSE
        RaiseErrIn(setitem, positionerr);
      END (*--if*);
    END (*--with*);
  ELSE
    RaiseErrIn(setitem, undefined);
  END (*--if*);
END SetItem;
(*-------------------------*)
```

(*

Construct forms an unbounded string from a standard Modula-2 string. If *theString* has not yet been created then *theSubstring* must not be empty for compatibility with the bounded form. If *theString* does exist and *theSubstring* is empty *Construct* clears *theString*. Otherwise the routine simply loops through *theSubstring* copying items from there to the target string and when done updating the string's length.
*)

```
PROCEDURE Construct (VAR theString  : String      (*--inout*);
                         theSubstring: ARRAY OF Item(*-- in *));

VAR   index     : CARDINAL; (*-- loop index over items *)
      lenSubstr : CARDINAL; (*-- # of items in substring *)
      newString : String;   (*-- new string, if necessary *)

BEGIN
  stringError := noerr;
  lenSubstr := LengthSubstr(theSubstring);
  IF (theString ≠ NIL) THEN
    IF (lenSubstr = 0) THEN
      Clear(theString);
      RETURN;
```

```
          END (*--if*);
      ELSIF (lenSubstr = 0) THEN
          RaiseErrIn(construct, positionerr);
      ELSE
          newString := Create();
          IF (stringError ≠ noerr) THEN
              RETURN;
          END (*--if*);
          theString := newString;
      END (*--if*);
      SetSize(theString^, lenSubstr, trashvalue);
      IF setSizeOK THEN
          WITH theString^ DO
              index := MIN(Position);
              WHILE (index ≤ lenSubstr) &
                  (theSubstring[index - 1] ≠ NullItem) DO
                  items^[index] := theSubstring[index - 1];
                  INC(index);
              END (*--while*);
          END (*--with*);
      ELSE
          RaiseErrIn(construct, overflow);
      END (*--if*);
  END Construct;
  (*--------------------------*)


  (*
```

10.2.6 Selectors

IsDefined tests the given string for a non-NIL value.

IsEmpty tests the given string's length for zero which is the value used to represent an empty string. While *LengthOf* returns the value of the given string's length.
```
  *)

  PROCEDURE IsDefined   (    theString : String   (*-- in    *))
                                        : BOOLEAN  (*-- out   *);
  BEGIN
      RETURN (theString ≠ NIL);
  END IsDefined;
  (*--------------------------*)

  PROCEDURE IsEmpty     (    theString : String   (*-- in    *))
                                        : BOOLEAN  (*-- out   *);
```

```
BEGIN
  stringError := noerr;
  IF (theString ≠ NIL) THEN
    RETURN theString^.length = 0;
  END (*--if*);
  RaiseErrIn(isempty, undefined);
  RETURN TRUE;
END IsEmpty;
(*--------------------------*)

PROCEDURE LengthOf   (    theString : String   (*-- in    *))
                                    : CARDINAL (*-- out   *);
BEGIN
  stringError := noerr;
  IF (theString ≠ NIL) THEN
    RETURN theString^.length;
  END (*--if*);
  RaiseErrIn(lengthof, undefined);
  RETURN 0;
END LengthOf;
(*--------------------------*)


(*
```

Compare returns the ordering relation between two strings such that "left Relation right" is True. If either or both strings are undefined then the *incomparable* relation is returned.

Initially we set up *minLength* with the smaller of the two string lengths, since reaching the end of a string is one condition that terminates the comparison. We also set *relOrder* to the correct result based on length — since the smaller of the strings is likely to be less than the other.

Once this initialization is done, the algorithm loops through the strings from the beginning examining each character item for the relation between them. The loop continues as long as the strings are equal or until the end of the smaller string is reached. The instant the left item at the current index is less than its counterpart in the right string the loop terminates and the relation *less* is returned. Likewise when the left item is greater than the right item, the relation *greater* is returned. For equal items the index is incremented, advancing the algorithm towards the terminating condition.

```
*)

PROCEDURE Compare    (    left    : String  (*-- in    *);
                          right   : String  (*-- in    *))
                                  : Relation (*-- out   *);

VAR  index      : CARDINAL; (*-- Index into items arrays *)
     minLength  : CARDINAL; (*-- Smaller of the two strings *)
     relOrder   : Relation; (*-- Most recent comparison result *)
```

```
BEGIN
  stringError := noerr;
  relOrder    := incomparable;
  IF (left ≠ NIL) & (right ≠ NIL) THEN
    WITH left^ DO
      IF (length = right^.length) THEN
        relOrder  := equal;
        minLength := length;
      ELSIF (length < right^.length) THEN
        relOrder  := less;
        minLength := length;
      ELSE
        relOrder  := greater;
        minLength := right^.length;
      END (*--if*);
    END (*--with*);
    index := MIN(Position);
    LOOP
      IF (index > minLength) THEN
        EXIT (*--loop*);
      END (*--if*);
      IF (left^.items^[index] < right^.items^[index]) THEN
        relOrder := less;
        EXIT (*--loop*);
      ELSIF (left^.items^[index] > right^.items^[index]) THEN
        relOrder := greater;
        EXIT (*--loop*);
      END (*--if*);
      INC(index);
    END (*--loop*);
  ELSE
    RaiseErrIn(compare, undefined);
  END (*--if*);
  RETURN relOrder;
END Compare;
(*--------------------------*)


(*
```

IsEqual scans both strings looking for the first mismatch (inequality) which indicates the strings are unequal, otherwise if the FOR loop completes the strings must be equal. This assumes that the strings have been defined and have the same length.

The first of these assumptions, if unfounded, raises the *undefined* exception; while the second is a simple determinant of inequality.
```
*)
```

```
PROCEDURE IsEqual     (     left     : String   (*-- in    *);
                            right    : String   (*-- in    *))
                                     : BOOLEAN  (*-- out   *);

VAR   index : CARDINAL; (*-- loop index over items *)

BEGIN
  stringError := noerr;
  IF (left ≠ NIL) & (right ≠ NIL) THEN
    WITH left^ DO
      IF (length = right^.length) THEN
        FOR index := MIN(Position) TO length DO
          IF (items^[index] ≠ right^.items^[index])
              THEN
            RETURN FALSE;
          END (*--if*);
        END (*--for*);
        RETURN TRUE;
      END (*--if*);
    END (*--with*);
  ELSE
    RaiseErrIn(isequal, undefined);
  END (*--if*);
  RETURN FALSE;
END IsEqual;
(*--------------------------*)
```

(*

ItemOf attempts to return the item of the string at the given index position. If
theIndex exceeds the length of the string the *positionerr* exception is raised. This
exception and also an undefined string causes the NullItem (0C) to be returned.
*)

```
PROCEDURE ItemOf      (     theString : String   (*-- in    *);
                            theIndex  : Position (*-- in    *))
                                      : Item     (*-- out   *);
BEGIN
  stringError := noerr;
  IF (theString ≠ NIL) THEN
    WITH theString^ DO
      IF (theIndex ≤ length) THEN
        RETURN items^[theIndex];
      END (*--if*);
    END (*--with*);
    RaiseErrIn(itemof, positionerr);
  ELSE
    RaiseErrIn(itemof, undefined);
  END (*--if*);
  RETURN NullItem;
END ItemOf;
(*--------------------------*)
```

(*

SliceOf extracts a portion of the given string returning the sequence of characters as a standard Modula-2 string. The range of index positions within the string, *fromIndex* and *toIndex* specify the portion of the string to be extracted. The target slice is indexed from zero and so must shift items from their positions within the source string into the appropriate positions in the target slice. Two preconditions must be met:

1. fromIndex ≤ toIndex ≤ source string length; and
2. number of items between the from and to indices, inclusive, ≤ target slice size.

If not, then the *positionerr* and *overflow* exceptions are raised, respectively. If necessary, the string terminator is added to the end of the slice.
*)

```
PROCEDURE SliceOf    (  theString  : String       (*-- in   *);
                         fromIndex  : Position     (*-- in   *);
                         toIndex    : Position     (*-- in   *);
                     VAR theSlice   : ARRAY OF Item (*-- out  *));

VAR    index     : CARDINAL; (*-- loop index over items *)
       sliceSize : CARDINAL; (*-- # items between from & to
                                  indexes *)

BEGIN
  stringError := noerr;
  IF (theString ≠ NIL) THEN
    WITH theString^ DO
      IF FromToOK(fromIndex, toIndex, length) THEN
        sliceSize := toIndex - fromIndex;
        IF (sliceSize ≤ VAL(CARDINAL, HIGH(theSlice))) THEN
          FOR index := fromIndex TO toIndex DO theSlice[index -
            fromIndex] := items^ [index];
          END (*--for*);
          IF (sliceSize < VAL(CARDINAL, HIGH (theSlice))) THEN
            theSlice[sliceSize + 1] := NullItem;
          END (*--if*);
        ELSE
          RaiseErrIn(sliceof, overflow);
        END (*--if*);
      ELSE
        RaiseErrIn(sliceof, positionerr);
      END (*--if*);
    END (*--with*);
  ELSE
    RaiseErrIn(sliceof, undefined);
  END (*--if*);
END SliceOf;
(*-------------------------------*)
```

```
(*
```

SubstringOf is similar to *SliceOf*, above, except that the whole string is re-turned. When the *Target* substring is too small for all the items in the *Source* string, overflow is raised and the target filled with as many items as will fit.

```
*)

PROCEDURE SubstringOf( theString  : String        (*-- in   *);
                   VAR toSubstring: ARRAY OF Item (*-- out  *));

VAR index      : CARDINAL; (*-- loop index over items *)
    copyLength : CARDINAL; (*-- # items to copy into substring*)

BEGIN
  stringError := noerr;
  IF (theString ≠ NIL) THEN
    WITH theString^ DO
      IF (length > VAL(CARDINAL, HIGH(toSubstring)) + 1) THEN
        RaiseErrIn(substringof, overflow);
        copyLength := HIGH(toSubstring) + 1;
      ELSE
        copyLength := length;
      END (*--if*);
      FOR index := MIN(Position) TO copyLength DO
        toSubstring[index - 1] := items^[index];
      END (*--for*);
      IF copyLength < VAL(CARDINAL, HIGH(toSubstring)) THEN
        toSubstring[copyLength + 1] := NullItem;
      END (*--if*);
    END (*--with*);
  ELSE
    RaiseErrIn(substringof, undefined);
  END (*--if*);
END SubstringOf;
(*-------------------------*)


(*
```

10.2.7 Iterators

The unbounded string iterators *LoopOver* and *LoopChange* share a common al-gorithm which is almost identical to that used with the bounded string, the dif-ference being that the items array must be dereferenced as we maintain a pointer to the dynamic structure. *StringError* is reset to *noerr* and a test made for the un-defined string, raising the *undefined* exception if such is the case. Then it loops through each item of the string passing it along to the given procedure for pro-cessing until either the end of the string is reached or the visiting process returns False indicating that the iteration be terminated.

The unbounded string iterators *Traverse* and *TravChange* use the same algorithm, which is almost identical to that used with the bounded string, the difference being that the items array must be dereferenced as we maintain a pointer to the dynamic structure. The *stringError* state is reset to *noerr* and a test made for the undefined string, raising the *undefined* exception if such is the case. Then simply loop through each item of the string passing it along to the given procedure for processing.
*)

```
PROCEDURE LoopOver    ( theString : String           (*-- in   *);
                        theProcess: LoopAccessProc (*-- in   *));

VAR   index : CARDINAL; (*-- loop index over items *)

BEGIN
  stringError := noerr;
  IF (theString ≠ NIL) THEN
    WITH theString^ DO
      FOR index := MIN(Position) TO length DO
        IF ¬theProcess(items^[index]) THEN
          RETURN;
        END (*--if*);
      END (*--for*);
    END (*--with*);
  ELSE
    RaiseErrIn(loopover, undefined);
  END (*--if*);
END LoopOver;
(*---------------------------*)


PROCEDURE LoopChange ( theString : String           (*-- in   *);
                       theProcess: LoopChangeProc (*-- in   *));

VAR   index : CARDINAL; (*-- loop index over items *)

BEGIN
  stringError := noerr;
  IF (theString ≠ NIL) THEN
    WITH theString^ DO
      FOR index := MIN(Position) TO length DO
        IF ¬theProcess(items^[index]) THEN
          RETURN;
        END (*--if*);
      END (*--for*);
    END (*--with*);
  ELSE
    RaiseErrIn(loopchange, undefined);
  END (*--if*);
END LoopChange;
(*---------------------------*)
```

```
PROCEDURE Traverse    ( theString : String        (*-- in   *);
                        theProcess: AccessProc     (*-- in   *));

VAR    index : CARDINAL; (*-- loop index over items *)

BEGIN
  stringError := noerr;
  IF (theString ≠ NIL) THEN
    WITH theString^ DO
      FOR index := MIN(Position) TO length DO
        theProcess(items^[index]);
      END (*--for*);
    END (*--with*);
  ELSE
    RaiseErrIn(traverse, undefined);
  END (*--if*);
END Traverse;
(*--------------------------*)


PROCEDURE TravChange ( theString : String        (*-- in   *);
                       theProcess: ChangeProc     (*-- in   *));

VAR    index : CARDINAL; (*-- loop index over items *)

BEGIN
  stringError := noerr;
  IF (theString ≠ NIL) THEN
    WITH theString^ DO
      FOR index := MIN(Position) TO length DO
        theProcess(items^[index]);
      END (*--for*);
    END (*--with*);
  ELSE
    RaiseErrIn(travchange, undefined);
  END (*--if*);
END TravChange;
(*--------------------------*)


(*
```

10.2.8 Module Initialization

Module initialization sets the local exception handler array variables to default handlers (*ExitOnError*) except for the *noerr* handler which is given the null handler. *stringError* is given the value *noerr* avoiding an undefined state.

```
*)
```

```
BEGIN
  SetHandler(noerr, nullHandler);
  FOR stringError := initfailed TO MAX(Exceptions) DO
    SetHandler(stringError, ExitOnError);
  END (*--for*);
  stringError := noerr;
END StringCSUMI.
```

References

[1] G. Booch, *Software Components With Ada Structures, Tools, and Subsystems*, Benjamin/Cummings, Menlo Park, CA, 1987, pp. 104-141.

[2] D. Knuth, *The Art of Computer Programming, Vol. 1, Fundamental Algorithms*, Addison-Wesley, Reading, MA 1973.

[3] R. Sedgewick, *Algorithms*, Addison-Wesley, Reading, MA 1983.

[4] T. Standish, *Data Structure Techniques*, Addison-Wesley, Reading, MA 1980.

[5] R. Wiener and R. Sincovec, *Data Structures Using Modula-2*, John Wiley & Sons, New York, NY 1986, pp. 461-469.

11 The Set Abstraction

Sets are fundamental mathematical entities having a powerful descriptive notation and strong theoretical basis. As such, sets have many uses in computer applications as well as in mathematics. Many abstract data types can be built upon set-theoretic foundations. Unfortunately, the set data type, when provided in a computer language, is often restricted to such an extent that it becomes a poor cousin to its mathematical counterpart. For example, character sets are often useful, yet Modula-2 implementations typically restrict set size precluding such declarations (often a maximum of 16 or 32 elements). Limitations on the base type of a set further confine the usefulness of the language-defined set. For example, graphs may be represented by sets of lists (for the vertices) and arcs. This chapter, and the next three chapters, attempt to remedy this by providing several example set implementations allowing arbitrary base types and expanded size of the set universe. Due to the many ways of implementing set components, only the basic set representations can be covered. To do otherwise would require a separate volume devoted solely to the subject of sets. Also, by definition, a set is an *unordered* collection, which is slightly different than a partially ordered set or ordered set.

11.1 Sets: Concepts and Definitions

11.1.1 Concepts

A set is an arbitrary collection of items without duplicates drawn from a class of values called *the universe*. When the items of the universe are bound by an ordering relationship between every item in the universe, the set is called a *partially ordered set*, or *poset*, for short. For example, sets of characters, sets of integers, etc. are posets, while sets of unordered lists are simple sets. This distinction is important in that there are several operations available for posets that are meaningless when applied to sets.

It is possible to construct sets whose items may themselves contain sets as well as individual items. A set of this kind is referred to as a *power set*. The set representations described here do not directly support this kind of set, which can be derived from the modules by declaring a set of sets.

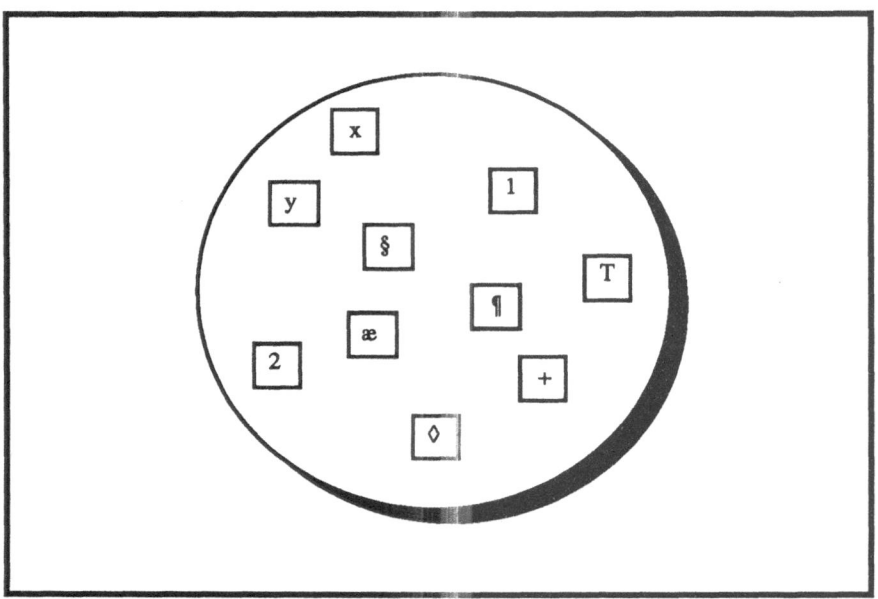

Figure 11.1 The Set Abstraction

11.1.2 Definitions

Set	Abstraction for an arbitrary collection of items without duplicates.
Universe	The class of values from which items are taken.
Extent	Also called the *cardinality* of a set, is a count of the number of items in a set.
Empty	Names a set whose extent is zero.

11.2 Applications of Sets

As mentioned above, sets are useful whenever one needs an unordered collection of (like) items without duplicates. Character sets are often used when programming to test whether a given character value is a member of some range or group of characters. For example, testing if a character is:

1. an alphabetic letter (upper or lower case),
2. a numeric digit,
3. a hexadecimal digit,
4. a punctuation symbol, etc.

Sets can represent other abstract data types, such as dictionaries and priority queues. Sets can be used to compute the reaching definitions of variables in data flow analysis of a program text [1, pp.110-113]. Many other uses could easily be added to this brief list.

11.3 Set Notation

Mathematical notation for expressing the value of a set and various set operations are provided below with a brief description of the notation's meaning. Where necessary, each set operation is also described formally using standard mathematical notation.

Notation	**Meaning**
$A = \{a,b,c,d\}$	denotes the set A with the items a, b, c, and d.
$\emptyset$	denotes the empty set.
$a \in A$	denotes that a is a member of the set A.
$g \notin A$	denotes that g is not a member of the set A.
$\#(A)$	denotes 'cardinality' of A, or the number of members in A.
$\{x \in N \mid x>0\}$	denotes an expression that establishes the criteria for set membership, in this case the set of positive integer numbers.
$A \subseteq B$	denotes that the set A is a subset of set B. $\{\forall x \in A \mid x \in B\}$
$B \supseteq A$	denotes that A is a superset of B. $\{\forall x \in B \mid x \in A\}$
$A \subset B$	denotes that A is a proper subset of B. $A \subseteq B \wedge A \neq B$
$A \supset B$	denotes that A is a proper superset of B. $A \supseteq B \wedge A \neq B$
$A \cup B$	denotes set union. $\{x \mid x \in A \vee x \in B\}$
$A \cap B$	denotes set intersection. $\{x \mid x \in A \wedge x \in B\}$
$A - B$	denotes set difference (the symbol \ is also seen). $\{x \mid x \in A \wedge x \notin B\}$
$A \vartriangle B$	denotes symmetric set difference. $\{A - B\} \cup \{B - A\}$
A'	denotes the complement of the set A. $\{x \mid \neg(x \in A)\}$
$A = B$	denotes set equality. $A \subseteq B \wedge B \subseteq A$

11.3.1 Examples

$\{1,2,3,4\} \cup \{4,5,6\} = \{1,2,3,4,5,6\}$	example of set union
$\{1,2,3,4\} \cap \{1,5,6\} = \{1\}$	example of set intersection
$\{1,2,3,4\} - \{1,5,6\} = \{2,3,4\}$	example of set difference
$\{1,2,3,4\} \triangle \{1,5,6\} = \{2,3,4,5,6\}$	example of set symmetric difference

11.3.2 Laws of Set Theory

These are taken from Mathematics in Computing [3], pg 17, Theorem 1.2.2.

For any sets A, B, and C

1. $A \cup B = B \cup A$
2. $A \cap B = B \cap A$
3. $A \cup A = A$
4. $A \cap A = A$
5. $A \cup (B \cup C) = (A \cup B) \cup C$
6. $A \cap (B \cap C) = (A \cap B) \cap C$
7. $A \cup (B \cap C) = (A \cup B) \cap (A \cup C)$
8. $A \cap (B \cup C) = (A \cap B) \cup (A \cap C)$
9. $A \cup A' =$ the Universe Set
10. $A \cap A' = \emptyset$
11. $(A \cup B)' = A' \cup B'$
12. $(A \cap B)' = A' \cap B'$

The operators
' ∩ ∪
are ranked from left to right with ' having the highest priority.

11.4 Set Constructor Operations

In the following notations, A, B, and C represent sets, while x represents a set element (Item).

11.4.1 Assign (↓SetA ↕SetB)

Requires	**nothing**
Modifies	**nothing**
Effects	Copies the items from one set to another, formally: B' := A.
Signals	Overflow **when** unable to create a new set B **ensuring modifies at most B**
Signals	Undefined **when** ¬IsDefined (SetA) **ensuring modifies nothing**

11.4.2 Clear (↕SetA)

Requires	**nothing**
Modifies	**at most A**
Effects	Removes all of the items, if any, from the set making the set empty. A' = ∅
Signals	Undefined **when** ¬IsDefined(SetA) **ensuring modifies nothing**

11.4.3 Create () ↑SetA

Requires	**nothing**
Modifies	**nothing**
Effects	Creates a new set variable, initialized to the empty set, afterwards both IsDefined(A') and IsEmpty(A') are true.
Signals	Overflow **when** unable to create a new set **ensuring** returns NullSet

11.4.4 Destroy (↕SetA)

Requires	**nothing**
Modifies	**at most SetA**
Effects	Destroys an existing set variable. After execution of this routine, A' is undefined.
Signals	Undefined **when** ¬IsDefined(A) **ensuring modifies nothing**

11.4.5 Complement (↓SetA ↕SetB)

Requires	The Universe for the set is known and finite.
Modifies	**at most** SetB
Effects	Returns the complement of a set, formally $\{x \mid \neg(x \in A)\} \rightarrow B'$. SetB is created if necessary, but in any case the previous contents of SetB are lost.
Signals	Overflow **when** unable to create a new set B **ensuring modifies at most** Set B
Signals	Undefined **when** ¬IsDefined(SetA) **ensuring modifies nothing**

11.4.6 Difference (↓SetA ↓SetB ↕SetC)

Requires	**nothing**
Modifies	**at most** SetC
Effects	Returns the set C whose elements are members of A and not members of B, formally: $A - B = C'$.
Signals	Overflow **when** unable to create a new set **ensuring modifies at most** SetC
Signals	Undefined **when** ¬IsDefined(SetA) ⏐ ¬IsDefined(SetB) **ensuring modifies nothing**

11.4.7 Exclude (↕Set ↓Item)

Requires	Item is a valid element of the Universal Set for A.
Modifies	**at most** Set
Effects	Removes an item as a member of the set, formally: $A - \{x\} = A'$
Signals	ItemNotInSet **when** ¬IsAMember(Set, Item) **ensuring modifies nothing**
Signals	Undefined **when** ¬IsDefined(Set) **ensuring modifies nothing**

11.4.8 Include (↕Set ↓Item)

Requires	Item is a valid element of the Universal Set for A
Modifies	**at most** Set
Effects	Inserts an item as a member of the set. $A' = A \cup \{x\}$

Signals	Overflow **when** unable to insert the item into the set A **ensuring modifies nothing**
Signals	ItemInSet **when** IsAMember(Set, Item) **ensuring modifies nothing**
Signals	Undefined **when** ¬IsDefined(Set) **ensuring modifies nothing**

11.4.9 Intersection (↓SetA ↓SetB ↕SetC)

Requires	**nothing**
Modifies	**at most** SetC
Effects	Given two sets, forms a set containing the items that are members of both sets, formally A ∩ B → C'
Signals	Overflow **when** unable to create a new set C' **ensuring modifies at most** SetC
Signals	Undefined **when** ¬IsDefined(SetA)	¬IsDefined(SetB) **ensuring modifies nothing**

11.4.10 SymmetricDifference (↓SetA ↓SetB ↕SetC)

Requires	**nothing**
Modifies	**at most** SetC
Effects	Given two sets, forms a set containing the items that are members of either the first set or the second set, but not both, formally A ▵ B → C
Signals	Overflow **when** unable to create a new set C' **ensuring modifies at most** SetC
Signals	Undefined **when** ¬IsDefined(SetA)	¬IsDefined(SetB) **ensuring modifies nothing**

11.4.11 Union (↓SetA ↓SetB ↕SetC)

Requires	**nothing**
Modifies	**at most** SetC
Effects	Given two sets, forms a set containing the items that are members of either the first set or the second set, formally: A ∪ B = C'
Signals	Overflow **when** unable to create a new set C' **ensuring modifies at most** SetC
Signals	Undefined **when** ¬IsDefined(SetA)	¬IsDefined(SetB) **ensuring modifies nothing**

11.5 Set Selector Operations

11.5.1 IsDefined (↓Set) ↑Boolean

Requires	**nothing**
Modifies	**nothing**
Effects	Returns TRUE ≡ the given set has been created and not yet destroyed, in other words, True if the set is a valid, active set object.
Signals	**nothing**

11.5.2 IsEmpty (↓Set) ↑Boolean

Requires	**nothing**
Modifies	**nothing**
Effects	Returns TRUE ≡ the given set contains no items, in other words True if the set = ∅.
Signals	Undefined **when** ¬IsDefined(Set) **ensuring** returns True

11.5.3 IsEqual (↓Left ↓Right ↑Boolean)

Requires	**nothing**
Modifies	**nothing**
Effects	Returns TRUE if the two given sets have the same items as members. True if Left = Right for all items and False otherwise.
	Formally: $\{\forall x \in A \mid x \in B\} \wedge \{\forall x \in B \mid x \in A\}$
Signals	Undefined **when** ¬IsDefined(Left) ❘ ¬IsDefined(Right) **ensuring** returns False

11.5.4 NumMembers (↓Set) ↑Cardinal

Requires	**nothing**
Modifies	**nothing**
Effects	Returns the number of items in a given set #A, and the result ≥ 0.
Signals	Undefined **when** ¬IsDefined(Set) **ensuring** returns zero

11.5.5 IsAMember (↓SetA ↓Item) ↑Boolean

Requires	**nothing**
Modifies	**nothing**
Effects	Returns TRUE ≡ the given item is a member of the set. (True → x ∈ A) ∨ (False → x ∉ A)
Signals	Undefined **when** ¬IsDefined(A) **ensuring** returns False

11.5.6 IsAProperSubset (↓Left ↓Right) ↑Boolean

Requires	**nothing**
Modifies	**nothing**
Effects	Returns true ≡ Left is a proper subset of Right. True if Left ⊂ Right and False otherwise.
Signals	Undefined **when** ¬IsDefined(Left)	¬IsDefined(Right) **ensuring** returns False

11.5.7 IsASubset (↓Left ↓Right) ↑Boolean

Requires	**nothing**
Modifies	**nothing**
Effects	Returns true ≡ Left is an improper subset of Right. True if Left ⊆ Right and False otherwise.
Signals	Undefined **when** ¬IsDefined(Left)	¬IsDefined(Right) **ensuring** returns False

11.6 Set Iterator Operations

11.6.1 LoopOver (↓Set ↓LoopAccessProcedure)

Requires	LoopAccessProcedure ≠ NIL
Where	LoopAccessProcedure = **procedure** (↓Item) ↑Continue? [Boolean]
Modifies	**nothing**

Effects   Invoke the LoopAccessProcedure for every item in the given set in
                   their order of occurrence in the set, or until the LoopAccessProce-
                   dure returns false, whichever occurs first.

Signals   Undefined **when** ¬IsDefined(SetA) **ensuring modifies noth-
                   ing**

11.6.2 Traverse (↓Set ↓AccessProcedure)

Requires   AccessProcedure ≠ NIL

Where   AccessProcedure = **procedure** (↓Item)

Modifies   **nothing**

Effects   Perform the given operation on every item in the set. Each and
                   every member item in the given set will be forwarded to the Ac-
                   cessProcedure for processing.

Signals   Undefined **when** ¬IsDefined(Set) **ensuring modifies nothing**

11.7   Undesired Events and Exceptions

11.7.1 Initialization Failed

This exception can be raised during module initialization. It represents all conditions where one or more prerequisites for the module's proper execution cannot
be met. Even if the implementation always succeeds in its initialization we define the exception for completeness and to minimize future changes in client
modules if it becomes necessary to add such an exception.

11.7.2 Domain Error

Each set may contain values defined over a given universe. When an item value
is not a member of this universal set the domain error exception may be raised.
An implementation is not required to support a specific domain, but the exception is provided for those implementations that do provide domains and domain
checking.

11.7.3 Item In Set

Attempting to add an item to a set that is already a member of the set can be considered an exception since the set abstraction only allows single entries for any given item value. In Modula-2 BITSETs and SETs, including an item that is already a set member is not treated as an exception since the set does not change. Whether this condition is considered an exception or not would appear to be a matter of personal preference.

11.7.4 Item Not In Set

Like the above exception, attempting to remove an item not currently a set member can be treated as an exception or an action to be quietly ignored.

11.7.5 Overflow

Memory allocation failed when creating a new set variable, or in attempting to add an item to a set. This error can also occur when operating on a bounded or discrete set, where it indicates that the set already contains as many items as the set's specified maximum size.

11.7.6 Undefined

The set variable has not been defined using *Create*, has already been destroyed, or is not a set. How the implementation determines undefined sets is left to the implementor, but at a minimum it is expected that NIL pointer values will not be allowed as legal set values.

11.8 Summary

11.8.1 Operations Summary

Below we summarize all of the set operations, categorized into Constructors, Selectors, and Iterators, and arranged alphabetically within each category.

Constructor
Operation

Assign	Set $\times$ Set $\rightarrow$ Set
Clear	Set $\rightarrow$ Set
Complement	Set $\rightarrow$ Set
Create	$\rightarrow$ Set
Destroy	Set $\rightarrow$ λ
Difference	Set $\times$ Set $\rightarrow$ Set
Exclude	Set $\times$ Item $\rightarrow$ Set
Include	Set $\times$ Item $\rightarrow$ Set
Intersection	Set $\times$ Set $\rightarrow$ Set
SymmetricDifference	Set $\times$ Set $\rightarrow$ Set
Union	Set $\times$ Set $\rightarrow$ Set

Selector
Operation

IsAMember	Set $\times$ Item $\rightarrow$ BOOLEAN
IsAProperSubset	Set $\times$ Set $\rightarrow$ BOOLEAN
IsASubset	Set $\times$ Set $\rightarrow$ BOOLEAN
IsDefined	Set $\rightarrow$ BOOLEAN
IsEmpty	Set $\rightarrow$ BOOLEAN
IsEqual	Set $\times$ Set $\rightarrow$ BOOLEAN
NumMembers	Set $\rightarrow$ CARDINAL

Iterator
Operation

| LoopOver | Set × Procedure |
| Traverse | Set × Procedure |

11.8.2 Exceptions Summary

Exception	*Raised By Operation*
DomainError	Include, Exclude
InitFailed	Module Initialization
ItemInSet	Include
ItemNotInSet	Exclude
Overflow	Assign, Complement, Create, Difference, Include, Intersection, SymmetricDifference, Union
TypeError	Difference, Intersection, IsEqual, SymmetricDifference, Union
Undefined	Assign, Clear, Complement, Destroy, Difference, Exclude, Include, Intersection, IsAMember, IsAProperSubset, IsASubset, IsEmpty, IsEqual, LoopOver, NumMembers, SymmetricDifference, Traverse, Union

Operation	*Raises Exception*
Assign	Overflow, Undefined
Clear	Undefined
Create	Overflow
Complement	Undefined
Destroy	Undefined
Difference	Overflow, TypeError, Undefined
Exclude	DomainError, ItemNotInSet, Undefined
Include	DomainError, ItemInSet, Overflow, Undefined
Initialization	Init Failed
Intersection	Overflow, TypeError, Undefined
IsAMember	DomainError, Undefined
IsAProperSubset	Undefined
IsASubset	Undefined
IsDefined	--

IsEmpty	Undefined
IsEqual	Undefined
LoopOver	Undefined
NumMembers	Undefined
SymmetricDifference	Overflow, TypeError, Undefined
Traverse	Undefined
Union	Overflow, TypeError, Undefined

References

[1]   A.V. Aho, J.E. Hopcroft, and J.D. Ullman, *Data Structures and Algorithms*, Addison-Wesley, Reading, MA 1983.

[2]   R. Courant and H. Robbins, *What Is Mathematics? An Elementary Approach to Ideas and Methods*, Oxford University Press, Oxford, England 1941 and 1969.

[3]   G.P. McKeown and V.J. Rayward-Smith, *Mathematics for Computing*, John Wiley & Sons, New York, NY 1982.

[4]   J.L. Mott, A. Kandel, and T.P. Baker, *Discrete Mathematics for Computer Scientists*, Reston Publishing Company, Reston, VA 1983.

[5]   N. Wirth, *Algorithms & Data Structures*, Prentice-Hall, Englewood Cliffs, NJ 1986.

[6]   N. Wirth, *Algorithms + Data Structures = Programs*, Prentice-Hall, Englewood Cliffs, NJ 1976.

12 The Bounded Set

This chapter presents the first of three implementations for the set abstraction described in the previous chapter. This particular form has the properties: Sequential, Bounded, Managed, and Iterator. These describe specific aspects of the implementation as follows:

Sequential   Can only be used in a non-tasking environment, or by only one task.

Bounded   The maximum size of a set is given when the set is created.

Managed   Memory space for items and objects is returned to the system when no longer needed.

Iterator   Provides routines for looping over each of a set's items.

As with the other abstractions, the interface to the module defining set operations and exceptions is included in Section 12.1. The bounded set interface follows in Section 12.2 while the actual implementation appears in Section 12.3.

12.1 Set Enumerations Interface

This module provides definitions of the standard set exceptions and operations.

```
DEFINITION MODULE SetEnum;
(*===========================================================
    Version  : 1.02 02 Jan 1988 C. Lins
    Compiler : TML Modula-2 Compiler for the Apple Macintosh
    Component: Set Enumerations Utility

    REVISION HISTORY
    v1.02 02 Jan 1988 C. Lins:
        Initial TML Modula-2 implementation.
=========================================================*)


        (*-------------------------------*)
        (*-------- SET OPERATIONS --------*)

TYPE Operations = (
                    (*-- Module Initialization *)
                     modinit,
                    (*-- Constructors *)
                     create, destroy, clear, assign, include,
                     exclude, inclrange, exclrange, union,
```

```
                    intersection, difference, symdifference,
                    merge, complement, construct,
                  (*-- Selectors *)
                    isdefined, isempty, isequal, sizeof, typeof,
                    nummembers, ismember, issubset,
                    ispropersubset, universeof, inuniverse,
                    minmember, maxmember,
                  (*-- Iterators *)
                    loopover, traverse,
                  (*-- Guarded Concurrent Operations *)
                    seize, release
                  );

TYPE Constructors = Operations [ create .. construct ];
TYPE Selectors    = Operations [ isdefined .. maxmember ];
TYPE Iterators    = Operations [ loopover .. traverse ];
TYPE GuardedOps   = Operations [ seize .. release ];


   (*--------------------------------*)
   (*-------- SET EXCEPTIONS ---------*)


TYPE Exceptions =(noerr,      (*-- Nothing went wrong, all's
                                  well.                    *)
                  initfailed,(*-- Module initialization
                                  failure.*)
                  domainerr, (*-- Item outside the Universe, or
                                  Set Universes mismatched, or
                                  Invalid Universe definition *)
                  iteminset, (*-- Item already exists in set  *)
                  notinset,  (*-- Item does not exist in set  *)
                  overflow,  (*-- Set cannot grow big enough for
                                  the requested operation.   *)
                  typeerror, (*-- TypeID mismatch between sets*)
                  undefined  (*-- Set has not been Created, or
                                  set has been Destroyed.    *)
                  );


TYPE ExceptionSet = SET OF Exceptions;

END SetEnum.
```

12.2 SetSBMI Interface

This module provides the interface to the bounded implementation Set abstraction for generic Items.

```
DEFINITION MODULE SetSBMI;
(*================================================================
   Version  : 1.02 02 Jan 1988 C. Lins
   Compiler : TML Modula-2 Compiler for the Apple Macintosh
   Component: Monolithic Structures - Set
              Sequential Bounded Managed Iterator

   REVISION HISTORY
   v1.02 02 Jan 1988 C. Lins
       Initial implementation for TML Modula-2.
================================================================*)

FROM Items IMPORT
  (*--Type*) Item, AccessProc, LoopAccessProc;

FROM ErrorHandling IMPORT
  (*--Proc*) HandlerProc;

FROM SetEnum IMPORT
  (*--Type*) Exceptions;

FROM TypeManager IMPORT
  (*--Type*) TypeID;

(*----------------------*)

TYPE  Set;
TYPE  SizeRange = [ 1 .. 8000 ];
CONST NullSet = VAL(Set, NIL);

(*
```

12.2.1 Exceptions

ModuleID   used by the exception handling mechanism to distinguish this module from other modules.

SetError   returns the exception code from the most recent bounded set operation. A result of *noerr* indicates successful completion of the operation.

GetHandler   returns the exception handler routine associated with a given exception. Though the routine is a function procedure returning a
procedure as its result, the *HandlerProc* may not be called from
within the *GetHandler* call itself. The procedure result must be
first assigned to a procedure variable before invocation. Exception
handlers are given an initial value of *ExitOnError* except for the
handler for *noerr* which is initialized to the null exception handler.

SetHandler   associates an exception handler routine with a given exception and
is the inverse of *GetHandler*. This routine may be used to override
the default settings for the exception handlers.

```
*)

CONST ModuleID = 200;

PROCEDURE SetError    ()               : Exceptions  (*-- out *);

PROCEDURE GetHandler ( theError    : Exceptions  (*-- in  *))
                                    : HandlerProc (*-- out *);

PROCEDURE SetHandler ( theError    : Exceptions  (*-- in  *);
                       theHandler : HandlerProc (*-- in  *));

(*
```

12.2.2 Constructors

Create   attempts to generate a new, empty set of a given maximum size
(*theSize*) and Item operations associated with a given data type
identifier (*theType*).

           The bounded form of set requires defining the maximum number
of desired items. This is done with *theSize* parameter.

           The *TypeID* supports Items of any data type. Using the *TypeID*,
the component can assign one item to another and release any dynamically allocated resources associated with an Item without
knowledge of the Item's internal composition. In this way, one
may create a set whose items consist of other (dynamically allocated) structures, as well as sets consisting of the basic data types.

           Create will return the new set upon successful completion of the
routine. If it not possible for the set to be created, the *overflow* exception is raised and the constant *NullSet* will be returned instead.

Destroy   clears a given set of its items, if any, and destroys the set itself.
Destroy is the inverse of *Create*, making the set undefined.

Clear   removes all items from a given set. It uses *theType* attribute of
                 the set (assigned when the set was created) to retrieve the item
                 deallocation routine for the items of the set. Clearing the set re-
                 turns it to the empty state.

Assign   attempts to generate a duplicate of the source set (*theSet*) in the
                 target set (*toSet*). It automatically creates the target set, if neces-
                 sary using the size and data type attributes of the source set. If this
                 step is unnecessary (the target set has already been previously
                 created), *Assign* clears the target of its present contents and sets its
                 data type to that of the source set leaving the size unchanged.

                 There is no guarantee that the client module would desire the target
                 set to be defined with the same size as the source. The minimum
                 requirement for the target set size is that it be capable of storing
                 all items present in the source set. It may be desirable that the tar-
                 get set size be greater than the source set size. Such a situation
                 could occur during error recovery of a bounded set overflow caused
                 by the set's cardinality encountering the set size. The client mod-
                 ule may effectively attempt to increase the set size using the as-
                 signment mechanism.

                 In order to permit Items of any data type, the *TypeID* of the
                 source set is used to assign the contents of one item to another
                 item.

Include   adds items to a given set. If the cardinality of the set is already at
                 its maximum size the *overflow* exception will be raised and the set
                 remains unchanged.

Exclude   removes the specified item from a given set. If the given set is
                 empty on entry to *Exclude*, or the given item is not a member of
                 the set the *notinset* exception may be raised and the set remains
                 unchanged.

Union, Intersection, Difference and *SymDifference* (symmetric difference) operations all implement the standard set operations of the same name.
*)

```
PROCEDURE Create          (    theSize : SizeRange (*-- in    *);
                               theType : TypeID    (*-- in    *))
                                       : Set       (*-- out   *);

PROCEDURE Destroy         (VAR theSet  : Set       (*-- inout *));

PROCEDURE Clear           (VAR theSet  : Set       (*-- inout *));

PROCEDURE Assign          (    theSet  : Set       (*-- in    *);
                           VAR toSet   : Set       (*-- inout *));

PROCEDURE Include         (    theItem : Item      (*-- in    *);
                           VAR inSet   : Set       (*-- inout *));
```

```
PROCEDURE Exclude         (     theItem : Item      (*-- in    *);
                          VAR fromSet : Set       (*-- inout *));

PROCEDURE Union           (     left    : Set       (*-- in    *);
                                right   : Set       (*-- in    *);
                          VAR toSet   : Set       (*-- inout *));

PROCEDURE Intersection    (     left    : Set       (*-- in    *);
                                right   : Set       (*-- in    *);
                          VAR toSet   : Set       (*-- inout *));

PROCEDURE Difference      (     left    : Set       (*-- in    *);
                                right   : Set       (*-- in    *);
                          VAR toSet   : Set       (*-- inout *));

PROCEDURE SymDifference   (     left    : Set       (*-- in    *);
                                right   : Set       (*-- in    *);
                          VAR toSet   : Set       (*-- inout *));
(*
```

12.2.3 Selectors

IsDefined	attempts to determine whether a given set is valid, e.g., has been created and not yet destroyed. How this is accomplished may be as simple or complicated as the implementor desires and the requirements of the application.
IsEmpty	returns true if the given set contains no items; in other words, its cardinality is zero. Undefined sets are considered to be empty.
IsEqual	returns true if the left and right sets contain the same items. Both must also have the same data type and have been created. An undefined set is not equal to any other set, including itself.
SizeOf *TypeOf*	and both return the values given the set when it was created, and both are provided so the user of the module need not maintain separate variables recording this information.
NumMembers	returns the number of items present on the given set. Undefined sets have a cardinality of zero.
IsAMember	returns true if the given item is present in a given set, and false otherwise.
IsSubset *IsProperSubset*	and both implement standard logical set operations as defined in the Set Abstraction (chapter 11).

*)

```
PROCEDURE IsDefined        (   theSet  : Set       (*-- in  *))
                               : BOOLEAN  (*-- out *);

PROCEDURE IsEmpty          (   theSet  : Set       (*-- in  *))
                               : BOOLEAN  (*-- out *);

PROCEDURE IsEqual          (   left    : Set       (*-- in  *);
                               right   : Set       (*-- in  *))
                               : BOOLEAN  (*-- out *);

PROCEDURE SizeOf           (   theSet  : Set       (*-- in  *))
                               : CARDINAL (*-- out *);

PROCEDURE TypeOf           (   theSet  : Set       (*-- in  *))
                               : TypeID   (*-- out *);

PROCEDURE NumMembers       (   theSet  : Set       (*-- in  *))
                               : CARDINAL (*-- out *);

PROCEDURE IsAMember        (   theItem : Item      (*-- in  *);
                               theSet  : Set       (*-- in  *))
                               : BOOLEAN  (*-- out *);

PROCEDURE IsSubset         (   left    : Set       (*-- in  *);
                               right   : Set       (*-- in  *))
                               : BOOLEAN  (*-- out *);

PROCEDURE IsProperSubset   (   left    : Set       (*-- in  *);
                               right   : Set       (*-- in  *))
                               : BOOLEAN  (*-- out *);

(*
```

12.2.4 Iterators

LoopOver   provides the facility for looping over some or all items of a set,
provides read-only access to each item. The routine's *theProcess*
procedure parameter returns a BOOLEAN function: TRUE permits
the iteration to proceed to the next item and FALSE causes the iteration to be terminated.

Traverse   provides the facility for looping over all items of a set, with read-
only access to each item.

Both iterators traverse a given set from the first item towards the last item in ascending order. Obviously, if given an empty set the processing procedure will
not be invoked.

Iterators allowing changes to an item's value are not provided since this would violate the abstraction (and increase the complexity of the implementation).
*)

```
PROCEDURE LoopOver (      theSet  : Set              (*-- in *);
                         process : LoopAccessProc  (*-- in *));

PROCEDURE Traverse (      theSet  : Set              (*-- in *);
                         process : AccessProc       (*-- in *));

END SetSBMI.
```

12.3 SetSBMI Implementation

This module provides the implementation of the bounded Set abstraction for generic Items using an ordered array.

```
IMPLEMENTATION MODULE SetSBMI;
(*=============================================================
   Version   : 1.02 04 Jan 1988 C. Lins
   Compiler  : TML Modula-2 Compiler for the Apple Macintosh
   Code Size: R- 4626 bytes
   Component: Monolithic Structures - Set
              Sequential Bounded Managed Iterator

   REVISION HISTORY
   v1.02 04 Jan 1988 C. Lins
       Initial implementation for TML Modula-2.
=============================================================*)

FROM MacSystem IMPORT
    (*--Proc*) Allocate, Deallocate;

FROM Items IMPORT
    (*--Type*) Item, AssignProc, CompareProc, DisposeProc,
AccessProc, LoopAccessProc;

FROM ErrorHandling IMPORT
    (*--Type*) HandlerProc,
    (*--Proc*) Raise, NullHandler, ExitOnError;

FROM Relations IMPORT
    (*--Type*) Relation;

FROM SetEnum IMPORT
    (*--Type*) Exceptions, Operations;
```

```
FROM TypeManager IMPORT
    (*--Cons*) NullType,
    (*--Type*) TypeID,
    (*--Proc*) AssignOf, CompareOf, DisposeOf;

    (*--------------------*)

(*
```

12.3.1 Internal Bounded Set Representation

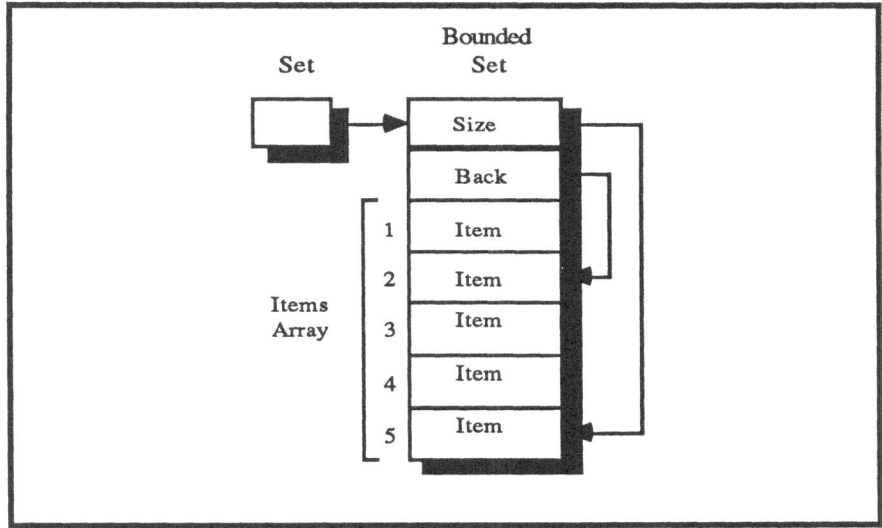

Figure 12.1 The Bounded Set

A bounded set is represented using a pointer to a record containing an array of items of a variable size, like the internal representations for the bounded stack and string. In addition, the structure holds the data type ID, physical array size (maximum number of items), and the current length (number of items currently present in the array). The representation invariants that must be enforced by the module are:

1. MIN(SizeRange) ≤ size ≤ MAX(SizeRange)
2. MIN(SizeRange) ≤ length ≤ size
3. items[x] < items[x+1], for all x such that x < length

The third invariant states that elements of the items array must be linearly ordered in ascending sequence.

Other representations are possible: unordered arrays, for example as given by
Booch [2]. The advantage of the representation used here is greater efficiency in
searching the set and binary set operations (*Union*, *Intersection*, etc.)
*)

```
TYPE ItemsArray = ARRAY SizeRange OF Item;
TYPE BoundedSet = RECORD
          dataID: TypeID;       (*-- defined data type *)
          size  : SizeRange;    (*-- defined Set size *)
          length: CARDINAL;     (*-- current Set length, := 0 *)
          items : ItemsArray;   (*-- ordered array [1..size] of Item*)
      END (*-- BoundedSet *);

TYPE Set = POINTER TO BoundedSet;

(*
```

12.3.2 Exceptions

Two variables are required to support the exception handling mechanism. The
first, *setError*, records the exception result from each operation; while *handlers* is
an array of exception handling procedures indexed by the exception result.

The definition module previously described the routines *SetError*, *GetHandler*,
and *SetHandler*, and their operation should be readily apparent. *RaiseErrIn* is a local routine used to set the *setError* variable and invoke the *Raise* routine of the
ErrorHandling module.
*)

```
VAR setError : Exceptions;
VAR handlers : ARRAY Exceptions OF HandlerProc;

    (*----------------------*)
PROCEDURE SetError () : Exceptions (*-- out *);
BEGIN
  RETURN setError;
END SetError;
(*--------------------*)

PROCEDURE GetHandler ( ofError   : Exceptions (*-- in  *))
                                 : HandlerProc (*-- out *);
BEGIN
  RETURN handlers[ofError];
END GetHandler;
(*--------------------*)

PROCEDURE SetHandler ( ofError   : Exceptions (*-- in  *);
                       toHandler : HandlerProc (*-- in  *));
```

```
BEGIN
  handlers[ofError] := toHandler;
END SetHandler;
(*--------------------*)

PROCEDURE RaiseErrIn ( theRoutine : Operations (*-- in  *);
                       theError   : Exceptions (*-- in  *));
BEGIN
  setError := theError;
  Raise(ModuleID, theRoutine, theError, handlers[theError]);
END RaiseErrIn;
(*--------------------*)

(*
```

12.3.3 Local Routines

12.3.3.1 CopySubset

Several set algorithms require the ability to copy all remaining items from a given set to a partially created target set. *CopySubset* performs this operation by looping through the *fromSet* beginning from a given index to the end of the *fromSet*, copying each item to the target set along the way. If during the copying process the target set size is insufficient for all of the items from the source set, *CopySubset* raises the overflow exception and aborts the operation. (A more efficient implementation for checking overflow would be to calculate the number of items to copy from the source (length - *fromIndex* + 1) and compare this to the number of available positions remaining in the target (size - length) and if the result is greater then invoke overflow).

12.3.3.2 Recreate

All routines that accept a target set as an inout parameter need to either clear the existing set of its contents (if the set already exists), or create a new, empty set. *Recreate* provides such a capability, returning true if successful. It should be noted that failure only occurs as a result when the set must be created.
```
*)

PROCEDURE CopySubset (     routine : Operations (*-- in    *);
                          fromSet : Set        (*-- in    *);
                            index : SizeRange  (*-- in    *);
                      VAR   toSet : Set        (*-- inout *));
```

```
VAR assignItem : AssignProc; (*-- Item assignment routine, if
any *)

BEGIN
  assignItem := AssignOf(fromSet^.dataID);
  WITH toSet^ DO
    WHILE (index ≤ fromSet^.length) DO
      IF (length < size) THEN
        INC(length);
        items[length] := assignItem(fromSet^.items [index]);
        INC(index);
      ELSE
        RaiseErrIn(routine, overflow);
        RETURN;
      END (*--if*);
    END (*--while*);
  END (*--with*);
END CopySubset;
(*--------------------*)

PROCEDURE Recreate (       theType : TypeID    (*-- in    *);
                           theSize : SizeRange (*-- in    *);
                       VAR theSet  : Set       (*-- inout *))
                                   : BOOLEAN   (*-- out   *);
BEGIN
  IF (theSet ≠ NIL) THEN
    Clear(theSet);
    theSet^.dataID := theType;
  ELSE
    theSet := Create(theSize, theType);
  END (*--if*);
  RETURN (setError = noerr);
END Recreate;
(*--------------------*)

(*
```

12.3.4 Constructors

Create begins by clearing the *setError* field under the assumption of a successful result.

The header for the set must then be allocated in a local variable since the function result cannot be manipulated but only returned. A key to this allocation step is the calculation of the number of bytes necessary for the items array based on the size of an individual item and the number of items requested. We must not forget the space for storing *theSize*, *theType*, and the *set length*. The constant *staticSize* accomplishes this regardless of the number and size of these 'static' fields. The calculation is unaffected by changes in the number or size of these fields that may come about due to future maintenance. If the bounded set could not be allocated, the *overflow* exception must be raised, and the *NullSet* returned.

The possibility of failure has now been avoided and the bounded set header can be initialized to its empty state, and the size limit and data type ID can be stored for this bounded set. Lastly, the new set can be returned to the caller.
*)

```
PROCEDURE Create (     theSize : SizeRange (*-- in *);
                       theType : TypeID     (*-- in *))
                             : Set         (*-- out *);

CONST staticSize = SIZE(BoundedSet) - SIZE(ItemsArray);
CONST itemSize   = SIZE(Item);

VAR newSet : Set;

BEGIN
  setError := noerr;
  Allocate(newSet, staticSize + itemSize * VAL(INTEGER,
        theSize));
  IF (newSet ≠ NIL) THEN
    WITH newSet^ DO
      size   := theSize;
      dataID := theType;
      length := 0;
    END (*--with*);
    RETURN newSet;
  END (*--if*);
  RaiseErrIn(create, overflow);
  RETURN NullSet;
END Create;
(*--------------------*)
```

(*
Destroy takes advantage that *Clear* sets *setError* to *noerr* and raises the *undefined* set exception. So if *Clear* succeeds, *Destroy* simply releases the allocated set header.
*)

```
PROCEDURE Destroy (VAR theSet : Set (*-- inout *));
BEGIN
  Clear(theSet);
  IF (setError = noerr) THEN
    Deallocate(theSet);
  END (*--if*);
END Destroy;
(*--------------------*)
```

```
(*
```
Clear sets *setError* to *noerr* and checks for an undefined set raising the *undefined*
set exception if necessary. After asserting a valid set, it retrieves the item disposal routine for the set, followed by the deallocation of every item in the set.
Once this has been taken care of, it adjusts the set length to the empty state.
```
*)

PROCEDURE Clear (VAR theSet : Set (*-- inout *));

VAR freeItem : DisposeProc;(*-- Item disposal routine, if any *)
    index    : CARDINAL;    (*-- Loop index over items *)

BEGIN
  setError := noerr;
  IF (theSet ≠ NIL) THEN
    WITH theSet^ DO
      freeItem := DisposeOf(dataID);
      FOR index := MIN(SizeRange) TO length DO
        freeItem(items[index]);
      END (*--for*);
      length := 0;
    END (*--with*);
  ELSE
    RaiseErrIn(clear, undefined);
  END (*--if*);
END Clear;
(*-------------------*)

(*
```
Assignment for bounded objects is simpler to implement than their unbounded
counterparts since the opportunity for overflow is restricted to when the target
object is being (re-)created.

If the target object exists and is capable of holding all of the source object's
items the target can be safely cleared and its data type updated appropriately. Otherwise, the *overflow* exception is raised and the assignment operation aborted.
When the target object is initially undefined it must be created using the data
type and size attributes of the source object. If overflow does not occur, the actual assignment can commence, otherwise it suffices to exit since *Create* has already raised the exception.

The assignment operator cannot copy the entire items array as only a slice of
the array's index range was actually allocated and who knows what other dynamically allocated objects follow in memory? Nor can assignment be used to copy
individual items as the data type of those items is unknown; using assignment
for dynamically allocated items would cause structural sharing of items, which is
not desired.
```
*)
```

```
PROCEDURE Assign (    theSet : Set (*-- in    *);
                  VAR toSet  : Set (*-- inout *));

VAR assignItem : AssignProc; (*-- Item assignment routine, if
                                             any *)
    index      : CARDINAL;    (*-- Loop index over items *)
BEGIN
  setError := noerr;
  IF (theSet ≠ NIL) THEN
    WITH theSet^ DO
      IF Recreate(dataID, size, toSet) THEN
        IF (length ≤ toSet^.size) THEN
          assignItem := AssignOf(dataID);
          FOR index := MIN(SizeRange) TO length DO
            toSet^.items[index] := assignItem(items [index]);
          END (*--for*);
          toSet^.length := length;
        ELSE
          RaiseErrIn(assign, overflow);
        END (*--if*);
      END (*--if*);
    END (*--with*);
  ELSE
    RaiseErrIn(assign, undefined);
  END (*--if*);
END Assign;
(*-------------------*)
```

(*
Include must add a given item to the set if it is not already a member or simply exit if the item *is* a member. (These semantics are compatible with Modula-2's INCL operation). We could use the *IsAMember* selector except the index where the item is not found is necessary to insert the item in its appropriate position within the ordered array of items. Once we have this position, we make room for the new item by shifting all items above the index position up by one index position in the array. Of course, there must be room for the new item in the set. Then the new item is inserted into its proper place.
*)

```
PROCEDURE Include ( theItem  : Item (*-- in    *);
                VAR inSet : Set  (*-- inout *));

VAR index       : CARDINAL;   (*-- Loop index in search for
                                            theItem *)
    jndex       : CARDINAL;   (*-- Loop index in shifting items*)
    compareItem: CompareProc; (*-- Item comparison routine *)
    itemOrder   : Relation;    (*-- Relation between items *)

BEGIN
  setError := noerr;
  IF (inSet ≠ NIL) THEN
```

```
       WITH inSet^ DO
          compareItem := CompareOf(dataID);
          index := MIN(SizeRange);
          LOOP
            IF (index > length) THEN
              EXIT (*--loop*);
            END (*--if*);
            itemOrder := compareItem(items[index], theItem);
            IF (itemOrder = equal) THEN
              RETURN;
            ELSIF (itemOrder = greater) THEN
              EXIT (*--loop*);
            END (*--if*);
            INC(index);
          END (*--loop*);
          IF (length < size) THEN
            FOR jndex := length TO index BY -1 DO
              items[jndex + 1] := items[jndex];
            END (*--for*);
            INC(length);
            items[index] := theItem;
          ELSE
            RaiseErrIn(include, overflow);
          END (*--if*);
        END (*--with*);
      ELSE
        RaiseErrIn(include, undefined);
      END (*--if*);
END Include;
(*--------------------*)


(*
```

Exclude undoes what *Include* did to add an item to the set. If the item is found then for all items above it in the array, *Exclude* shifts downward one position and updates the set length to reflect removal of the item. If the item is not found the routine simply exits to be compatible with Modula-2's EXCL operation.
```
*)

PROCEDURE Exclude (    theItem : Item (*-- in    *);
                   VAR fromSet : Set  (*-- inout *));

VAR index      : CARDINAL;    (*-- Loop index over items *)
    compareItem : CompareProc; (*-- Item comparison routine *)
    itemOrder   : Relation;    (*-- Relation between items *)

BEGIN
  setError := noerr;
  IF (fromSet ≠ NIL) THEN
    WITH fromSet^ DO
      compareItem := CompareOf(dataID);
      index := MIN(SizeRange);
      LOOP
        IF (index > length) THEN
```

```
                RETURN;
             END (*--if*);
              itemOrder := compareItem(items[index], theItem);
             IF (itemOrder = equal) THEN
                EXIT (*--loop*);
             ELSIF (itemOrder = greater) THEN RETURN;
             END (*--if*);
              INC(index);
          END (*--loop*);
          WHILE (index < length) DO
             INC(index);
             items[index - 1] := items[index];
          END (*--while*);
          DEC(length);
       END (*--with*);
    ELSE
       RaiseErrIn(exclude, undefined);
    END (*--if*);
END Exclude;
(*-------------------*)


(*
```

Union computes the set containing all members of left and right, for example,
```
         x IN toSet iff (x IN left) OR (x IN right).
```

The algorithm used is a variation on the array merge from Augenstein and Tenbaum [3, pg. 414] and the set *intersection* algorithm presented in Aho, Hopcroft, and Ullman [1, pg. 117].

The algorithm loops over items of the left and right sets until reaching the end of either. On each iteration it compares items for the ordering relation between them. This is used to determine from which set an item is copied to the target set and which indexes to advance. In this manner all items are processed only once and duplicate items in the target set are avoided. The *toSet* length is used as the running index for adding the resulting items of the union.

The last step is to copy the remaining items, if any, from either the left set or the right set to the destination set.
```
*)

PROCEDURE Union (    left  : Set (*-- in    *);
                     right : Set (*-- in    *);
               VAR toSet : Set (*-- inout *));

VAR leftIndex   : CARDINAL;   (*-- Loop index over left set *)
    rightIndex  : CARDINAL;   (*-- Loop index over right set *)
    compareItem : CompareProc; (*-- Item comparison routine *)
    order       : Relation;   (*-- Ordering relation between
                                    items *)
    assignItem  : AssignProc; (*-- Item assignment routine *)
```

```
BEGIN
  setError := noerr;
  IF (left = NIL) OR (right = NIL) THEN
    RaiseErrIn(union, undefined);
    RETURN;
  ELSIF (left^.dataID ≠ right^.dataID) THEN
    RaiseErrIn(union, typeerror);
    RETURN;
  ELSIF ¬Recreate(left^.dataID, left^.size, toSet) THEN
    RETURN;
  END (*--if*);
  WITH toSet^ DO
    compareItem := CompareOf(dataID);
    assignItem := AssignOf(dataID);
  END (*--with*);
  leftIndex  := MIN(SizeRange);
  rightIndex := MIN(SizeRange);
  WHILE (leftIndex ≤ left^.length) & (rightIndex ≤
        right^.length) DO
    order := compareItem(left^.items[leftIndex],
                         right^.items[rightIndex]);
    WITH toSet^ DO
      IF (length < size) THEN
        INC(length);
      ELSE
        RaiseErrIn(union, overflow);
        RETURN;
      END (*--if*);
      IF (order = less) THEN
        items[length] := assignItem(left^.items
            [leftIndex]);
        INC(leftIndex);
      ELSIF (order = equal) THEN
        items[length] := assignItem(left^.items
            [leftIndex]);
        INC(leftIndex);
        INC(rightIndex);
      ELSE
        items[length] := assignItem(right^.items
                [rightIndex]);
        INC(rightIndex);
      END (*--if*);
    END (*--with*);
  END (*--while*);
  IF (leftIndex > left^.length) THEN
    CopySubset(union, right, rightIndex, toSet);
  ELSIF (rightIndex > right^.length) THEN
    CopySubset(union, left, leftIndex, toSet);
  END (*--if*);
END Union;
(*--------------------*)
```

```
( *
```
Intersection computes the set containing all members in both left and right sets, for example,
```
            x IN toSet iff (x IN left) AND (x IN right).
```

The algorithm is similar to the set *intersection* algorithm given in Aho, Hopcroft, and Ullman [1, pg. 117] for ordered lists.

The algorithm loops over the items of the left and right sets until reaching the end of either. On each iteration, the items are compared for the ordering relation between them. Equal items are copied to the target set and both indexes are advanced, otherwise the index to the smaller item is advanced. In this manner, all items are processed only once and duplicate items in the target set are avoided. The *toSet* length is used as the running index for adding the resulting items of the intersection.
```
*)

PROCEDURE Intersection (     left : Set (*-- in    *);
                            right : Set (*-- in    *);
                        VAR toSet : Set (*-- inout *));

VAR leftIndex : CARDINAL;    (*-- Loop index over left set *)
    rightIndex : CARDINAL;   (*-- Loop index over right set *)
    compareItem: CompareProc; (*-- Item comparison routine *)
    order      : Relation;   (*-- Ordering relation between
                                      items *)
    assignItem : AssignProc; (*-- Item assignment routine *)

BEGIN
  setError := noerr;
  IF (left = NIL) OR (right = NIL) THEN
    RaiseErrIn(intersection, undefined);
    RETURN;
  ELSIF (left^.dataID ≠ right^.dataID) THEN
    RaiseErrIn(intersection, typeerror);
    RETURN;
  ELSIF ¬Recreate(left^.dataID, left^.size, toSet) THEN
    RETURN;
  END (*--if*);
  WITH toSet^ DO
    compareItem := CompareOf(dataID);
    assignItem := AssignOf(dataID);
  END (*--with*);
  leftIndex  := MIN(SizeRange);
  rightIndex := MIN(SizeRange);
  WHILE (leftIndex ≤ left^.length) & (rightIndex ≤
          right^.length) DO
    order := compareItem(left^.items[leftIndex],
                         right^.items[rightIndex]);
    IF (order = equal) THEN
      WITH toSet^ DO
```

```
      IF (length < size) THEN
         INC(length);
         items[length] :=assignItem(left^.items
            [leftIndex]);
      ELSE
         RaiseErrIn(intersection, overflow);
         RETURN;
      END (*--if*);
    END (*--with*);
    INC(leftIndex);
    INC(rightIndex);
  ELSIF (order = less) THEN
    INC(leftIndex);
  ELSE
    INC(rightIndex);
  END (*--if*);
 END (*--while*);
END Intersection;
(*-------------------*)
```

(*

Difference computes the set containing all members of the left set that are not members of the right set, e.g.,

```
      x IN toSet iff (x IN left) & ¬(x IN right)
```

The algorithm is similar to the above algorithm for *intersection*.

The algorithm loops over the items of the left and right sets until reaching the end of either. On each iteration, it compares items for the ordering relation between them. Equal items are skipped and both indexes advanced, otherwise the index to the smaller item is advanced. When the item from the left set is less than that of the right set we know that it is not present in the right set and can copy that item over to the target set. The *toSet* length is used as the running index for adding the resulting items of the difference. The last step is to copy the remaining items, if any, from the left set to the destination set.
*)

```
PROCEDURE Difference (    left  : Set (*-- in    *);
                          right : Set (*-- in    *);
                      VAR toSet : Set (*-- inout *));

VAR leftIndex   : CARDINAL;    (*-- Loop index over left set *)
    rightIndex  : CARDINAL;    (*-- Loop index over right set *)
    compareItem : CompareProc; (*-- Item comparison routine *)
    order       : Relation;    (*-- Ordering relation between
                                    items *)
    assignItem  : AssignProc;  (*-- Item assignment routine *)

BEGIN
  setError := noerr;
  IF (left = NIL) OR (right = NIL) THEN
    RaiseErrIn(difference, undefined);
```

```
      RETURN;
   ELSIF (left^.dataID ≠ right^.dataID) THEN
      RaiseErrIn(difference, typeerror);
      RETURN;
   ELSIF ¬Recreate(left^.dataID, left^.size, toSet) THEN
      RETURN;
   END (*--if*);
   WITH toSet^ DO
      compareItem := CompareOf(dataID);
      assignItem  := AssignOf(dataID);
   END (*--with*);
   leftIndex   := MIN(SizeRange);
   rightIndex  := MIN(SizeRange);
   WHILE (leftIndex ≤ left^.length) & (rightIndex ≤
       right^.length) DO
      order := compareItem(left^.items[leftIndex],
                           right^.items[rightIndex]);
      IF (order = equal) THEN
         INC(leftIndex);
         INC(rightIndex);
      ELSIF (order = less) THEN
         WITH toSet^ DO
            IF (length < size) THEN
               INC(length);
               items[length] := assignItem(left^.items [leftIndex]);
            ELSE
               RaiseErrIn(difference, overflow);
               RETURN;
            END (*--if*);
         END (*--with*);
         INC(leftIndex);
      ELSE
         INC(rightIndex);
      END (*--if*);
   END (*--while*);
   CopySubset(difference, left, leftIndex, toSet);
END Difference;
(*--------------------*)
```

(*

SymDifference computes the set containing all members of the left or right set that are not members of both sets, for example,

```
          x IN toSet iff (x IN left) ≠ (x IN right)
```

The algorithm is similar to that given above for *union* and *difference*.

The algorithm loops over the items of the left and right sets until the end of either is reached. On each iteration, items are compared for the ordering relation between them. Equal items are skipped and both indexes advanced, otherwise the index to the smaller item is advanced. When the items between the two sets are unequal we can then copy the smaller of the two items over to the target set. The *toSet* length is used as the running index for adding the resulting items of the

symmetric difference. The last step is to copy the remaining items, if any, from
either the left or right set, whichever has items remaining, to the target set.
*)

```
PROCEDURE SymDifference (      left : Set (*-- in    *);
                              right : Set (*-- in    *);
                        VAR toSet : Set (*-- inout *));

VAR leftIndex    : CARDINAL;     (*-- Loop index over left set *)
    rightIndex   : CARDINAL;     (*-- Loop index over right set *)
    compareItem  : CompareProc;  (*-- Item comparison routine *)
    order        : Relation;     (*-- Ordering relation between
                                      items *)
    assignItem   : AssignProc;   (*-- Item assignment routine *)

BEGIN
  setError := noerr;
  IF (left = NIL) OR (right = NIL) THEN
    RaiseErrIn(symdifference, undefined);
    RETURN;
  ELSIF (left^.dataID ≠ right^.dataID) THEN
    RaiseErrIn(symdifference, typeerror);
    RETURN;
  ELSIF ¬Recreate(left^.dataID, left^.size, toSet) THEN
    RETURN;
  END (*--if*);
  WITH toSet^ DO
    compareItem := CompareOf(dataID);
    assignItem := AssignOf(dataID);
  END (*--with*);
  leftIndex  := MIN(SizeRange);
  rightIndex := MIN(SizeRange);
  WHILE (leftIndex ≤ left^.length) & (rightIndex ≤
         right^.length) DO
    order := compareItem(left^.items[leftIndex],
                         right^.items[rightIndex]);
    IF (order = equal) THEN
      INC(leftIndex);
      INC(rightIndex);
    ELSE
      WITH toSet^ DO
        IF (length < size) THEN
          INC(length);
        ELSE
          RaiseErrIn(symdifference, overflow);
          RETURN;
        END (*--if*);
        IF (order = less) THEN
          items[length] := assignItem(left^.items
                  [leftIndex]);
          INC(leftIndex);
        ELSE
          items[length] := assignItem(right^.items[rightIndex]);
```

```
          INC(rightIndex);
        END (*--if*);
      END (*--with*);
    END (*--if*);
  END (*--while*);
  IF (leftIndex > left^.length) THEN
    CopySubset(symdifference, right, rightIndex, toSet);
  ELSIF (rightIndex > right^.length) THEN
    CopySubset(symdifference, left, leftIndex, toSet);
  END (*--if*);
END SymDifference;
(*--------------------*)


(*
```

12.3.5 Selectors

IsDefined returns true if a given set is non-NIL, which is the simplest test for a defined set object.
```
*)

PROCEDURE IsDefined (    theSet : Set      (*-- in  *))
                               : BOOLEAN (*-- out *);


BEGIN
  RETURN (theSet ≠ NIL);
END IsDefined;
(*--------------------*)

(*
```
IsEmpty (as always) returns the logical condition as to the state of the set's length, which if zero indicates an empty set.
```
*)

PROCEDURE IsEmpty (    theSet : Set      (*-- in  *))
                             : BOOLEAN (*-- out *);
BEGIN
  setError := noerr;
  IF (theSet ≠ NIL) THEN
    RETURN (theSet^.length = 0);
  END (*--if*);
  RaiseErrIn(isempty, undefined);
  RETURN TRUE;
END IsEmpty;
(*--------------------*)

(*
```
Sizeof returns the defined size for a given set or a default value for an undefined set. *TypeOf* is similar except that it deals with the set's data type ID.
```
*)
```

```
PROCEDURE SizeOf ( theSet : Set      (*-- in  *))
                         : CARDINAL (*-- out *);

BEGIN
  setError := noerr;
  IF (theSet ≠ NIL) THEN
    RETURN theSet^.size;
  END (*--if*);
  RaiseErrIn(sizeof, undefined);
  RETURN 0;
END SizeOf;
(*-------------------*)

PROCEDURE TypeOf ( theSet : Set      (*-- in  *))
                         : TypeID   (*-- out *);

BEGIN
  setError := noerr;
  IF (theSet ≠ NIL) THEN
    RETURN theSet^.dataID;
  END (*--if*);
  RaiseErrIn(typeof, undefined);
  RETURN NullType;
END TypeOf;
(*-------------------*)
```

(*

IsEqual returns true if the two given sets each contain the same items. After en
forcing required preconditions, *IsEqual* compares the lengths of the sets in a sim
ple test for inequality. If lengths are equal it is possible for the sets to be equa
so we loop over each item of both sets returning false upon encountering th
first inequality between two items. The routine returns true when the loop com
pletes without finding any mismatched items.
*)

```
PROCEDURE IsEqual (     left  : Set       (*-- in *);
                       right : Set       (*-- in *))
                             : BOOLEAN   (*-- out *);

VAR index : CARDINAL; (*-- Loop index over items *)

BEGIN
  setError := noerr;
  IF (left ≠ NIL) & (right ≠ NIL) THEN
    IF (left^.dataID = right^.dataID) THEN
      IF (left^.length = right^.length) THEN
        FOR index := MIN(SizeRange) TO left^.length DO
          IF (left^.items[index] ≠ right^.items [index]) THEN
            RETURN FALSE;
          END (*--if*);
        END (*--for*);
        RETURN TRUE;
```

```
      END (*--if*);
    ELSE
      RaiseErrIn(isequal, typeerror);
    END (*--if*);
  ELSE
    RaiseErrIn(isequal, undefined);
  END (*--if*);
  RETURN FALSE;
END IsEqual;
(*--------------------------*)
```

(*

NumMembers needs to simply return the current set length or for an undefined
set return zero as it is impossible to have any members in such a set.
*)

```
PROCEDURE NumMembers ( theSet : Set       (*-- in  *))
                                : CARDINAL (*-- out *);

BEGIN
  setError := noerr;
  IF (theSet ≠ NIL) THEN
    RETURN theSet^.length;
  END (*--if*);
  RaiseErrIn(nummembers, undefined);
  RETURN 0;
END NumMembers;
(*--------------------------*)
```

(*

IsAMember seeks to determine whether a given item is a member of a given set
by scanning each of the items in the set in turn. Two conditions could cause the
loop to terminate prior to reaching the last item:

1. the item and a set item match indicating that the item is a member
    of the set, and
2. the item is greater than a set item indicating non-membership since
    the set items are linearly ordered.

If the end of the loop is reached without exiting with a match then, by implication, the item is not present.
*)

```
PROCEDURE IsAMember (theItem : Item       (*-- in *);
theSet
                             : Set        (*-- in *))
                             : BOOLEAN    (*-- out *);

VAR index       : CARDINAL;    (*-- Loop index over items *)
    compareItem : CompareProc; (*-- Item comparison routine *)
    order       : Relation;    (*-- Ordering relation between
                                    items *)
```

```
BEGIN
  setError := noerr;
  IF (theSet ≠ NIL) THEN
    WITH theSet^ DO
      compareItem := CompareOf(dataID);
      FOR index := MIN(SizeRange) TO length DO
        IF (theItem = items[index]) THEN
          RETURN TRUE;
        ELSE
          order := compareItem(items[index], theItem);
          IF (order = greater) THEN
            RETURN FALSE;
          END (*--if*);
        END (*--if*);
      END (*--for*);
    END (*--with*);
  ELSE
    RaiseErrIn(ismember, undefined);
  END (*--if*);
  RETURN FALSE;
END IsAMember;
(*--------------------------*)
```

(*

IsSubset ensures that the required preconditions are met and loops through the
items of the left and right sets attempting to determine if every member of the
left set is also a member of the right set. Because items of the array are linearly
ordered in ascending sequence, inequality can be determined more quickly than
with a completely unordered set implementation. When an item of the left set is
less than its counterpart in the right, the routine immediately returns false knowing that that item is not present in the right set. If the left item is greater then
the right, the routine advances the index into the right set since the item may yet
be found further into the array. When items are equal both indexes are advanced.
When the end of the loop is reached without premature exit, the left set can only
be a subset of the right if we have examined beyond the end of the left set.
*)

```
PROCEDURE IsSubset (left  : Set        (*-- in  *);
                    right : Set        (*-- in  *))
                          : BOOLEAN    (*-- out *);

VAR leftIndex   : CARDINAL;    (*-- Loop index over left set *)
    rightIndex  : CARDINAL;    (*-- Loop index over right set *)
    compareItem : CompareProc; (*-- Item comparison routine *)
    order       : Relation;    (*-- Ordering relation between
                                   items *)
```

```
BEGIN
  setError := noerr;
  IF (left = NIL) OR (right = NIL) THEN
    RaiseErrIn(issubset, undefined);
    RETURN FALSE;
  ELSIF (left^.dataID ≠ right^.dataID) THEN
    RaiseErrIn(issubset, typeerror);
    RETURN FALSE;
  END (*--if*);
  compareItem:= CompareOf(left^.dataID);
  leftIndex  := MIN(SizeRange);
  rightIndex := MIN(SizeRange);
  WHILE (leftIndex ≤ left^.length) & (rightIndex ≤
          right^.length) DO
    order := compareItem(left^.items[leftIndex],
                         right^.items[rightIndex]);
    IF (order = equal) THEN
      INC(leftIndex);
      INC(rightIndex);
    ELSIF (order = less) THEN
      RETURN FALSE;
    ELSE
      INC(rightIndex);
    END (*--if*);
  END (*--while*);
  RETURN (leftIndex > left^.length);
END IsSubset;
(*--------------------------*)

PROCEDURE IsProperSubset( left  : Set      (*-- in *);
                          right : Set      (*-- in *))
                                : BOOLEAN  (*-- out *);

BEGIN
  RETURN IsSubset(left, right) & (left^.length < right^.length);
END IsProperSubset;
(*--------------------------*)

(*
```

12.3.6 Iterators

Both iterators simply loop over each item in a given set. *LoopOver* may terminate before reaching the last item in the set if the access procedure returns false.
```
*)

PROCEDURE LoopOver (    theSet  : Set             (*-- in *);
                       process : LoopAccessProc  (*-- in *));

VAR index : CARDINAL; (*-- Loop index over items *)
```

```
BEGIN
  setError := noerr;
  IF (theSet ≠ NIL) THEN
    WITH theSet^ DO
      FOR index := MIN(SizeRange) TO length DO
        IF ¬process(items[index]) THEN
          RETURN;
        END (*--if*);
      END (*--for*);
    END (*--with*);
  ELSE
    RaiseErrIn(loopover, undefined);
  END (*--if*);
END LoopOver;
(*---------------------------*)

PROCEDURE Traverse (    theSet  : Set        (*-- in *);
                        process : AccessProc (*-- in *));

VAR index : CARDINAL; (*-- Loop index over items *)

BEGIN
  setError := noerr;
  IF (theSet ≠ NIL) THEN
    WITH theSet^ DO
      FOR index := MIN(SizeRange) TO length DO
        process(items[index]);
      END (*--for*);
    END (*--with*);
  ELSE
    RaiseErrIn(traverse, undefined);
  END (*--if*);
END Traverse;
(*---------------------------*)

(*
```

12.3.7 Module Initialization

Module initialization sets the local exception handlers array variables to default
handlers (*ExitOnError*) except for the *noerr* handler which is given the null handler. *setError* is given the value *noerr* avoiding an undefined state.

```
*)

BEGIN
  FOR setError := MIN(Exceptions) TO MAX(Exceptions) DO
    handlers[setError] := ExitOnError;
  END (*--for*);
  handlers[noerr] := NullHandler;
  setError := noerr;
END SetSBMI.
```

References

[1]   A. Aho, J. Hopcroft and J. Ullman, *Data Structures and Algorithms*, Addison-Wesley, Reading, MA 1983.

[2]   G. Booch, *Software Components with Ada Strucures, Tools and Subsystems*, Benjamin/Cummings, Menlo Park, CA 1987.

[3]   A.M. Tenenbaum and M.J. Augenstein, *Data Structures Using Pascal*, Prentice-Hall, Englewood Cliffs, NJ 1981.

13 The Unbounded Set

This chapter presents the unbounded implementation of the set abstraction described in Chapter 11. As with the other unbounded modules previously described, the size of the set structure will vary dynamically as items are added and removed. This particular form has the properties: Sequential, Unbounded, Managed, and Iterator. These describe specific aspects of the implementation as follows:

Sequential   Can only be used in a non-tasking environment, or by only one task.

Unbounded   The size of a set varies dynamically as items are added and removed from the set.

Managed   Memory space for items and objects is returned to the system when no longer needed.

Iterator   Routines for looping over each of the set items are provided.

The unbounded set interface follows in Section 13.1; the actual implementation appears in Section 13.2.

13.1 SetSUMI Interface

```
DEFINITION MODULE SetSUMI;
(*=============================================================
   Version  : 1.01 02 Jan 1988 C. Lins
   Compiler : TML Modula-2 Compiler for the Apple Macintosh
   Component: Monolithic Structures - Set
              Sequential Unbounded Managed Iterator

   INTRODUCTION
   This module provides the interface for the unbounded Set
   abstraction for generic Items.

   REVISION HISTORY
   v1.01 02 Jan 1988 C. Lins
       Initial implementation for TML Modula-2.
=============================================================*)

FROM SYSTEM IMPORT
    (*--Proc*) VAL;
```

```
FROM ErrorHandling IMPORT
    (*--Proc*) HandlerProc;

FROM SetEnum IMPORT
    (*--Type*) Exceptions;

FROM TypeManager IMPORT
    (*--Type*) TypeID;
    (*----------------------*)

TYPE  Set;
CONST NullSet = VAL(Set, NIL);

(*
```

13.1.1 Exceptions

ModuleID   distinguishes this module from all other modules.

SetError   returns the exception code from the most recent set operation. A
               result of *noerr* indicates successful completion of the operation.

GetHandler   returns the exception handler routine associated with a given ex-
               ception. Though the routine is a function procedure returning a
               procedure as its result, the *HandlerProc* may not be called from
               within the *GetHandler* call itself. The procedure result must be
               first assigned to a procedure variable before invocation. Exception
               handlers are given an initial value of *ExitOnError* except for the
               handler for *noerr* which is initialized to the null exception handler.

SetHandler   associates an exception handler routine with a given exception and
               is the inverse of *GetHandler*. This routine may override the default
               settings for the exception handlers.

```
*)

CONST ModuleID = 201;

PROCEDURE SetError    ()              : Exceptions  (*-- out  *);

PROCEDURE GetHandler ( ofError    : Exceptions  (*-- in   *))
                                   : HandlerProc (*-- out  *);

PROCEDURE SetHandler ( ofError    : Exceptions  (*-- in   *);
                       toHandler : HandlerProc (*-- in *));
```

```
(*
```

13.1.2 Constructors

Create	attempts to define a new, empty unbounded set of a given type, raising the *overflow* exception if it is unable to successfully complete the set.
Destroy	clears the given set of any items, and then destroys the set itself. Where *Create* makes a defined set, *Destroy* is its inverse, making the set undefined.
Clear	removes all items from a given set. *theType* attribute of the set (assigned when the set was created) retrieves the item deallocation routine for the items of the set. *Clear*ing the set returns it to the empty state.
Assign	attempts to generate a duplicate of the source set (*theSet*) in the target set (*toSet*). The target set is automatically created using the data type attribute of the source set, if necessary. If this step is unnecessary, (the target set has been previously created), the target is cleared of its present contents, and its data type is changed to that of the source set.
Include	adds a given item to the given set. If the routine is unable to expand the set for the new item the *overflow* exception will be raised and the set remains unchanged. If the item is already a member of the set the *iteminset* exception is quietly ignored.
Exclude	removes the specified item from the given set. If the given set is empty on entry to *Exclude*, or the given item is not a member of the set the *notinset* exception is silently ignored and the set remains unchanged.
Union, Intersection, Difference and *SymDifference*	(symmetric difference) all implement the standard set operations of the same name as defined in the set abstraction chapter (11).

```
*)

PROCEDURE Create        (    theType : TypeID (*-- in    *))
                             : Set    (*-- out   *);

PROCEDURE Destroy       (VAR theSet  : Set     (*-- inout *));

PROCEDURE Clear         (VAR theSet  : Set     (*-- inout *));

PROCEDURE Assign        (    theSet  : Set     (*-- in    *);
                         VAR toSet   : Set     (*-- inout *));
```

```
PROCEDURE Include       (     theItem : Item   (*-- in    *);
                         VAR inSet    : Set    (*-- inout *));

PROCEDURE Exclude       (     theItem : Item   (*-- in    *);
                         VAR fromSet  : Set    (*-- inout *));

PROCEDURE Union         (     left    : Set    (*-- in    *);
                              right   : Set    (*-- in    *);
                         VAR toSet    : Set    (*-- inout *));

PROCEDURE Intersection  (    'left    : Set    (*-- in    *);
                              right   : Set    (*-- in    *);
                         VAR toSet    : Set    (*-- inout *));

PROCEDURE Difference    (     left    : Set    (*-- in    *);
                              right   : Set    (*-- in    *);
                         VAR toSet    : Set    (*-- inout *));

PROCEDURE SymDifference (     left    : Set    (*-- in    *);
                              right   : Set    (*-- in    *);
                         VAR toSet    : Set    (*-- inout *));

(*
```

13.1.3 Selectors

IsDefined   attempts to determine whether a given set is valid — that is, has been created and not yet destroyed. How this is accomplished may be as simple or complicated as the implementor desires and the requirements of the application.

IsEmpty   returns true if a given set contains no items; in other words, its cardinality is zero. Undefined sets are always considered empty.

IsEqual   returns true if the left and right sets contain the same items. Both must also have the same data type and have been created. An undefined set is not equal to any other set, including itself.

TypeOf   returns the current *TypeID* value given the set when it was created or assigned; is provided so the user of the module need not maintain a separate variable recording this information.

NumMembers   returns the number of items present in a given set. Undefined sets are considered to have no members.

IsAMember   returns true if a given item is present in a given set; false otherwise.

IsSubset   and
IsProperSubset both implement standard logical set operations as defined in the Set Abstraction (chapter 11).

*)

```
PROCEDURE IsDefined      (      theSet  : Set      (*-- in  *))
                                        : BOOLEAN (*-- out *);

PROCEDURE IsEmpty        (      theSet  : Set      (*-- in  *))
                                        : BOOLEAN (*-- out *);

PROCEDURE IsEqual        (      left    : Set      (*-- in  *);
                                right   : Set      (*-- in  *))
                                        : BOOLEAN (*-- out *);

PROCEDURE TypeOf         (      theSet  : Set      (*-- in  *))
                                        : TypeID   (*-- out *);

PROCEDURE NumMembers     (      theSet  : Set      (*-- in  *))
                                        : CARDINAL (*-- out *);

PROCEDURE IsAMember      (      theItem : Item     (*-- in  *);
                                theSet  : Set      (*-- in  *))
                                        : BOOLEAN (*-- out *);

PROCEDURE IsSubset       (      left    : Set      (*-- in  *);
                                right   : Set      (*-- in  *))
                                        : BOOLEAN (*-- out *);

PROCEDURE IsProperSubset (      left    : Set      (*-- in  *);
                                right   : Set      (*-- in  *))
                                        : BOOLEAN (*-- out *);
(*
```

13.1.4 Iterators

LoopOver   provides the facility for looping over some or all items of a set, with read-only access to each item. *theProcess* procedure parameter to this routine returns a BOOLEAN function result where TRUE allows the iteration to proceed to the next item and FALSE causes the iteration to be terminated.

Traverse   provides the facility for looping over all items of a set, granting read-only access to each item.

Both iterators traverse a given set from the first item towards the last item in ascending order. Obviously, if given an empty set the processing procedure will not be invoked.
```
*)

PROCEDURE LoopOver (    theSet  : Set            (*-- in *);
                       process : LoopAccessProc (*-- in *));

PROCEDURE Traverse (    theSet  : Set            (*-- in *);
                       process : AccessProc     (*-- in *));

END SetSUMI.
```

13.2 SetSUMI Implementation

```
IMPLEMENTATION MODULE SetSUMI;
(*=============================================================
Version  : 1.02 02-04 Jan 1988 C. Lins
Compiler : TML Modula-2 Compiler for the Apple Macintosh
Code Size: R- 4452 bytes
Component: Monolithic Structures - Set
           Sequential Unbounded Managed Iterator

INTRODUCTION
This module implements the unbounded Set abstraction for
generic Items using a linearly ordered list.

REVISION HISTORY
v1.02 04 Jan 1988 C. Lins
    Initial implementation for TML Modula-2.
=============================================================*)

FROM MacSystem IMPORT
  (*--Proc*) Allocate, Deallocate;

FROM Items IMPORT
  (*--Type*) Item, AssignProc, CompareProc, DisposeProc,
             AccessProc, LoopAccessProc;

FROM ErrorHandling IMPORT
  (*--Type*) HandlerProc,
  (*--Proc*) Raise, NullHandler, ExitOnError;

FROM Relations IMPORT
  (*--Type*) Relation;

FROM SetEnum IMPORT
  (*--Type*) Exceptions, Operations;

FROM TypeManager IMPORT
  (*--Cons*) NullType,
  (*--Type*) TypeID,
  (*--Proc*) AssignOf, CompareOf, DisposeOf;

  (*--------------------*)
```

(*

13.2.1 Internal Unbounded Set Representation

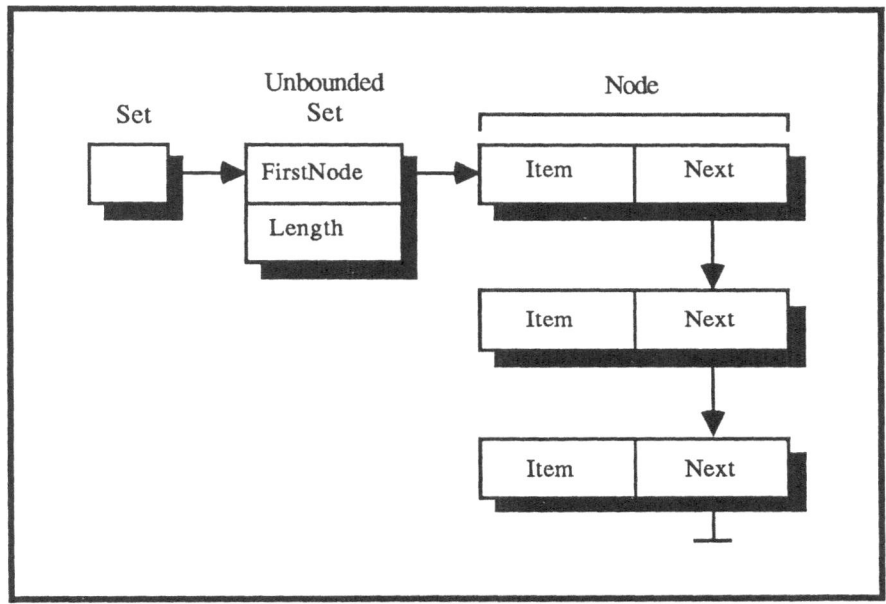

Figure 13.1 The Unbounded Set

The internal representation of an unbounded set uses a linear linked list, as shown above in Figure 13.1. Each item of the set is stored in a *node* which is linked to its immediate successor. The unbounded set header maintains the data type ID of the set, its current length, and the link to the first node of the list of set member items.

Representation Invariants:

1. when length = 0, first = NIL
2. when length > 0, first ≠ NIL
3. each item node is linked to its successor and the last item node has a *next* of NIL
4. first^.item < first^.next^.item and item < item.next^.item
5. length contains the number of nodes in the list

The fourth Invariant describes the property that the linked list is linearly ordered in ascending sequence based on item values.
*)

```
TYPE Link = POINTER TO Node;
TYPE Node = RECORD    (*-- a set item node *)
        item : Item; (*-- the item nodes' data *)
        next : Link; (*-- link to next node in list *)
     END (*-- Node *);

TYPE UnboundedSet = RECORD (*-- set header *)
        dataID : TypeID;    (*-- defined data type *)
        length : CARDINAL; (*-- current set length, := 0 *)
        first  : Link;      (*-- link to first Item node *)
     END (*-- UnboundedSet *);

TYPE Set = POINTER TO UnboundedSet;

(*
```

13.2.2 Exceptions

To support the exception handling mechanism two variables are needed. The first, *setError*, is used to record the exception code from each operation; while *handlers* is an array of exception handling procedures indexed by the exception code.

The routines *SetError*, *GetHandler*, and *SetHandler* have been previously described in the definition module, and their operation should be readily apparent. *RaiseErrIn* is a local routine used to set the *setError* variable and invoke the *Raise* routine of the ErrorHandling module.
*)

```
VAR setError : Exceptions;
VAR handlers : ARRAY Exceptions OF HandlerProc;

  (*-----------------------*)

PROCEDURE SetError () : Exceptions (*-- out *);
BEGIN
  RETURN setError;
END SetError;
(*-------------------*)

PROCEDURE GetHandler ( ofError    : Exceptions  (*-- in  *))
                                  : HandlerProc (*-- out *);

BEGIN
  RETURN handlers[ofError];
END GetHandler;
(*-------------------*)

PROCEDURE SetHandler ( ofError    : Exceptions  (*-- in  *);
                       toHandler : HandlerProc (*-- in  *));
```

```
BEGIN
  handlers[ofError] := toHandler;
END SetHandler;
(*--------------------*)

PROCEDURE RaiseErrIn ( theRoutine: Operations   (*-- in *);
                       theError   : Exceptions   (*-- in *));

BEGIN
  setError := theError;
  Raise(ModuleID, theRoutine, theError, handlers[theError]);
END RaiseErrIn;
(*--------------------*)

(*
```

13.2.3 Local Routines

Many set routines need to create new item nodes and *NewNode* performs this; setting the *item* and *link* fields to the new node which is returned. Two state variables are used by *NewNode*: *setRoutine* and *assignItem*, when raising the overflow exception and when copying item values, respectively. A routine, such as *Union*, may call *NewNode* many times throughout its execution and it would be quite inefficient to repeatedly pass these as parameters.

Several set algorithms require the ability to copy all remaining items from a given set to a partially created target set. *CopySubset* does this by looping through *fromSet*, beginning from a given index to the end of the source set, copying each item to the target set along the way.

All routines that accept a target set as an inout parameter need to either clear the set of its present contents (if the set already exists) or create a new, empty set to be target of the operation. The *Recreate* routine provides such a capability, returning true if successful. It should be noted that failure only occurs as a result when the set must be created.

```
*)

VAR setRoutine : Operations; (*-- Routine calling NewNode *)
VAR assignItem : AssignProc; (*-- Item assignment routine *)

PROCEDURE NewNode (    theItem : Item (*-- in *);
                       theNext : Link (*-- in *))
                             : Link (*-- out *);

VAR newLink : Link;

BEGIN
  Allocate(newLink, SIZE(Node));
  IF (newLink = NIL) THEN
    RaiseErrIn(setRoutine, overflow);
```

```
        ELSE
          WITH newLink^ DO
            item := assignItem(theItem);
            next := theNext;
          END (*--with*);
        END (*--if*);
        RETURN newLink;
      END NewNode;
      (*-------------------*)

      PROCEDURE CopySubset (    fromIndex : Link (*-- in    *);
                                toIndex   : Link (*-- in    *);
                            VAR toSet     : Set  (*-- inout *));

      VAR tempNode : Link;

      BEGIN
        LOOP
          IF (fromIndex = NIL) THEN
            EXIT (*--loop*);
          ELSE
            tempNode := NewNode(fromIndex^.item, NIL);
            IF (tempNode = NIL) THEN
              EXIT (*--loop*);
            END (*--if*);
            INC(toSet^.length);
            IF (toSet^.first = NIL) THEN
              toSet^.first := tempNode;
            ELSE
              toIndex^.next := tempNode;
            END (*--if*);
            toIndex := tempNode;
            fromIndex := fromIndex^.next;
          END (*--if*);
        END (*--loop*);
      END CopySubset;
      (*-------------------*)

      PROCEDURE Recreate (    theType : TypeID  (*-- in    *);
                          VAR theSet  : Set     (*-- inout *))
                                      : BOOLEAN (*-- out   *);

      BEGIN
        IF (theSet ≠ NIL) THEN
          Clear(theSet);
          theSet^.dataID := theType;
        ELSE
          theSet := Create(theType);
        END (*--if*);
        RETURN (setError = noerr);
      END Recreate;
      (*-------------------*)

      (*
```

13.2.4 Constructors

Create attempts to allocate a new, empty unbounded set header which, if successful, initializes the set to an empty state with a given data type ID, a *length* of
zero and a pointer to the *first* item node of NIL. If unable to allocate the header,
it raises the *overflow* exception and returns the *NullSet*.
*)

```
PROCEDURE Create (    theType : TypeID (*-- in  *))
                            : Set    (*-- out *);

VAR newSet : Set; (*-- new set variable being created *)

BEGIN
  setError := noerr;
  Allocate(newSet, SIZE(UnboundedSet));
  IF (newSet ≠ NIL) THEN
    WITH newSet^ DO
      dataID := theType;
      length := 0;
      first := NIL;
    END (*--with*);
    RETURN newSet;
  END (*--if*);
  RaiseErrIn(create, overflow);
  RETURN NullSet;
END Create;
(*--------------------*)
```

(*
Destroy takes advantage that *Clear* sets *setError* to *noerr* and raises the *undefined*
set exception. If *Clear* succeeds, *Destroy* releases the allocated set header.
*)

```
PROCEDURE Destroy (VAR theSet : Set (*-- inout *));

BEGIN
  Clear(theSet);
  IF (setError = noerr) THEN
    Deallocate(theSet);
  END (*--if*);
END Destroy;
(*--------------------*)
```

(*
Clear sets *setError* to *noerr* and then ensures a valid set object, raising the *undefined* exception, if necessary. Then it traverses the set nodes in order —
deallocating each item and then its node. The representation invariants state that
when length is zero, first must be NIL, and so we repeatedly adjust *first* since
our last step will be to set *length* to zero. The loop is guaranteed to terminate as
the last item node must have a *next* of NIL.
*)

```
PROCEDURE Clear (VAR theSet : Set (*-- inout *));

VAR freeItem : DisposeProc;(*-- Item disposal routine, if any *)
    theNode  : Link;        (*-- Set node to be deallocated *)

BEGIN
  setError := noerr;
  IF (theSet ≠ NIL) THEN
    WITH theSet^ DO
      freeItem := DisposeOf(dataID);
      WHILE (first ≠ NIL) DO
        theNode := first;
        first := first^.next;
        freeItem(theNode^.item);
        Deallocate(theNode);
      END (*--while*);
      length := 0;
    END (*--with*);
  ELSE
    RaiseErrIn(clear, undefined);
  END (*--if*);
END Clear;
(*--------------------*)
```

(*
Assign attempts to duplicate the items of the source set in the target set, avoiding the useless operation of assigning a set to itself and recreating the target set if necessary. To simplify the assignment, the routine initially copies the first node from the source to the target and then loops through any remaining item nodes. This maintains the elements of the target in the same order as they appeared in the source.
*)

```
PROCEDURE Assign (    theSet : Set (*-- in    *);
                  VAR toSet  : Set (*-- inout *));

VAR fromIndex : Link; (*-- Loop index over source set items *)
    toIndex   : Link; (*-- Loop index over target set items *)

BEGIN
  setError := noerr;
  IF (theSet ≠ NIL) THEN
    IF (toSet = theSet) OR ¬Recreate(theSet^.dataID, toSet)
         THEN
      RETURN;
    END (*--if*);
    WITH theSet^ DO
      IF (first = NIL) THEN
        RETURN;
      END (*--if*);
      assignItem := AssignOf(dataID);
    END (*--with*);
    setRoutine := assign;
```

```
    WITH toSet^ DO
      first := NewNode(theSet^.first^.item, NIL);
      IF (setError = overflow) THEN
        RETURN;
      END (*--if*);
      toIndex := first;
      fromIndex := theSet^.first;
    END (*--with*);
    WHILE (fromIndex^.next ≠ NIL) DO
      fromIndex := fromIndex^.next;
      toIndex^.next := NewNode(fromIndex^.item, NIL);
      IF (setError = overflow) THEN
        RETURN;
      END (*--if*);
      toIndex := toIndex^.next;
    END (*--while*);
    toSet^.length := theSet^.length;
  ELSE
    RaiseErrIn(assign, undefined);
  END (*--if*);
END Assign;
(*--------------------*)
```

```
(*
```
Include adds a given item to the set if it is not already a member or simply exits
if the item *is* already a member. (The semantics are compatible with Modula-2's
INCL operation.) We could use the *IsAMember* selector except when the item is
not found in the set it must be inserted in its appropriate index position within
the ordered list. Once we have this position, we add the new item using the standard ordered linked list insertion algorithm.
```
*)
```

```
PROCEDURE Include (    theItem : Item (*-- in    *);
                      VAR inSet   : Set  (*-- inout *));

VAR current      : Link;        (*-- Loop index in search of
                                           theItem *)
    previous     : Link;        (*-- Previous node examined *)
    newNode      : Link;        (*-- For new node to add *)
    compareItem : CompareProc; (*-- Item comparison routine *)
    itemOrder    : Relation;    (*-- Ordering relation between
                                              items *)

BEGIN
  setError := noerr;
  IF (inSet ≠ NIL) THEN
    compareItem := CompareOf(inSet^.dataID);
    current  := inSet^.first;
    previous := NIL;
    LOOP
      IF (current = NIL) THEN
        EXIT (*--loop*);
```

```
    END (*--if*);
      itemOrder := compareItem(current^.item, theItem);
      IF (itemOrder = equal) THEN
        RETURN;
        ELSIF (itemOrder = greater) THEN EXIT (*--loop*);
      END (*--if*);
      previous := current;
      current  := current^.next;
    END (*--loop*);
    (*-- Insert the new item *)
    Allocate(newNode, SIZE(Node));
    IF (newNode = NIL) THEN
      RaiseErrIn(include, overflow);
    ELSE
      newNode^.item := theItem;
      IF (previous = NIL) THEN
        newNode^.next := inSet^.first;
        inSet^.first  := newNode;
      ELSE
        newNode^.next  := current;
        previous^.next := newNode;
      END (*--if*);
      INC(inSet^.length);
    END (*--if*);
  ELSE
    RaiseErrIn(include, undefined);
  END (*--if*);
END Include;
(*--------------------*)


(*
```

Exclude undoes what *Include* did in adding an item to the set. The first step is to determine if a given item is present in the set. If the item is not found the routine exits to be compatible with Modula-2's EXCL operation. When the item *is* found, it updates the list by relinking nodes using the standard ordered linked list node deletion algorithm. The removed node and its item are both deallocated and the set length is updated to reflect the removal of the item.
```
*)

PROCEDURE Exclude (    theItem : Item (*-- in    *);
                   VAR fromSet : Set  (*-- inout *));

VAR current     : Link;         (*-- Loop index over items *)
    previous    : Link;         (*-- Previous node examined *)
    compareItem : CompareProc;  (*-- Item comparison routine *)
    itemOrder   : Relation;     (*-- Relation between items *)
    freeItem    : DisposeProc;  (*-- Item disposal routine *)

BEGIN
  setError := noerr;
  IF (fromSet ≠ NIL) THEN
    compareItem := CompareOf(fromSet^.dataID);
```

```
current      := fromSet^.first;
previous     := NIL;
LOOP
  IF (current = NIL) THEN
    RETURN;
  END (*--if*);
  itemOrder := compareItem(current^.item, theItem);
  IF (itemOrder = equal) THEN
    EXIT (*--loop*);
  ELSIF (itemOrder = greater) THEN
    RETURN;
  END (*--if*);
  previous := current;
  current  := current^.next;
END (*--loop*);
(*-- "current" points to the node to be deleted. *)
IF (previous = NIL) THEN
  fromSet^.first := current^.next;
ELSE
  previous^.next := current^.next;
END (*--if*);
freeItem := DisposeOf(fromSet^.dataID);
freeItem(current^.item);
Deallocate(current);
DEC(fromSet^.length);
ELSE
  RaiseErrIn(exclude, undefined);
END (*--if*);
END Exclude;
(*--------------------*)
```

```
(*
```

Union computes the set containing all members of the left and right sets, for example,

```
            x IN toSet iff (x IN left) OR (x IN right).
```

The algorithm is a variation on the array merge from reference [2], pg. 414 and the ordered list set intersection algorithm presented in Aho, Hopcroft, and Ullman [1, pg. 117]. It is similar to the algorithm used in the previous chapter on the bounded set converted to work with ordered linear linked lists.

The algorithm loops over the items of the left and right sets until reaching the end of either. Each iteration compares the items for the ordering relation between them. This is used to determine the set from which an item is copied to the target set and the indexes to advance. In this way, all items are processed only once and duplicate items in the target set are avoided.

The last step copies the remaining items, if any, from either the left set or the right set to the destination set.
```
*)
```

```
PROCEDURE Union (    left  : Set (*-- in *);
                     right : Set (*-- in *);
                 VAR toSet : Set (*-- inout *));
```

```
VAR leftIndex   : Link;          (*-      index over left set *)
    rightIndex  : Link;          (*-      index over right set *)
    toIndex     : Link;          (*-      of target set nodes *)
    tempNode    : Link;          (*-      rary node *)
    compareItem : CompareProc;   (*-      comparison routine *)
    order       : Relation;      (*-      ing relation between
                                           *)

BEGIN
  setError := noerr;
  IF (left = NIL) OR (right = NIL)
    RaiseErrIn(union, undefined);
    RETURN;
  ELSIF (left^.dataID ≠ right^.dataID) THEN
    RaiseErrIn(union, typeerror);
    RETURN;
  ELSIF ¬Recreate(left^.dataID, toSet) THEN
    RETURN;
  END (*--if*);
  WITH toSet^ DO
    compareItem := CompareOf(dataID);
    assignItem  := AssignOf(dataID);
  END (*--with*);
  setRoutine := union;
  leftIndex   := left^.first;
  rightIndex  := right^.first;
  WHILE (leftIndex ≠ NIL) & (rightIndex ≠ NIL) DO
    order := compareItem(leftIndex^.item, rightIndex^.item);
    Allocate(tempNode, SIZE(Node));
    IF (tempNode = NIL) THEN
      RaiseErrIn(union, overflow);
      RETURN;
    END (*--if*);
    tempNode^.next := NIL;
    INC(toSet^.length);
    IF (order = less) THEN
      tempNode^.item := assignItem(leftIndex^.item);
      leftIndex := leftIndex^.next;
    ELSIF (order = equal) THEN
      tempNode^.item := assignItem(leftIndex^.item);
      leftIndex  := leftIndex^.next;
      rightIndex := rightIndex^.next;
    ELSE
      tempNode^.item := assignItem(rightIndex^.item);
      rightIndex := rightIndex^.next;
    END (*--if*);
    (*-- Update the linked list *)
    IF (toSet^.first = NIL) THEN
      toSet^.first := tempNode;
    ELSE
      toIndex^.next := tempNode;
    END (*--if*);
    toIndex := tempNode;
  END (*--while*);
  IF (leftIndex = NIL) THEN
    CopySubset(rightIndex, toIndex, toSet);
  ELSIF (rightIndex = NIL) THEN
```

```
      CopySubset(leftIndex, toIndex, toSet);
  END (*--if*);
END Union;
(*--------------------*)
```

(*
Intersection computes the set containing all members in both left and right sets
— for example,

```
            x IN toSet iff (x IN left) AND (x IN right).
```

The algorithm, derived from that given by Aho, Hopcroft, and Ullman [1, pg. 117], loops over the items of the left and right sets until reaching the end of either. Each iteration compares the items for the ordering relation between them. It copies equal items to the target set and advances both indexes, otherwise the index to the smaller item is advanced. In this manner, all items are processed only once and duplicate items in the target set are avoided.
*)

```
PROCEDURE Intersection (     left : Set (*-- in    *);
                            right : Set (*-- in    *);
                        VAR toSet : Set (*-- inout *));

VAR leftIndex   : Link;       (*-- Loop link over left set *)
    rightIndex  : Link;       (*-- Loop link over right set *)
    toIndex     : Link;       (*-- List of target set nodes *)
    compareItem : CompareProc; (*-- Item comparison routine *)
    order       : Relation;    (*-- Ordering relation between
                                    items *)

BEGIN
  setError := noerr;
  IF (left = NIL) OR (right = NIL) THEN
    RaiseErrIn(intersection, undefined);
    RETURN;
  ELSIF (left^.dataID ≠ right^.dataID) THEN
    RaiseErrIn(intersection, typeerror);
    RETURN;
  ELSIF ¬Recreate(left^.dataID, toSet) THEN
    RETURN;
  END (*--if*);
  WITH toSet^ DO
    compareItem := CompareOf(dataID);
    assignItem  := AssignOf(dataID);
  END (*--with*);
  setRoutine := intersection;
  leftIndex  := left^.first;
  rightIndex := right^.first;
  WHILE (leftIndex ≠ NIL) & (rightIndex ≠ NIL) DO
    order := compareItem(leftIndex^.item, rightIndex^.item);
    IF (order = equal) THEN
      IF (toSet^.first = NIL) THEN
        toSet^.first := NewNode(leftIndex^.item, NIL);
```

```
      toIndex := toSet^.first;
    ELSE
      toIndex^.next := NewNode(leftIndex^.item, NIL);
      toIndex := toIndex^.next;
    END (*--if*);
    IF (setError = overflow) THEN
      RETURN;
    END (*--if*);
    INC(toSet^.length);
    leftIndex := leftIndex^.next;
    rightIndex := rightIndex^.next;
  ELSIF (order = less) THEN
    leftIndex := leftIndex^.next;
  ELSE
    rightIndex := rightIndex^.next;
  END (*--if*);
  END (*--while*);
END Intersection;
(*--------------------*)


(*
```

Difference computes the set containing all members of the left set that are not
members of the right set — for example,

```
      x IN toSet iff (x IN left) & ¬(x IN right)
```

The algorithm, similar to that given above for *union* and *intersection*, loops over
the items of the left and right sets until reaching the end of either. Each iteration
compares the items for the ordering relation between them. It skips equal items
and advances both indexes, otherwise the index to the smaller item is advanced.
When the item from the left set is less than that of the right set it is not present
in the right set and that item can then be copied to the target set. The last step
copies remaining items, if any, from the left set to the destination set.
```
*)

PROCEDURE Difference (     left  : Set (*-- in *);
                          right : Set (*-- in *);
                     VAR toSet : Set (*-- inout *));

VAR leftIndex   : Link;       (*-- Loop index over left set *)
    rightIndex  : Link;       (*-- Loop index over right set *)
    toIndex     : Link;       (*-- List of target set nodes *)
    compareItem : CompareProc; (*-- Item comparison routine *)
    order       : Relation;    (*-- Ordering relation between
                                      items *)

BEGIN
  setError := noerr;
  IF (left = NIL) OR (right = NIL) THEN
    RaiseErrIn(difference, undefined);
    RETURN;
  ELSIF (left^.dataID ≠ right^.dataID) THEN
    RaiseErrIn(difference, typeerror);
```

```
        RETURN;
      ELSIF ¬Recreate(left^.dataID, toSet) THEN
         RETURN;
     END (*--if*);
    WITH toSet^ DO
      compareItem := CompareOf(dataID);
      assignItem  := AssignOf(dataID);
    END (*--with*);
     setRoutine := difference;
    leftIndex  := left^.first;
    rightIndex := right^.first;
    WHILE (leftIndex ≠ NIL) & (rightIndex ≠ NIL) DO
      order := compareItem(leftIndex^.item, rightIndex^.item);
      IF (order = equal) THEN
         leftIndex  := leftIndex^.next;
         rightIndex := rightIndex^.next;
      ELSIF (order = less) THEN
         IF (toSet^.first = NIL) THEN
           toSet^.first := NewNode(leftIndex^.item, NIL);
           toIndex := toSet^.first;
         ELSE
           toIndex^.next := NewNode(leftIndex^.item, NIL);
           toIndex := toIndex^.next;
         END (*--if*);
         IF (setError = overflow) THEN
           RETURN;
         END (*--if*);
         INC(toSet^.length);
         leftIndex := leftIndex^.next;
      ELSE
         rightIndex := rightIndex^.next;
      END (*--if*);
    END (*--while*);
   CopySubset(leftIndex, toIndex, toSet);
  END Difference;
  (*--------------------*)


  (*
```

SymDifference computes the set containing all members of the left or right set that are not members of the both sets, for example,

```
        x IN toSet iff (x IN left) ≠ (x IN right)
```

The algorithm, similar to that given above for *union* and *difference*, loops over the items of the left and right sets until reaching the end of either. Each iteration compares the items for the ordering relation between them. It skips equal items and advances both indexes, otherwise the index to the smaller item is advanced. When items between the two sets are unequal the routine copies the smaller of the two items to the target set. The last step copies the remaining items, if any, from either the left or right set, whichever has items remaining, to the target set.
```
  *)
```

```
PROCEDURE SymDifference (      left  : Set (*-- in      *);
                               right : Set (*-- in      *);
                          VAR toSet  : Set (*-- inout *));

VAR leftIndex    : Link;          (*-- Loop index over left set *)
    rightIndex   : Link;          (*-- Loop index over right set *)
     toIndex     : Link;          (*-- List of target set nodes *)
     tempNode    : Link;          (*-- Temporary node *)
    compareItem : CompareProc; (*-- Item comparison routine *)
    order        : Relation;      (*-- Ordering relation between
                                      items *)

BEGIN
  setError := noerr;
  IF (left = NIL) OR (right = NIL) THEN
    RaiseErrIn(symdifference, undefined);
    RETURN;
  ELSIF (left^.dataID ≠ right^.dataID) THEN
    RaiseErrIn(symdifference, typeerror);
    RETURN;
  ELSIF ¬Recreate(left^.dataID, toSet) THEN
    RETURN;
  END (*--if*);
  WITH toSet^ DO
    compareItem := CompareOf(dataID);
    assignItem := AssignOf(dataID);
  END (*--with*);
  setRoutine := symdifference;
  leftIndex  := left^.first;
  rightIndex := right^.first;
  WHILE (leftIndex ≠ NIL) & (rightIndex ≠ NIL) DO
    order := compareItem(leftIndex^.item, rightIndex^.item);
    IF (order = equal) THEN
      leftIndex  := leftIndex^.next;
      rightIndex := rightIndex^.next;
    ELSE
      Allocate(tempNode, SIZE(Node));
      IF (tempNode = NIL) THEN
        RaiseErrIn(symdifference, overflow);
        RETURN;
      END (*--if*);
      INC(toSet^.length);
      IF (order = less) THEN
        tempNode^.item := assignItem(leftIndex^.item);
        leftIndex := leftIndex^.next;
      ELSE
        tempNode^.item := assignItem(rightIndex^.item);
        rightIndex      := rightIndex^.next;
      END (*--if*);
      IF (toSet^.first = NIL) THEN
        toSet^.first := tempNode;
      ELSE
        toIndex^.next := tempNode;
      END (*--if*);
      toIndex := tempNode;
```

```
      END (*--if*);
    END (*--while*);
    IF (leftIndex = NIL) THEN
      CopySubset(rightIndex, toIndex, toSet);
    ELSIF (rightIndex = NIL) THEN
      CopySubset(leftIndex, toIndex, toSet);
    END (*--if*);
END SymDifference;
(*-------------------*)


(*
```

13.2.5 Selectors

IsDefined returns true if a given set is not NIL and false otherwise, which is the
simple test for a defined set object.
```
*)

PROCEDURE IsDefined ( theSet : Set      (*-- in  *))
                             : BOOLEAN (*-- out *);

BEGIN
  RETURN (theSet ≠ NIL);
END IsDefined;
(*-------------------*)


(*
```
IsEmpty (as always) returns the logical condition as to the state of the set's
length, which if zero indicates an empty set.
```
*)

PROCEDURE IsEmpty ( theSet : Set      (*-- in  *))
                           : BOOLEAN (*-- out *);

BEGIN
  setError := noerr;
  IF (theSet ≠ NIL) THEN
    RETURN (theSet^.length = 0);
  END (*--if*);
  RaiseErrIn(isempty, undefined);
  RETURN TRUE;
END IsEmpty;
(*-------------------*)

PROCEDURE TypeOf ( theSet : Set      (*-- in  *))
                          : TypeID (*-- out *);

BEGIN
  setError := noerr;
  IF (theSet ≠ NIL) THEN
    RETURN theSet^.dataID;
  END (*--if*);
```

```
        RaiseErrIn(typeof, undefined);
        RETURN NullType;
END TypeOf;
(*--------------------*)
```

(*

IsEqual returns true if two given sets contain the same items. After enforcing the
required preconditions (cf. Chapter 11), the routine compares the lengths of sets
in a simple test for inequality. If lengths are equal it is possible for sets to be
equal so the procedure loops over each item of both sets returning false upon encountering a mismatch between two items. It returns true when the loop completes without finding any mismatched items. Note, because the lengths are
equal, both indexes will simultaneously reach the end of their respective set.
*)

```
PROCEDURE IsEqual ( left  : Set     (*-- in  *);
                    right : Set     (*-- in  *))
                          : BOOLEAN (*-- out *);

VAR leftIndex : Link; (*-- Loop index over left set items *)
    rightIndex: Link; (*-- Loop index over right set items *)

BEGIN
  setError := noerr;
  IF (left ≠ NIL) & (right ≠ NIL) THEN
    IF (left^.dataID = right^.dataID) THEN
      IF (left^.length = right^.length) THEN
        leftIndex := left^.first;
        rightIndex:= right^.first;
        WHILE (leftIndex ≠ NIL) DO
          IF (leftIndex^.item ≠ rightIndex^.item) THEN
            RETURN FALSE;
          END (*--if*);
          leftIndex := leftIndex^.next;
          rightIndex:= rightIndex^.next;
        END (*--while*);
        RETURN TRUE;
      END (*--if*);
    ELSE
      RaiseErrIn(isequal, typeerror);
    END (*--if*);
  ELSE
    RaiseErrIn(isequal, undefined);
  END (*--if*);
  RETURN FALSE;
END IsEqual;
(*-------------------------*)
```

(*

NumMembers returns the current set length or, for an undefined set, returns zero
since it is impossible to have any members in such a set.
*)

```
PROCEDURE NumMembers ( theSet : Set        (*-- in  *))
                               : CARDINAL (*-- out *);

BEGIN
  setError := noerr;
  IF (theSet ≠ NIL) THEN
    RETURN theSet^.length;
  END (*--if*);
  RaiseErrIn(nummembers, undefined);
  RETURN 0;
END NumMembers;
(*---------------------------*)
```

(*

IsAMember determines whether a given item is a member of the given set by
scanning each item in the set in turn. Two conditions terminate the loop prior to
reaching the last item: the item and a set item match indicating that the item is a
member of the set, and the item is greater than a set item indicating non-
membership since the set items are linearly ordered. If the end of the loop is
reached and the routine has not exited with a match then by implication the item
is not present.
*)

```
PROCEDURE IsAMember ( theItem : Item       (*-- in  *);
                      theSet  : Set        (*-- in  *))
                              : BOOLEAN (*-- out *);

VAR index       : Link;        (*-- Loop index over items   *)
    compareItem : CompareProc; (*-- Item comparison routine *)

BEGIN
  setError := noerr;
  IF (theSet ≠ NIL) THEN
    WITH theSet^ DO
      compareItem := CompareOf(dataID);
      index := first;
    END (*--with*);
    WHILE (index ≠ NIL) DO
      IF (theItem = index^.item) THEN
        RETURN TRUE;
      ELSIF (compareItem(index^.item, theItem) = greater)THEN
        RETURN FALSE;
      END (*--if*);
      index := index^.next;
    END (*--while*);
  ELSE
    RaiseErrIn(ismember, undefined);
  END (*--if*);
  RETURN FALSE;
END IsAMember;
(*---------------------------*)
```

(*

IsSubset ensures that required preconditions are met and loops through items of the left and right sets attempting to determine if every member of the left set is also a member of the right set. Because items of the lists are linearly ordered in ascending sequence, inequality can be determined more quickly than with a completely unordered set implementation. When an item of the left set is less than its counterpart in the right set we immediately return false knowing that the item is not present in the right set. If the left item is greater we know that we must advance the index into the right set since the item may yet be found further into the list. When items are equal both indexes are advanced. When the end of the loop is reached without premature exit, the left set can only be a subset of the right if we have examined beyond the end of the left set.
*)

```
PROCEDURE IsSubset (    left  : Set      (*-- in  *);
                        right : Set      (*-- in  *))
                              : BOOLEAN  (*-- out *);

VAR leftIndex   : Link;       (*-- Loop index over left set  *)
    rightIndex  : Link;       (*-- Loop index over right set *)
    compareItem : CompareProc; (*-- Item comparison routine   *)
    order       : Relation;   (*-- Ordering relation between
                                  items *)

BEGIN
  setError := noerr;
  IF (left = NIL) OR (right = NIL) THEN
    RaiseErrIn(issubset, undefined);
    RETURN FALSE;
  ELSIF (left^.dataID ≠ right^.dataID) THEN
    RaiseErrIn(issubset, typeerror);
    RETURN FALSE;
  END (*--if*);
  compareItem:= CompareOf(left^.dataID);
  leftIndex  := left^.first;
  rightIndex := right^.first;
  WHILE (leftIndex ≠ NIL) & (rightIndex ≠ NIL) DO
    order := compareItem(leftIndex^.item, rightIndex^.item);
    IF (order = equal) THEN
      leftIndex  := leftIndex^.next;
      rightIndex := rightIndex^.next;
    ELSIF (order = less) THEN
      RETURN FALSE;
    ELSE
        rightIndex := rightIndex^.next;
    END (*--if*);
  END (*--while*);
  RETURN (leftIndex = NIL);
END IsSubset;
(*--------------------------------*)

PROCEDURE IsProperSubset( left  : Set      (*-- in  *);
                          right : Set      (*-- in  *))
                                : BOOLEAN  (*-- out *);
```

```
BEGIN
  RETURN IsSubset(left,          & (left^.length < right^.length);
END IsProperSubset;
(*--------------------          *)


(*
```

13.2.6 Iterators

Both *LoopOver* and *Traverse* loop through a given set's list of items from the
first to the end of the list passing the item to the given processing procedure parameter.
```
*)

PROCEDURE LoopOver ( theSet  : Set              (*-- in *);
                     process : LoopAccessProc (*-- in *));

VAR theNode : Link; (*-- Loop index over items *)

BEGIN
  setError := noerr;
  IF (theSet ≠ NIL) THEN
    theNode := theSet^.first;
    WHILE (theNode ≠ NIL) DO
      IF ¬process(theNode^.item) THEN
        RETURN;
      END (*--if*);
      theNode := theNode^.next;
    END (*--while*);
  ELSE
    RaiseErrIn(loopover, undefined);
  END (*--if*);
END LoopOver;
(*--------------------------*)

PROCEDURE Traverse ( theSet  : Set          (*-- in *);
                     process : AccessProc (*-- in *));

VAR theNode : Link; (*-- Loop index over items *)

BEGIN
  setError := noerr;
  IF (theSet ≠ NIL) THEN
    theNode := theSet^.first;
    WHILE (theNode ≠ NIL) DO
      process(theNode^.item);
      theNode := theNode^.next;
    END (*--while*);
  ELSE
    RaiseErrIn(traverse, undefined);
  END (*--if*);
END Traverse;
(*--------------------------*)
```

```
(*
```

13.2.7 Module Initialization

Module initialization sets the local exception handlers array variables to default handlers (*ExitOnError*) except for the *noerr* handler which is given the null handler. *setError* is given the value *noerr* avoiding an undefined state.
```
*)
```

```
BEGIN
  FOR setError := MIN(Exceptions) TO MAX(Exceptions) DO
    handlers[setError] := ExitOnError;
  END (*--for*);
  handlers[noerr] := NullHandler;
  setError := noerr;
END SetSUMI.
```

References

[1]   A.V. Aho, J.E. Hopcroft, and J.D. Ullman, *Data Structures and Algorithms*, Addison-Wesley, Reading, MA, 1983, pg. 118.

[2]   A.M. Tenenbaum and M.J. Augenstein, *Data Structures Using Pascal*, Prentice-Hall, Englewood Cliffs, NJ 1981.

14 The Discrete Bounded Set

Before leaving the subject of sets we will examine a set implementation for the Modula-2 CHAR data type. Because we are dealing with a scalar data type, we can use this information to our advantage and permit optimizing the implementation in ways that would not be possible with the generic form.

14.1 SetCSBMI Interface

Three differences between the generic bounded set and the discrete form are presented here:

Create   does not require a size parameter, since this value is constant;

SizeOf   is not necessary for the same reason; and

Complement   can be provided, since the universal set for characters is known and finite.

In all other respects, the definition is identical with that for the bounded set.

```
DEFINITION MODULE SetCSBMI;
(*================================================================
    Version  : 2.01 05 Jan 1988 C. Lins
    Compiler : TML Modula-2 Compiler for the Apple Macintosh
    Component: Monolithic Structures - Set
               Discrete Sequential Bounded Managed Iterator

    INTRODUCTION
    This module supports the abstract data type set for
    discrete values of ASCII CHARs.

    REVISION HISTORY
    v2.01 05 Jan 1988 C. Lins
        Initial implementation for TML Modula-2.
================================================================*)

FROM CharItems IMPORT
  (*--Type*) Item, AccessProc, LoopAccessProc;

FROM ErrorHandling IMPORT
  (*--Proc*) HandlerProc;

FROM SetEnum IMPORT
  (*--Type*) Exceptions;

  (*-----------------------*)
```

```
TYPE Set;

TYPE SizeRange = [1..256];

CONST NullSet = VAL(Set, NIL);

(*
```

14.1.1 Exceptions

ModuleID   is used by the exception handling mechanism to distinguish this module from all other modules.

SetError   returns the exception code from the most recent discrete set operation. A *noerr* result indicates successful completion of the operation.

GetHandler   returns the exception handler routine associated with a given exception. The routine is a function procedure returning a procedure as its result but the *HandlerProc* may not be called from within the *GetHandler* call itself. Before invocation the procedure result must be first assigned to a procedure variable. Exception handlers are given an initial value of *ExitOnError* except for the handler for *noerr* which is initialized to the null exception handler.

SetHandler   the inverse of *GetHandler*, associates an exception handler routine with a given exception. The routine may override the default settings for the exception handlers.

```
*)

CONST ModuleID = 250;

PROCEDURE SetError    ()              : Exceptions  (*-- out *);

PROCEDURE GetHandler ( ofError    : Exceptions  (*-- in  *))
                                    : HandlerProc (*-- out *);

PROCEDURE SetHandler ( ofError    : Exceptions  (*-- in  *);
                       toHandler : HandlerProc (*-- in  *));
```

(*

14.1.2 Constructors

Create   attempts to generate a new, empty character set. The *TypeID* is
                 unnecessary since we are dealing directly with characters and incor-
                 porating such knowledge into the implementation. A similar state-
                 ment can be made regarding the maximum size of the set since
                 characters form a small, discrete ranges of values.

                 Upon successful completion of the routine, *Create* returns the new
                 set. If it is not possible for the set to be created, the routine raises
                 the *overflow* exception and returns the constant *NullSet*.

Destroy   clears the items from a given set and then destroys the set. *De-
                 stroy*, the inverse of *Create*, makes the set undefined rather than (as
                 with *Create*) defining it.

Clear   removes the items from a given set, returning the set to the empty
                 state.

Assign   attempts to generate a duplicate of the source set (*theSet*) in the
                 target set (*toSet*). It creates the target set, if necessary, otherwise it
                 clears the target of its present contents before the assignment. All
                 character sets are given the same maximum size.

Include   adds items to a given set. If the item is already a member of the
                 set it ignores the exception condition.

Exclude   removes the specified item from a given set. If the given set is
                 empty on entry to *Exclude*, or a given item is not a member of the
                 set, *Exclude* ignores the *notinset* exception and the set remains un-
                 changed.

Union, Intersection, Difference, SymDifference (symmetric difference), and *Complement* operations all implement the standard set operations of the same name
as defined in the set abstraction (Chapter 11).
*)

```
PROCEDURE Create     ()            : Set  (*-- out    *);

PROCEDURE Destroy    (VAR theSet   : Set  (*-- inout *));

PROCEDURE Clear      (VAR theSet   : Set  (*-- inout *));

PROCEDURE Assign     (    theSet   : Set  (*-- in     *);
                      VAR toSet    : Set  (*-- inout *));

PROCEDURE Include    (    theItem  : Item (*-- in     *);
                      VAR inSet    : Set  (*-- inout *));
```

```
PROCEDURE Exclude        (     theItem : Item (*-- in    *);
                          VAR fromSet : Set  (*-- inout *));

PROCEDURE Union          (     left    : Set  (*-- in    *);
                               right   : Set  (*-- in    *);
                          VAR toSet   : Set  (*-- inout *));

PROCEDURE Intersection (     left    : Set  (*-- in    *);
                               right   : Set  (*-- in    *);
                          VAR toSet   : Set  (*-- inout *));

PROCEDURE Difference     (     left    : Set  (*-- in    *);
                               right   : Set  (*-- in    *);
                          VAR toSet   : Set  (*-- inout *));

PROCEDURE SymDifference(     left    : Set  (*-- in    *);
                               right   : Set  (*-- in    *);
                          VAR toSet   : Set  (*-- inout *));

PROCEDURE Complement     (     theSet  : Set  (*-- in    *);
                          VAR toSet   : Set  (*-- inout *));

(*
```

14.1.3 Selectors

IsDefined   attempts to determine whether a given set is valid — for ex-
                       ample, has been created and not yet destroyed. How this is
                       accomplished may be as simple or complicated as the im-
                       plementors desire and the applications require.

IsEmpty   returns true if a given set contains no items (i.e. its cardi-
                       nality is zero). It always considers undefined sets empty.

IsEqual   returns true if the left and right sets contain the same items.
                       Obviously, both must also have been created. An undefined
                       set is not equal to any other set, including itself.

NumMembers   returns the number of items present in a given set. Unde-
                       fined sets are considered to have no members.

IsAMember   returns true if a given item is present in a given set, and
                       false otherwise.

IsSubset and
IsProperSubset   both implement standard logical set operations as defined in
                       the Set Abstraction (chapter 11).
*)

```
PROCEDURE IsDefined       (     theSet : Set    (*-- in  *))
                                       : BOOLEAN (*-- out *);
```

```
PROCEDURE IsEmpty        (    theSet : Set     (*-- in  *))
                              : BOOLEAN (*-- out *);

PROCEDURE IsEqual        (    left   : Set     (*-- in  *);
                              right  : Set     (*-- in  *))
                              : BOOLEAN (*-- out *);

PROCEDURE NumMembers     (    theSet : Set     (*-- in  *))
                              : CARDINAL(*-- out *);

PROCEDURE IsAMember      (    theItem: Item    (*-- in  *);
                              theSet : Set     (*-- in  *))
                              : BOOLEAN (*-- out *);

PROCEDURE IsSubset       (    left   : Set     (*-- in  *);
                              right  : Set     (*-- in  *))
                              : BOOLEAN (*-- out *);

PROCEDURE IsProperSubset(    left   : Set     (*-- in  *);
                              right  : Set     (*-- in  *))
                              : BOOLEAN (*-- out *);

(*
```

14.1.4 Iterators

LoopOver   provides the facility for looping over some or all items of a set, with read-only access to each item. *theProcess* procedure parameter to this routine returns a BOOLEAN function result where TRUE allows the iteration to proceed to the next item and FALSE terminates the iteration.

Traverse   provides the facility for looping over all items of a set, with read-only access to each item.

Both iterators traverse a given set from the first item towards the last item in ascending order. If given an empty set the processing procedure will obviously not be invoked.

```
*)
PROCEDURE LoopOver    ( theSet  : Set            (*-- in *);
                        process : LoopAccessProc (*-- in *));

PROCEDURE Traverse    ( theSet  : Set            (*-- in *);
                        process : AccessProc     (*-- in *));

END SetCSBMI.
```

14.2 SetCSBMI Implementation

```
IMPLEMENTATION MODULE SetCSBMI;
(*================================================================
   Version   : 2.01 05 Jan 1988 C. Lins
   Compiler  : TML Modula-2 Compiler for the Apple Macintosh
   Code Size: R- 2454 bytes
   Component: Monolithic Structure - Set
              Discrete Sequential Bounded Managed Iterator


   INTRODUCTION
   This module supports the abstract data type set for
   discrete values of CHARs.


   REVISION HISTORY
   v2.01 05 Jan 1988 C. Lins:
       Initial TML Modula-2 implementation.
================================================================*)

FROM MacSystem IMPORT
   (*--Proc*) Allocate, Deallocate;

FROM CharItems IMPORT
   (*--Type*) Item, AccessProc, LoopAccessProc;

FROM SetEnum IMPORT
   (*--Type*) Exceptions, Operations;

FROM ErrorHandling IMPORT
   (*--Type*) HandlerProc,
   (*--Proc*) NullHandler, Raise, ExitOnError;

   (*-----------------------*)

(*
```

14.2.1 Internal Discrete Set Representation

The internal representation of the discrete (character) set uses a bit vector of items, where an item at the appropriate index has a value of one if the item is a member of the set and a value of zero if not. To save space and to enable the use of the standard Modula-2 bitset operations, the modula stores the bit vector as an array of BITSETs, thus requiring only 16 words (rather than 256) per character set. It indexes the array of bitsets from zero to 15 inclusive, as shown in the calculation of the maximum value for the *BitsetsPerSet* subrange. In effect, this constant expression reduces to:

$$(16 \text{ DIV } 16) - 1 = (16 - 1) = 15.$$

The space savings is purchased at the cost of increased execution time used in calculating an item's bitset index and bit offset within the bitset.

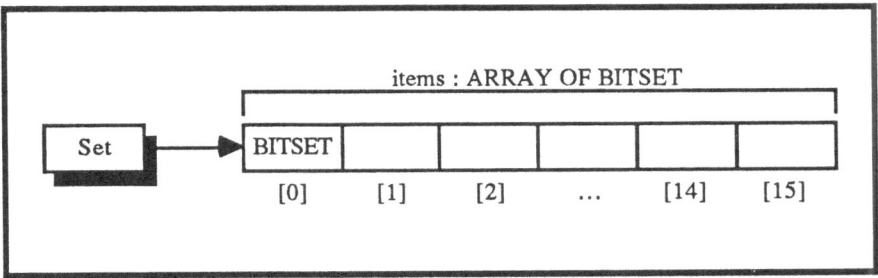

Figure 14.1 The Discrete Bounded Set (CHARs)

```
*)

CONST bitsPerBitset = 16;
CONST maxSetSize    = MAX(SizeRange);
TYPE  BitsetsPerSet = [0 .. (maxSetSize DIV bitsPerBitset) -1 ];
TYPE  BitIndex      = [0 .. bitsPerBitset - 1 ];
TYPE  ItemsArray    = ARRAY BitsetsPerSet OF BITSET;
TYPE  DiscreteSet   = RECORD
        items : ItemsArray; (*-- Bit vector of items *)
      END (*-- DiscreteSet *);
TYPE  Set = POINTER TO DiscreteSet;
    (*------------------------*)

VAR theEmptySet : ItemsArray; (*-- Predefined set, initialized
                 to ø *)

(*
```

14.2.2 Exceptions

Two variables are required to support the exception handling mechanism. The first, *setError*, records the exception result from each operation; while *handlers* is an array of exception handling procedures indexed by the exception result.

The definition module has previously described the routines *SetError*, *GetHandler* and *SetHandler*, and their operation should be readily apparent. *RaiseErrIn* is a local routine used to set the setError variable and invoke the *Raise* routine of the *ErrorHandling* module.

```
*)

VAR setError : Exceptions;
VAR handlers : ARRAY Exceptions OF HandlerProc;

    (*------------------------*)
```

```
PROCEDURE SetError      ()              : Exceptions   (*-- out *);

BEGIN
  RETURN setError;
END SetError;
(*---------------------------*)

PROCEDURE GetHandler   ( ofError  : Exceptions  (*-- in  *))
                                   : HandlerProc (*-- out *);

BEGIN
  RETURN handlers[ofError];
END GetHandler;
(*---------------------------*)

PROCEDURE SetHandler   ( ofError   : Exceptions  (*-- in *);
                         toHandler : HandlerProc (*-- in *));

BEGIN
  handlers[ofError] := toHandler;
END SetHandler;
(*---------------------------*)

PROCEDURE RaiseErrIn ( theRoutine : Operations (*-- in  *);
                       theError   : Exceptions (*-- in  *));

BEGIN
  setError := theError;
  Raise(ModuleID, theRoutine, theError, handlers[theError]);
END RaiseErrIn;
(*---------------------------*)

PROCEDURE Recreate (VAR theSet    : Set        (*-- inout *))
                                   : BOOLEAN    (*-- out   *);

BEGIN
  IF (theSet = NIL) THEN
    theSet := Create();
  END (*--if*);
  RETURN (theSet ≠ NIL);
END Recreate;
(*---------------------------*)

(*
```

14.2.3 Constructors

Create allocates a new array of bitsets and raises the *overflow* exception if unable to do so. Otherwise, it clears the newly created set using array assignment of the predefined empty character set.
```
*)
```

```
PROCEDURE Create () : Set (*-- out *);

VAR newSet : Set;

BEGIN
  setError := noerr;
  Allocate(newSet, SIZE(DiscreteSet));
  IF (newSet ≠ NIL) THEN
    newSet^.items := theEmptySet;
    RETURN newSet;
  END (*--if*);
  RaiseErrIn(create, overflow);
  RETURN NullSet;
END Create;
(*--------------------------*)
```

```
(*
```
Destroy takes advantage that *Clear* sets *setError* to *noerr* and raises the *undefined* exception. So if *Clear* succeeds, *Destroy* releases the allocated set header.
```
*)

PROCEDURE Destroy (VAR theSet : Set (*-- inout *));

BEGIN
  setError := noerr;
  IF (theSet ≠ NIL) THEN
    Deallocate(theSet);
  ELSE
    RaiseErrIn(destroy, undefined);
    theSet := NullSet;
  END (*--if*);
END Destroy;
(*--------------------------*)
```

```
(*
```
Clear sets *setError* to *noerr*. If necessary, it checks for an undefined set and raises the *undefined* exception. After asserting a valid set, it is sufficient to overwrite the existing items with the predefined empty set.
```
*)

PROCEDURE Clear (VAR theSet : Set (*-- inout *));

BEGIN
  setError := noerr;
  IF (theSet ≠ NIL) THEN
    theSet^.items := theEmptySet;
  ELSE
    RaiseErrIn(clear, undefined);
  END (*--if*);
END Clear;
(*--------------------------*)
```

```
(*
```
Assign creates the target set if necessary and uses array assignment to duplicate
the source bitset array within the target.
```
*)

PROCEDURE Assign (    theSet : Set (*-- in    *); .
                  VAR toSet  : Set (*-- inout *));

BEGIN
  setError := noerr;
  IF (theSet ≠ NIL) THEN
    IF Recreate(toSet) THEN
      toSet^.items := theSet^.items;
    END (*--if*);
  ELSE
    RaiseErrIn(assign, undefined);
  END (*--if*);
END Assign;
(*--------------------------*)


(*
```
Include and *Exclude* simply calculate the bitset number and bit offset and use the
Modula-2 set inclusion and exclusion operations to set and clear the appropriate
bits.
```
*)

PROCEDURE Include (    theItem : Item (*-- in    *);
                   VAR inSet   : Set  (*-- inout *));

BEGIN
  setError := noerr;
  IF (inSet ≠ NIL) THEN
    INCL(inSet^.items[VAL(CARDINAL, ORD(theItem)) DIV
        bitsPerBitset],
    VAL(CARDINAL, ORD(theItem)) MOD bitsPerBitset);
  ELSE
    RaiseErrIn(include, undefined);
  END (*--if*);
END Include;
(*--------------------------*)

PROCEDURE Exclude (    theItem : Item (*-- in    *);
                   VAR fromSet : Set  (*-- inout *));

BEGIN
  setError := noerr;
  IF (fromSet ≠ NIL) THEN
    EXCL(fromSet^.items[VAL(CARDINAL, ORD(theItem)) DIV
        bitsPerBitset],
    VAL(CARDINAL, ORD(theItem)) MOD bitsPerBitset);
  ELSE
    RaiseErrIn(exclude, undefined);
  END (*--if*);
END Exclude;
(*--------------------------*)
```

```
(*
Union, Intersection, Difference, and SymDifference all simply loop over the bit-
sets of the left and right sets using the corresponding Modula-2 set operators to
form the target set. Complement is similar except that it takes the difference of
the universal set from the given set.
*)

PROCEDURE Union (      left  : Set (*-- in    *);
                       right : Set (*-- in    *);
                   VAR toSet : Set (*-- inout *));

VAR index : BitsetsPerSet; (*-- loop index over bitsets *)

BEGIN
  setError := noerr;
  IF (left ≠ NIL) & (right ≠ NIL) THEN
    IF Recreate(toSet) THEN
      WITH toSet^ DO
        FOR index := MIN(BitsetsPerSet) TO MAX(BitsetsPerSet) DO
          items[index] := left^.items[index] + right^.items
              [index];
          END (*--for*);
        END (*--with*);
      END (*--if*);
    ELSE
      RaiseErrIn(union, undefined);
    END (*--if*);
END Union;
(*---------------------------*)

PROCEDURE Intersection (    left  : Set (*-- in *);
                            right : Set (*-- in *);
                        VAR toSet : Set (*-- inout *));

VAR index : BitsetsPerSet; (*-- loop index over bitsets *)

BEGIN
  setError := noerr;
  IF (left ≠ NIL) & (right ≠ NIL) THEN
    IF Recreate(toSet) THEN
      WITH toSet^ DO
        FOR index := MIN(BitsetsPerSet) TO MAX(BitsetsPerSet) DO
          items[index] := left^.items[index] * right^.items
              [index];
          END (*--for*);
        END (*--with*);
      END (*--if*);
    ELSE
      RaiseErrIn(intersection, undefined);
    END (*--if*);
END Intersection;
(*---------------------------*)
```

```
PROCEDURE Difference (      left  : Set (*-- in    *);
                            right : Set (*-- in    *);
                        VAR toSet : Set (*-- inout *));

VAR index : BitsetsPerSet; (*-- loop index over bitsets *)

BEGIN
  setError := noerr;
  IF (left ≠ NIL) & (right ≠ NIL) THEN
    IF Recreate(toSet) THEN
      WITH toSet^ DO
        FOR index := MIN(BitsetsPerSet) TO MAX(BitsetsPerSet) DO
          items[index] := left^.items[index] - right^.items
              [index];
        END (*--for*);
      END (*--with*);
    END (*--if*);
  ELSE
    RaiseErrIn(difference, undefined);
  END (*--if*);
END Difference;
(*--------------------------*)

PROCEDURE SymDifference (    left  : Set (*-- in    *);
                            right : Set (*-- in    *);
                        VAR toSet : Set (*-- inout *));

VAR index : BitsetsPerSet; (*-- loop index over bitsets *)

BEGIN
  setError := noerr;
  IF (left ≠ NIL) & (right ≠ NIL) THEN
    IF Recreate(toSet) THEN
      WITH toSet^ DO
        FOR index := MIN(BitsetsPerSet) TO MAX(BitsetsPerSet) DO
          items[index] :=left^.items[index]/right^.items[index];
        END (*--for*);
      END (*--with*);
    END (*--if*);
  ELSE
    RaiseErrIn(symdifference, undefined);
  END (*--if*);
END SymDifference;
(*--------------------------*)

PROCEDURE Complement (    theSet : Set (*-- in    *);
                      VAR toSet  : Set (*-- inout *));

VAR index : BitsetsPerSet; (*-- loop index over bitsets *)

BEGIN
  setError := noerr;
  IF (theSet ≠ NIL) THEN
    IF Recreate(toSet) THEN
```

```
          WITH theSet^ DO
            FOR index := MIN(BitsetsPerSet) TO MAX(BitsetsPerSet) DO
              toSet^.items[index] := BITSET{0..15} - items[index];
            END (*--for*);
          END (*--with*);
      END (*--if*);
    ELSE
      RaiseErrIn(complement, undefined);
    END (*--if*);
  END Complement;
  (*---------------------------*)


  (*
```

14.2.4   Selectors

IsDefined returns true if a given set is not NIL and false otherwise — the simple
test for a defined set object.
```
  *)

  PROCEDURE IsDefined ( theSet : Set      (*-- in *))
                                 : BOOLEAN (*-- out *);

  BEGIN
    RETURN (theSet ≠ NIL);
  END IsDefined;
  (*---------------------------*)


  (*
```
IsEmpty loops through the bitsets, returning false if any are non-empty. The
function should directly compare a given bitset array with the empty set array
but Modula-2 does not support array comparison.
```
  *)

  PROCEDURE IsEmpty ( theSet  : Set      (*-- in  *))
                                 : BOOLEAN (*-- out *);

  VAR index : BitsetsPerSet; (*-- loop index over bitsets *)

  BEGIN
    setError := noerr;
    IF (theSet ≠ NIL) THEN
      WITH theSet^ DO
        FOR index := MIN(BitsetsPerSet) TO MAX(BitsetsPerSet) DO
          IF (items[index] ≠ BITSET{}) THEN
            RETURN FALSE;
          END (*--if*);
        END (*--for*);
      END (*--with*);
```

```
    ELSE
       RaiseErrIn(isempty, undefined);
    END (*--if*);
    RETURN TRUE;
END IsEmpty;
(*--------------------------*)
```

```
(*
```
IsEqual loops over the set's bitset arrays, returning false on the first inequality.
If the loop completes without premature exit then the two sets must be equal.
```
*)
```

```
PROCEDURE IsEqual ( left  : Set      (*-- in *);
                    right : Set      (*-- in *))
                          : BOOLEAN (*-- out *);
VAR index : BitsetsPerSet; (*-- loop index over bitsets *)

BEGIN
    setError := noerr;
    IF (left ≠ NIL) & (right ≠ NIL) THEN
       WITH left^ DO
          FOR index := MIN(BitsetsPerSet) TO MAX(BitsetsPerSet) DO
             IF (items[index] ≠ right^.items[index]) THEN
                RETURN FALSE;
             END (*--if*);
          END (*--for*);
       END (*--with*);
       RETURN TRUE;
    ELSE
       RaiseErrIn(isequal, undefined);
    END (*--if*);
    RETURN FALSE;
END IsEqual;
(*--------------------------*)
```

```
(*
```
NumMembers calculates the number of member items of the set by looping over
the individual bitsets and summing to the number of 'on' bits. A simple BIT-
SET comparison with the empty bitset permits the routine to skip over groups
of empty items. As always, undefined sets return zero.
```
*)
```

```
PROCEDURE NumMembers ( theSet : Set      (*-- in  *))
                              : CARDINAL (*-- out *);

VAR eachWord: BitsetsPerSet; (*-- loop index over bitsets *)
    eachBit : BitIndex;      (*-- loop index over bits *)
    count   : CARDINAL;      (*-- working sum of items in the
                                     set *)
```

```
BEGIN
  setError := noerr;
  count := 0;
  IF (theSet ≠ NIL) THEN
    WITH theSet^ DO
      FOR eachWord :=MIN(BitsetsPerSet) TO MAX(BitsetsPerSet) DO
        IF (items[eachWord] ≠ BITSET{}) THEN
          FOR eachBit := MIN(BitIndex) TO MAX(BitIndex) DO
            IF (eachBit IN items[eachWord]) THEN
              INC(count);
            END (*--if*);
          END (*--for*);
        END (*--if*);
      END (*--for*);
    END (*--with*);
  ELSE
    RaiseErrIn(nummembers, undefined);
  END (*--if*);
  RETURN count;
END NumMembers;
(*--------------------------*)
```

```
(*
```
IsAMember calculates the set number and bit offset into the character set and uses Modula-2 bitset inclusion to determine if a given item is a member of the set. Undefined sets cause false to be returned.
```
*)
```

```
PROCEDURE IsAMember ( theItem : Item      (*-- in  *);
                      theSet  : Set       (*-- in  *))
                              : BOOLEAN (*-- out *);

BEGIN
  setError := noerr;
  IF (theSet ≠ NIL) THEN
    RETURN (VAL(CARDINAL, ORD(theItem)) MOD bitsPerBitset)
        IN theSet^.items[VAL(CARDINAL, ORD(theItem)) DIV
        bitsPerBitset];
  ELSE
    RaiseErrIn(ismember, undefined);
  END (*--if*);
  RETURN FALSE;
END IsAMember;
(*--------------------------*)
```

```
(*
```
The *IsSubset* implementation takes advantage of the equivalence of A ⊆ B with A ∩ B = A, in other words A - B = ∅.
```
*)
```

```
PROCEDURE IsSubset ( left  : Set      (*-- in  *);
                     right : Set      (*-- in  *))
                           : BOOLEAN (*-- out *);
```

```
VAR index : BitsetsPerSet; (*-- loop index over bitsets *)

BEGIN
  setError := noerr;
  IF (left ≠ NIL) & (right ≠ NIL) THEN
    WITH left^ DO
      FOR index := MIN(BitsetsPerSet) TO MAX(BitsetsPerSet) DO
        IF (items[index] - right^.items[index]) ≠ BITSET{} THEN
          RETURN FALSE;
        END (*--if*);
      END (*--for*);
    END (*--with*);
    RETURN TRUE;
  ELSE
    RaiseErrIn(issubset, undefined);
  END (*--if*);
  RETURN FALSE;
END IsSubset;
(*---------------------------*)

PROCEDURE IsProperSubset ( left  : Set     (*-- in  *);
                           right : Set     (*-- in  *))
                                 : BOOLEAN (*-- out *);

BEGIN
  RETURN IsSubset(left, right) & ¬IsEqual(left, right);
END IsProperSubset;
(*---------------------------*)

(*
```

14.2.5 Iterators

LoopOver   scans each bitset within the character set, passing items to the pro-
              cessing procedure parameter. Rather than examining every single
              bit an optimization permits the routine to skip over an empty bit-
              set. Only bitsets with at least one present member are examined
              further to determine the individual items that are members.

Traverse   operates in the same manner.
`*)`

```
PROCEDURE LoopOver (theSet  : Set            (*-- in *);
                    process : LoopAccessProc (*-- in *));

VAR eachWord : BitsetsPerSet; (*-- loop index over bitsets *)
    eachBit  : BitIndex;      (*-- loop index over bits in
                                   bitset *)
```

```
BEGIN
  setError := noerr;
  IF (theSet ≠ NIL) THEN
    WITH theSet^ DO
      FOR eachWord := MIN(BitsetsPerSet) TO MAX
              (BitsetsPerSet) DO
        IF items[eachWord] ≠ BITSET{} THEN
          FOR eachBit := MIN(BitIndex) TO MAX(BitIndex) DO
            IF (eachBit IN items[eachWord]) THEN
              IF ¬process(CHR(eachWord * bitsPerBitset +
                  eachBit))THEN
                RETURN;
              END (*--if*);
            END (*--if*);
          END (*--for*);
        END (*--if*);
      END (*--for*);
    END (*--with*);
  ELSE
    RaiseErrIn(loopover, undefined);
  END (*--if*);
END LoopOver;
(*--------------------------*)


PROCEDURE Traverse ( theSet  : Set        (*-- in *);
                     process : AccessProc (*-- in *));

VAR eachWord : BitsetsPerSet; (*-- loop index over bitsets *)
    eachBit  : BitIndex;       (*-- loop index over bits in
                                       bitset *)

BEGIN
  setError := noerr;
  IF (theSet ≠ NIL) THEN
    WITH theSet^ DO
      FOR eachWord := MIN(BitsetsPerSet) TO MAX
            (BitsetsPerSet)DO
        IF items[eachWord] ≠ BITSET{} THEN
          FOR eachBit := MIN(BitIndex) TO MAX(BitIndex) DO
            IF (eachBit IN items[eachWord]) THEN
              process(CHR (eachWord * bitsPerBitset + eachBit));
            END (*--if*);
          END (*--for*);
        END (*--if*);
      END (*--for*);
    END (*--with*);
  ELSE
    RaiseErrIn(traverse, undefined);
  END (*--if*);
END Traverse;
(*--------------------------*)
```

```
(*
```

14.2.6 Module Initialization

The module initialization fills the predefined discrete set for the empty set (∅)
with empty values and sets the local exception handlers array variables to default
handlers (*ExitOnError*) except for the *noerr* handler which is given the null handler. *setError* is given the value *noerr* avoiding an undefined state.
```
*)
```

```
VAR index : BitsetsPerSet; (*-- loop index over bitsets *)

BEGIN
  FOR index := MIN(BitsetsPerSet) TO MAX(BitsetsPerSet) DO
    theEmptySet[index] := BITSET{};
  END (*--for*);
  FOR setError := MIN(Exceptions) TO MAX(Exceptions) DO
    handlers[setError] := ExitOnError;
  END (*--for*);
  handlers[noerr] := NullHandler;
  setError := noerr;
END SetCSBMI.
```

References

[1] G. Booch, *Software Components in Ada Structures, Tools and Subsystems*,
     Benjamin/Cummings, Menlo Park, CA, 1987, pp. 40-43, 250-295.

[2] R. Gleaves, *Modula-2 for Pascal Programmers*, Springer-Verlag, New York,
     NY, 1984, PowerSets Module, pg. 60.

[3] R. Ford and R.S. Wiener, *Modula-2: A Software Development Approach*,
     John Wiley and Sons, New York, NY, 1985.

[4] G.P. McKeown and V.J. Rayward-Smith, *Mathematics for Computing*, Hal-
     stead Press, Wokingham, England, 1982, Section 1.2, Set Theory, pp. 9-
     18.

[5] Modula Corporation, *Macintosh Modula-2 System Reference Manual, Ver-
     sion 4.1 Supplement*, Provo, UT, 1985, LongSets Module definition mod-
     ule.

[6] N. Wirth, *Programming in Modula-2*, 3rd ed., Springer-Verlag, Berlin Hei-
     delberg, 1985.

A Modula-2 Syntax Diagrams

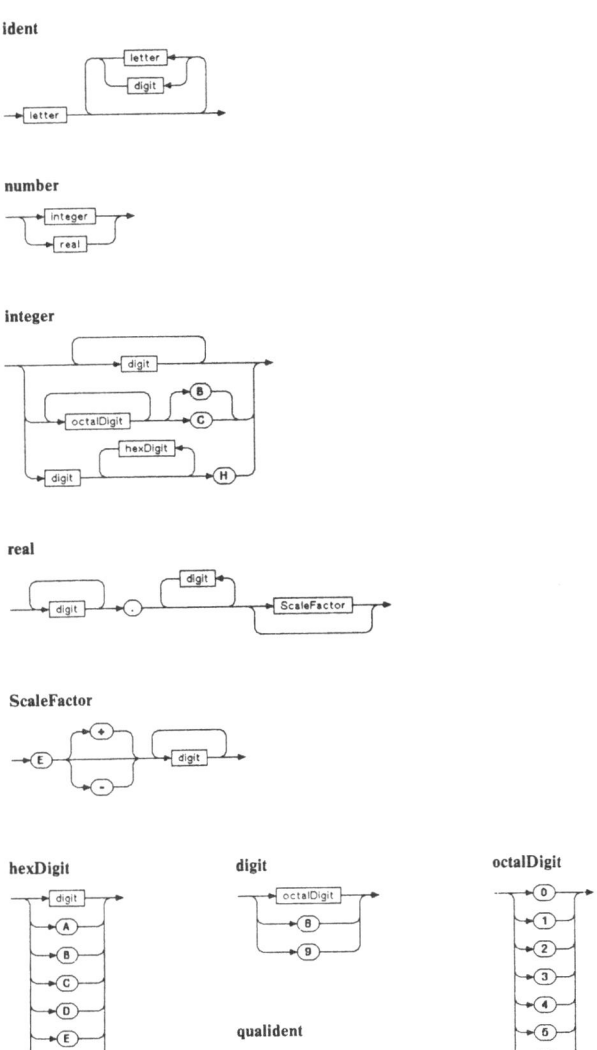

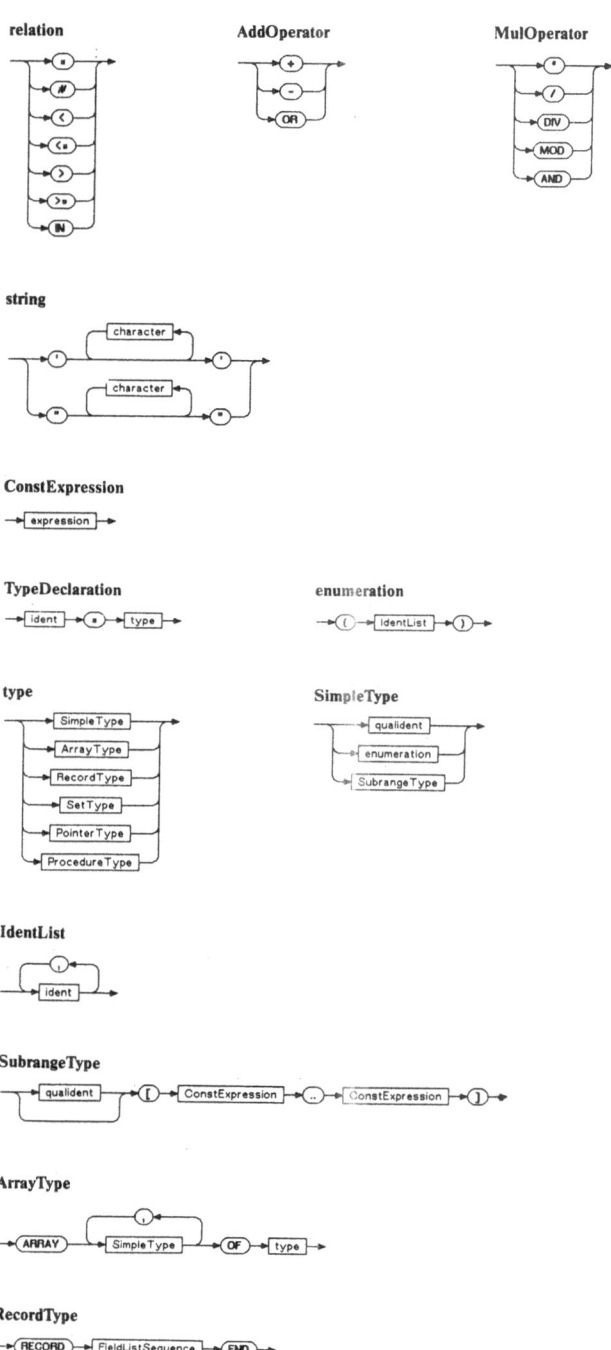

FieldListSequence

FieldList

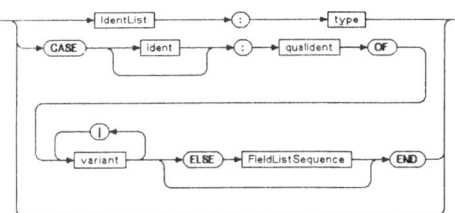

variant

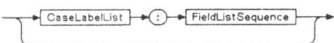

CaseLabelList

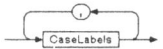

CaseLabels

SetType

PointerType

→(POINTER)→(TO)→ type →

ProcedureType

→(PROCEDURE)→ FormalTypeList →

FormalTypeList

VariableDeclaration

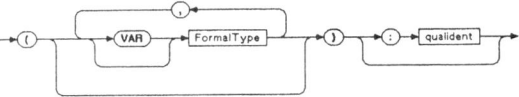

designator

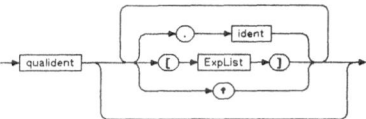

ExpList

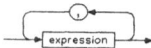

expression

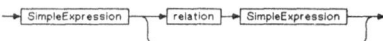

SimpleExpression

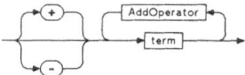

term

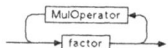

factor

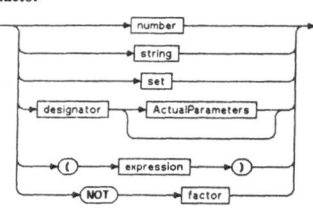

statement

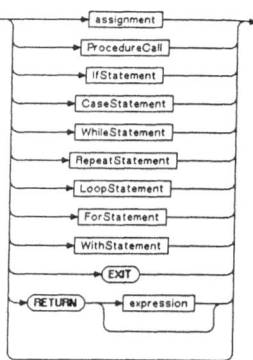

set

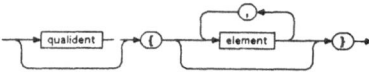

element

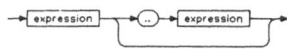

ActualParameters

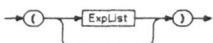

assignment

ProcedureCall

StatementSequence

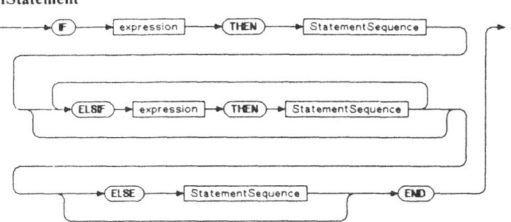

IfStatement

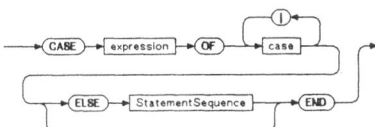

CaseStatement

case

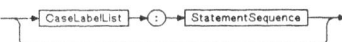

WhileStatement

RepeatStatement

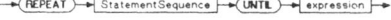

ForStatement

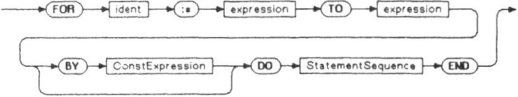

LoopStatement

WithStatement

ProcedureDeclaration

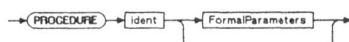

ProcedureHeading

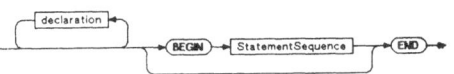

block

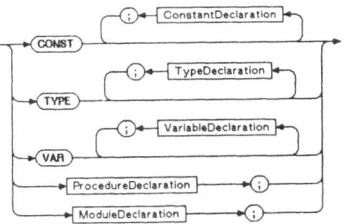

declaration

FormalParameters

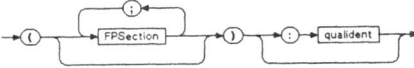

FPSection

FormalType

priority

→⓪→| ConstExpression |→⓪→

ModuleDeclaration

———→(MODULE)→| ident |→| priority |→;———→

| import |

| export |→| block |→| ident |

export

→(EXPORT)→(QUALIFIED)→| identList |→;→

import

→(FROM)→| ident |→(IMPORT)→| IdentList |→;→

DefinitionModule

———→(DEFINITION)———→(MODULE)→| ident |→;———→

| import | | definition |

(END)→| ident |→.

definition

;←| ConstantDeclaration |

→(CONST)————————————————→

→(TYPE)→| ident |→=→| type |→;

;←| VariableDeclaration |

→(VAR)

→| ProcedureHeading |→;

ProgramModule

———→(MODULE)→| ident |→| priority |→;———→

| import |

| block |→| ident |→.

CompilationUnit

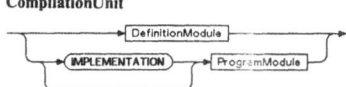

B Standard Modula-2 Routines

B.1 Standard Procedures

The following is a quick reference list of the standard Modula-2 procedures, arranged alphabetically, as implemented in the TML Modula-2 compiler.

DEC(x)

Decrements x by one.

DEC(x, i)

Decrements x by i. It is equivalent to the statement "x := x - i".

EXCL(s, x)

Removes the element x from the set s. If x is not a member of the set, then does nothing.

HALT

Calls the Macintosh debugger trap "_Debugger". The Modula-2 report states that HALT causes program termination. Due to the particular implementation, it may be possible for the program to *continue* execution following a call to this routine.

INC(x)

Increments x by one.

INC(x, i)

Increments x by i. It is equivalent to the statement "x := x + i".

INCL(s, x)

Includes the element x to the set s. If x is already a member of the set, then does nothing.

B.2   Standard Functions

The following is a quick reference list of the standard Modula-2 function procedures, arranged alphabetically, as implemented in the TML Modula-2 compiler.

ABS(x)

Returns the absolute value of x.

CAP(c)

If c, a CHAR value, is a lowercase letter then its uppercase equivalent is returned, otherwise the input value is returned.

CHR(x)

Returns the character corresponding to the given ordinal value, x. CHR is equivalent to VAL(CHAR, x).

FLOAT(x)

Returns the equivalent REAL value for the given x, where the base type for x may be an INTEGER, CARDINAL, LONGINT, or LONGCARD.

FLOATD(x)

Returns the equivalent LONGREAL value for the given x, where the base type for x may be an INTEGER, CARDINAL, LONGINT, or LONGCARD.

HIGH(a)

Returns the maximum index for the given array type, a.

MAX(T)

Returns the maximum value for the given type T.

MIN(T)

Returns the minimum value for the given type T.

ODD(x)

Returns TRUE if x is odd, and FALSE otherwise.

ORD(x)

Converts a scalar value to an INTEGER. (The Modula-2 Report states that ORD returns a CARDINAL.)

SIZE(T)

Returns the size in bytes of the given type or variable.

TRUNC(x)

Truncates the given REAL value, x, to an INTEGER value.

TRUNCD(x)

Truncates the given LONGREAL value, x, to a LONGINT value.

VAL(T, x)

This is a replacement for the type transfer functions, (e.g., INTEGER(x)). It is globally defined, but it may also be imported from module SYSTEM (for compatability with other compilers).

C Modula-2 Compilers

C.1 Sources of Selected Modula-2 Compilers

In the interest of promoting Modula-2 the following list of some vendors providing Modula-2 compilers is given. This list is not comprehensive, and is meant to be a representative sample. Inclusion in this compendium of a specific compiler is not an endorsement of any kind for the given product. Readers must make their own decision regarding the products' suitability with due consideration to their personal requirements.

<name>	Version	Edition of *Programming in Modula-2*	Hardware
MacMETH Modula-2 Modula Corporation 1673 West 820 North Provo, UT, USA 84601 (801) 375-7400	2.0	3rd	Macintosh
or			
Werner Heiz Neugasse 71 CH-8005 Zürich Switzerland	2.3	3rd	Macintosh
TML Modula-2 TML Systems, Inc. 4241 Baymeadows Road, Suite 23 Jacksonville, FL, USA 32217 (904) 636-8592	1.10	3rd	Macintosh under MPW
Sempersoft Modula-2 Semper Software P.O. Box 225 Glen Ellyn, IL, USA 60138 (312) 790-1253	1.0	3rd	Macintosh under MPW

MacLogimo Modula-2 2nd   Macintosh
Tim Meyers
79E 600N
Orem, UT, USA   84057

Logitech Modula-2 3.0   3rd   IBM pc, VAX
Logitech, Inc.
6505 Kaiser Drive
Fremont, CA, USA   94555
(415) 795-8500

C.2   Comments on Compiler Variations

Niklaus Wirth's book *Programming in Modula-2* is presently in its 3rd edition and there are differences in the language defined therein from its predecessor. All of the modules presented in this book have been based on the 3rd edition. Further, the language is evolving and (minor) changes have been made which are reflected in Modula-2 compilers being produced at ETH Zürich. The most important of these changes are summarized below, though the best source for this kind of information is the reference manual provided with your compiler.

VAL is a globally defined replacement for type transfer functions. Being globally defined means that an operation need not be imported from any other module; this is like the standard Modula-2 routines such as HIGH, MIN, MAX, etc. For compatability with other compilers VAL may be imported from module SYSTEM if desired. In this book we have excluded the import statement.

The TML Modula-2 compiler allows the following symbols as replacements for the standard operators of the language. These take advantage of the Macintosh extended character set and have been used throughout the book in the interest of readability except for the abbreviation for DIV which most likely will be unfamiliar to most readers.

TMLModula-2	*Standard Modula-2*	*Meaning*
≠	#	not equal
≤	<=	less than or equal to
≥	>=	greater than or equal to
¬	NOT	logical not, negation
÷	DIV	integer division

In TML Modula-2, the ADDRESS data type is compatible with the data type LONGINT.

D ASCII Table

DEFINITION MODULE ASCII;
(*===
    Version : 1.00   17 Dec 1987   C. Lins
    Compiler: TML Modula-2 Compiler for the Apple Macintosh

    REVISION HISTORY
    v1.00   17 Dec 1987   C. Lins
      Initial TML Modula-2 implementation.

    INTRODUCTION
    This module provides standard mnemonics for the ISO/ASCII
    control characters and non-alphanumeric characters common
    to most keyboards.

    INTERFACE DESIGN ISSUES
    • The mnemonic names are given in all lowercase letters for
      compatibility with other Modula-2 systems.

    • Should the names for non-alphanumeric characters be
      capitalized? The decision was to not capitalize, and use
      all lowercase letters.
        + Easier to enter without using Shift-Key.
        + Consistant with mnemonics for control characters.
===*)

(*-- Mnemonics for the non-printing ASCII control codes --*)

```
CONST   nul = 000C; (*-- null                     *)
        soh = 001C; (*-- start of header          *)
        stx = 002C; (*-- start of text            *)
        etx = 003C; (*-- end of text              *)
        eot = 004C; (*-- end of transmission      *)
        enq = 005C; (*-- enquiry                  *)
        ack = 006C; (*-- acknowledge              *)
        bel = 007C; (*-- bell                     *)

        bs  = 010C; (*-- backspace                *)
        ht  = 011C; (*-- horizontal tab           *)
        lf  = 012C; (*-- line feed                *)
        vt  = 013C; (*-- vertical tab             *)
        ff  = 014C; (*-- form feed                *)
        cr  = 015C; (*-- carriage return          *)
        so  = 016C; (*-- shift out                *)
        si  = 017C; (*-- shift in                 *)
```

```
      dle = 020C; (*-- data link escape        *)
      dc1 = 021C; (*-- device-control 1        *)
      dc2 = 022C; (*-- device-control 2        *)
      dc3 = 023C; (*-- device-control 3        *)
      dc4 = 024C; (*-- device-control 4        *)
      nak = 025C; (*-- negative acknowledge    *)
      syn = 026C; (*--                         *)
      etb = 027C; (*-- end transmission block  *)

      can = 030C; (*-- cancel                  *)
      em  = 031C; (*-- end of message          *)
      sub = 032C; (*--                         *)
      esc = 033C; (*-- escape                  *)
      fs  = 034C; (*-- file seperator          *)
      gs  = 035C; (*-- group seperator         *)
      rs  = 036C; (*-- record seperator        *)
      us  = 037C; (*-- unit seperator          *)

      del = 177C; (*-- delete                  *)


(*-- Mnemonics for the non-alphanumeric ASCII codes --*)

CONST   space      = ' ';

        ampersand  = '&' ;
        asterisk   = '*' ;
        atsign     = '@' ;

        backslash  = '\' ;
        bar        = '|' ;

        circumflex = '^' ;
        colon      = ':' ;
        comma      = ',' ;

        dollar     = '$' ;

        equalsign  = '=' ;
        exclam     = '!' ;

        grave      = '`' ;
        gtrsign    = '>' ;

        lesssign   = '<' ;
        lbrace     = '{' ;
        lbracket   = '[' ;
        lparen     = '(' ;

        minussign  = '-' ;
```

```
                percent    = '%' ;
                period     = '.' ;
                plussign   = '+' ;

                query      = '?' ;
                quote      = "'" ;
                quotequote = '"' ;

                rbrace     = '}' ;
                rbracket   = ']' ;
                rparen     = ')' ;

                semicolon  = ';' ;
                sharp      = '#' ;
                slash      = '/' ;

                tilde      = '~' ;

                underscore = '_' ;

END ASCII.
```

E   Import Graphs

The following diagrams graphically depict the static dependency between modules. Diagrams show modules on three levels:

- higher level modules are near the top,
- lower level modules extend towards the bottom of the diagram, and
- system intrinsic modules such as SYSTEM and interface modules for the underlying hardware and operating system are at the lowest level.

E.1 Support Definition Module Import Graphs

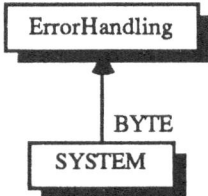

FIGURE E.1 ErrorHandling.DEF Import Graph

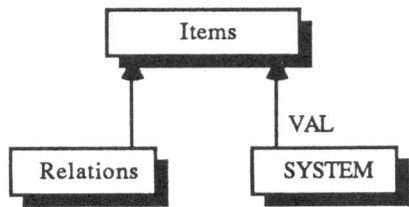

FIGURE E.2 Items.DEF Import Graph

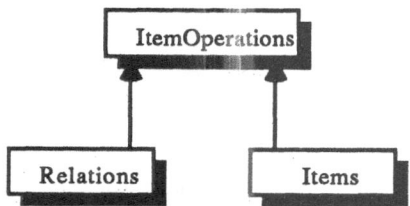

FIGURE E.3 ItemOperations.DEF Import Graph

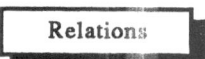

FIGURE E.4 Relations.DEF Import Graph

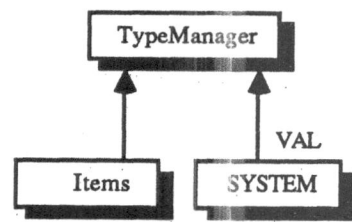

FIGURE E.5 TypeManager.DEF Import Graph

E.2 Support Implementation Module Import Graphs

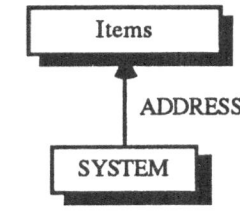

FIGURE E.6 Items.IMP Import Graph

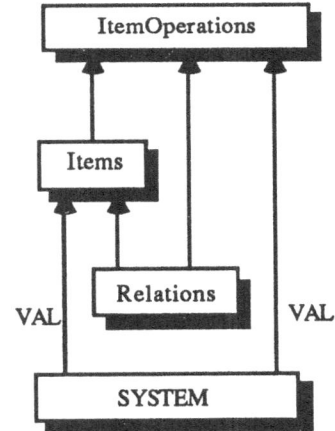

FIGURE E.7 ItemOperations.IMP Import Graph

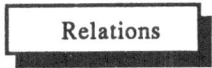

FIGURE E.8 Relations.IMP Import Graph

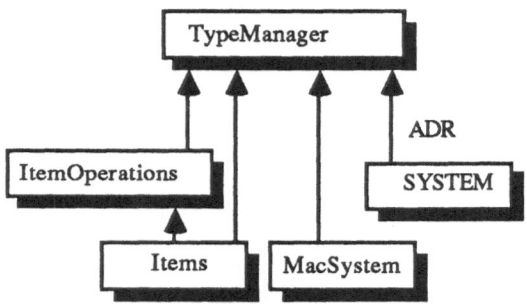

FIGURE E.9 TypeManager.IMP Import Graph

Bibliography

Aho, A.V., Hopcroft, J.E., Ullman, J.D.: *Data Structures and Algorithms*. Reading (MA): Addison-Wesley 1983

Aho, A.V., Sethi, R., Ullman, J.D.: *Compilers: Principles, Techniques, and Tools*, Reading (MA): Addison-Wesley 1986

Apple Computer: *Inside Macintosh*, Volume I. Reading (MA): Addison-Wesley 1985

Apple Computer: *Inside Macintosh*, Volume II. Reading (MA): Addison-Wesley 1985

Apple Computer: *Inside Macintosh*, Volume III. Reading (MA): Addison-Wesley 1985

Apple Computer: *Inside Macintosh*, Volume IV. Reading (MA): Addison-Wesley 1986

Barnard, H.J., Metz, R.F., Price, A.L.: "A Recommended Practice for Describing Software Designs: IEEE Standards Project 1016." *IEEE Transactions on Software Engineering* SE-12:2, 258-263 (Feb. 1986)

Bastani, F.B., Iyengar, S.S.: "The Effect of Data Structures on the Logical Complexity of Programs," *Communications of the ACM* 30, 250-259 (Mar. 1987)

Bauer, F.L. (ed.), *Software Engineering: An Advanced Course*. Berlin: Springer-Verlag 1975

Bentley, J.: *Programming Pearls*. Reading (MA): Addison-Wesley 1986

Berry, D.M.: "Towards a Formal Basis for the Formal Development Method and the Ina Jo Specification Language." *IEEE Transactions on Software Engineering* SE-13:2, 184-201 (Feb. 1987)

Booch, G.: "Object-Oriented Development." *IEEE Transactions on Software Engineering* SE-12, 211-221 (Feb. 1986)

Booch, G.: *Software Components With Ada Structures, Tools, and Subsystems*. Menlo Park (CA): Benjamin/Cummings 1987

Brown, M.H., Sedgewick R.: "Techniques for Algorithm Animation." *IEEE Software* 2:1, 28-39 (Jan. 1985)

Bruckner, J., Harp J.: "Implementing Opaque Types in Generic Data Structures in Modula-2." *Journal of Pascal, Ada, & Modula-2* 6:4, 14-30 (Jul./Aug. 1987)

Bruckner, J., Harp J.: "Macro Modules in Modula-2." *Journal of Pascal, Ada, & Modula-2* 6:6, 5-10 (Nov./Dec. 1987)

Campbell, R.R., et. al.: *Macintosh Programmer's Workshop TML Modula-2 Reference*. Jacksonville (FL): TML Systems, Inc. 1987

Card, D.N., Church, V.E., Agresti, W.W.: "An Empirical Study of Software Design Practices." *IEEE Transactions on Software Engineering* SE-12:2, 264-271 (Feb. 1986)

Card, D.N., McGarry, F.E., Page, G.T.: "Evaluating Software Engineering Technologies." *IEEE Transactions on Software Engineering* SE-13:7, 845-851 (Jul. 1987)

Christian, K.: *A Guide to Modula-2*. New York (NY): Springer-Verlag 1986

Clements, P.C., Faulk, S.R., Parnas, D.L.: *Interface Specifications for the SCR (A7-E) Application Data Types Module*, (NRL Report 8734). Washington, D.C.: Naval Research Laboratory 1983

Clements, P.C., Parker, R.A., Parnas, D.L., Shore, J.: *A Standard Organization for Specifying Abstract Interfaces*, (NRL Report 8815). Washington, D.C.: Naval Research Laboratory 1984

Crawford, A.L.: "An Extension to Modula-2 For Generic Types." *Journal of Pascal, Ada, & Modula-2* 6:6, 11-16 (Nov/Dec 1987)

Freeman, P.: "A Conceptual Analysis of the Draco Approach to Constructing Software Systems." *IEEE Transactions on Software Engineering* SE-13:7, 830-844 (Jul. 1987)

Gannon, J.D., Hamlet, R.G., Mills, H.D.: "Theory of Modules." *IEEE Transactions on Software Engineering* SE-13:7, 820-829 (Jul. 1987)

Gehani N., McGettrick, A.D.: *Software Specification Techniques*. Reading (MA): Addison-Wesley 1986

Gonnet, G.H.: *Handbook of Algorithms and Data Structures*. London: Addison-Wesley 1984

Gougen, J.: "Parameterized Programming." *IEEE Transactions on Software Engineering* SE-10:5, 528-543 (Sept. 1984)

Gough, K.J.: "Writing Generic Utilities in Modula-2." *Journal of Pascal, Ada, & Modula-2* 5:3, 53-62 (May/Jun. 1986)

Habermann, A.N., Notkin, D.: Gandalf: "Software Development Environments." *IEEE Transactions on Software Engineering* SE-12:12, 1117-1127 (Dec. 1986)

Hansen, P.B.: *Brinch Hansen on Pascal Compilers*. Englewood Cliffs (NJ): Prentice-Hall 1985

Hoare, C.A.R.: *Communicating Sequential Processes*. Englewood Cliffs (NJ): Prentice-Hall International 1985

Horowitz, E., Munson, J.B.: "An Expansive View of Reusable Software." *IEEE Transactions on Software Engineering* SE-10:5, 477-487 (Sept. 1984)

Horowitz, E., Williamson, R.C.: "SODOS: A Software Documentation Environment - Its Use." *IEEE Transactions on Software Engineering* SE-12:11, 1076-1087 (Nov. 1986)

Hunter, R.: *Compilers: Their Design and Construction Using Pascal*. New York (NY): John Wiley and Sons 1985

Jones, T.C.: "Reusability in Programming: A Survey of the State of the Art." *IEEE Transactions on Software Engineering* SE-10:5, 488-494 (Sept. 1984)

Knudsen, J.L.: "Better Exception-Handling in Block-Structured Systems." *IEEE Software* 4:3, 40-49 (May 1987)

Knuth, D.E.: *The Art of Computer Programming, Fundamental Algorithms*, Vol. 1. Reading (MA): Addison-Wesley 1972

Kopetz, H.: *Software Reliability*. Berlin: Springer-Verlag 1979

Korsh, J., Laison, G.: "A Multiple-Stack Manipulation Procedure." *Communications of the ACM* 26:11, 921-923 (Nov. 1983)

Liskov, B., Guttag, J.: *Abstraction and Specification in Program Development*. Cambridge (MA): The MIT Press 1986

Liskov, B., Zilles, S.N.: "Specification Techniques for Data Abstraction." *IEEE Transactions of Software Engineering* SE-1:1, 7-19 (Mar. 1975) (In "Tutorial on Software Design Techniques," 4th ed., P. Freeman and A. I. Wasserman, (eds.), IEEE Computer Society Press, 1983.)

Matsumura, K., Mizutani, H., Arai, M.: "An Application of Structural Modeling to Software Requirements and Design." *IEEE Transactions on Software Engineering* SE-13:4 461-471 (Apr. 1987)

Milenkovic, M.: *Operating Systems: Concepts and Design*. New York (NY): McGraw-Hill 1987

Moore, J., McKay, K.: *Modula-2 Text and Reference*. Englewood Cliffs (NJ): Prentice-Hall, 1987

Musa, J.D., Iannino, A., Okumoto, K.: *Software Reliability Measurement, Prediction, Application*. New York (NY): McGraw-Hill, 1987

Oktaba, H., Berber, R.: "Crafting Reusable Software in Modula-2." *BYTE* 12:10, 123-128 (Sept. 1987)

Parnas, D.L.: "On the Criteria To Be Used in Decomposing Systems into Modules." Tutorial on Software Design Techniques Fourth Edition (P. Freeman and A.I. Wasserman, eds.). Silver Spring (MD): IEEE Computer Society Press, 1983 (Reprinted from Communications of the ACM, December 1972, pp. 1053-1058)

Parnas, D.L.: "Designing Software for Ease of Extension and Contraction." *Tutorial on Software Design Techniques Fourth Edition* (P. Freeman and A.I. Wasserman, eds.). Silver Spring (MD): IEEE Computer Society Press, 1983 (Reprinted from *IEEE Transactions on Software Engineering*, Vol. SE-5, No. 2, March 1979, pp. 128-138)

Parnas D.L., Britton, K.H.: *A-7E Software Module Guide* (NRL Memorandum Report 4702), Washington D.C.: Naval Research Laboratory 1981

Parnas D.L., Clements, P.C.: "A Rational Design Process: How and Why to Fake It." *IEEE Transactions on Software Engineering* SE-12:2, 251-257 (Feb. 1986)

Pomberger, G.: *Software Engineering and Modula-2*. New York (NY): Prentice-Hall International 1984

Pressman, R.S.: *Software Engineering: A Practitioner's Approach*. New York (NY): McGraw-Hill 1982

Rajlich, V.: "Refinement Methodology for Ada." *IEEE Transactions on Software Engineering* SE-13:4, 472-478 (Apr. 1987)

Reynolds, C.: "On Implementing Generic Data Structures in Modula-2." *Journal of Pascal, Ada, & Modula-2* 6:5, 26-38 (Sept./Oct. 1987)

Sale, A.: *Modula-2 Disciple and Design.* Wokingham (England): Addison-Wesley 1986

Schildt, H.: *Modula-2 Made Easy*, Berkeley (CA): Osborne McGraw-Hill 1986

Sedgewick, R.: *Algorithms.* Reading (MA): Addison-Wesley 1983

Silberman, G.: "Stack Processing Techniques in Delayed-Staging Storage Hierarchies." *Communications of the ACM* 26:11, 999-1007 (Nov. 1983)

Sommerville, I.: *Software Engineering, Second Edition.* Reading (MA): Addison-Wesley 1985

Standish, T.A.: *Data Structure Techniques.* Reading (MA): Addison-Wesley 1980

Standish, T.A.: "An Essay on Software Reuse." *IEEE Transactions on Software Engineering* SE-10:5, 494-497 (Sept. 1984)

Tenenbaum, A., Augenstein, M.: *Data Structures Using Pascal.* Englewood Cliffs (NJ):Prentice-Hall 1981

Vick, C.R., Ramamoorthy, C.V. (eds.): *Handbook of Software Engineering.* New York (NY): Van Nostrand Reinhold, 1984

Waite, W., Goos, G.: *Compiler Construction.* New York (NY):Springer-Verlag 1984

Wallace, R.H., Stockenberg J.E., Charette, R.N.: *A Unified Methodology for Developing Systems*, New York (NY): Intertext Publications, Inc. 1987

Welsh, J., Hay, A.: *A Model Implementation of Standard Pascal.* Prentice-Hall International (UK) Ltd. 1986

Wiener, R.S., Ford, G.: *Modula-2 A Software Development Approach.* New York (NY): John Wiley & Sons 1985

Wiener, R.S., Sincovec, R.F.: *Data Structures Using Modula-2.* New York (NY): John Wiley & Sons 1985

Wiener, R.S., Sincovec, R.F.: *Software Engineering with Modula-2 and Ada.* New York (NY): John Wiley & Sons 1985

Wirth, N.: *Programming in Modula-2*, 3rd. ed. New York (NY): Springer-Verlag 1985

Wirth, N.: *Algorithms and Data Structures.* Englewood Cliffs (NJ): Prentice-Hall 1986

Yun Yeh, D., Munakata, T.: "Dynamic Initial Allocation and Local Reallocation Procedures for Multiple Stacks." *Communications of the ACM* 29:2, 134-141 (Feb. 1986)

"Unified Terminology for Exception Handling," *IEEE Software*, Vol. 4 (3), (May 1987), pp. 46-47.